SCRIPTURAL TRACES

CRITICAL PERSPECTIVES ON THE RECEPTION AND INFLUENCE OF THE BIBLE

17

Editors
Claudia V. Camp, Texas Christian University
Matthew A. Collins, University of Chester
Andrew Mein, Durham University

Editorial board
Michael J. Gilmour, David Gunn, James Harding, Jorunn Økland

Published under

LIBRARY OF HEBREW BIBLE/ OLD TESTAMENT STUDIES

684

Formerly Journal for the Study of the Old Testament Supplement Series

Editors
Claudia V. Camp, Texas Christian University
Andrew Mein, Durham University

Founding Editors
David J. A. Clines, Philip R. Davies, and David M. Gunn

Editorial Board
Alan Cooper, John Goldingay,
Norman K. Gottwald, James E. Harding, John Jarick, Carol Meyers,
Francesca Stavrakopoulou, Daniel L. Smith-Christopher, James W. Watts,
Susan Gillingham

STORYTELLING THE BIBLE AT THE CREATION MUSEUM, ARK ENCOUNTER, AND MUSEUM OF THE BIBLE

Paul Thomas

LONDON • NEW YORK • OXFORD • NEW DELHI • SYDNEY

T&T CLARK

Bloomsbury Publishing Plc

50 Bedford Square, London, WC1B 3DP, UK
1385 Broadway, New York, NY 10018, USA
29 Earlsfort Terrace, Dublin 2, Ireland

BLOOMSBURY, T&T CLARK and the T&T Clark logo are trademarks of
Bloomsbury Publishing Plc

First published in Great Britain 2020
This paperback edition published in 2021

Copyright © Paul Thomas, 2020

Paul Thomas has asserted his right under the Copyright, Designs and Patents Act,
1988, to be identified as Author of this work.

For legal purposes the Acknowledgments on p. xiii constitute an extension
of this copyright page.

Cover design: Charlotte James
Cover image © Mark Cornelison/Lexington Herald-Leader/MCT via Getty Images

All rights reserved. No part of this publication may be reproduced or transmitted
in any form or by any means, electronic or mechanical, including photocopying,
recording, or any information storage or retrieval system, without prior
permission in writing from the publishers.

Bloomsbury Publishing Plc does not have any control over, or responsibility for, any
third-party websites referred to or in this book. All internet addresses given in this
book were correct at the time of going to press. The author and publisher regret any
inconvenience caused if addresses have changed or sites have ceased to exist,
but can accept no responsibility for any such changes.

A catalogue record for this book is available from the British Library.

Library of Congress Control Number: 2019956639

ISBN: HB: 978-0-5676-8713-5
PB: 978-0-5677-0503-7
ePDF: 978-0-5676-8714-2

Series: Library of Hebrew Bible/Old Testament Studies, ISSN 2513-8758, volume 684
Scriptural Traces, volume 17

Typeset by Deanta Global Publishing Services, Chennai, India

To find out more about our authors and books visit www.bloomsbury.com and
sign up for our newsletters.

For Gabriella Smith and Jade Thomas
my guiding voices

"And when you turn to the right or when you turn to the left, your ears shall hear a word behind you saying, 'This is the way; walk in it.'"

CONTENTS

Preface	ix
Acknowledgments	xiii
A note on text/translation	xiv
Abbreviations	xv

Chapter 1
RECEPTION STUDIES: AN INITIATION … 1

Chapter 2
HAMMING IT UP WITH ANSWERS IN GENESIS … 21

Chapter 3
MOON POOLS AND POOP CHUTES … 37

Chapter 4
BIBLICAL HIRAETH AND STORIES OF HOME … 55

Chapter 5
DRAGONS, DINOS, AND TECH … 73

Chapter 6
SOMETHING TERRIBLE IS COMING … 85

Chapter 7
NOAH STOPS A KNIFE FIGHT … 99

Chapter 8
THE FAKE ARK DELUGION … 109

Chapter 9
ADAM IS TOO SEXY! … 123

Chapter 10
EXPECTING SOME FLATBREAD SANDWICHES … 137

Chapter 11
PLAYING IT SAFE AT THE MUSEUM OF THE BIBLE 149

Chapter 12
STRANGERS IN THEIR OWN LAND 163

Bibliography 169
Index 179

PREFACE

Writing about the Kentucky Creation Museum and the Ark Encounter has been a wild ride, to say the least. For many years I have nurtured an interest in how the Bible is used in novel ways by marginal groups in marginal contexts. In recent years this pursuit has taken me from twentieth-century feminism to extraterrestrial-inspired religions, demonstrating that the Bible can be found just about everywhere. When I started this project, I assumed that the manner in which the Bible is used by Answers in Genesis (AiG hereafter) would be a bit more sober than some of the materials I have recently examined. I am delighted to say that I was wrong. This research has taken me on a journey through the pitfalls of storybook and cartoon depictions of Noah's Ark to cryptozoology (a pseudoscience focused on the study of cryptids, creatures of folklore, and myths like the Sasquatch). Along the way I have encountered dragons and ancient Middle Eastern "goth" girls, and have grappled with the question of Adam's sexy body.

Likewise, I have a long-standing interest in the Genesis narratives, particularly Gen 1–12. This part of Genesis, known as the primeval history, contains fascinating material, those things that some have called the most mythological elements of the Bible (in order to distinguish these narratives from the "history" that commences with the introduction of Abraham and his family), including the creation narratives, the first humans, the first murders, the expansion of civilization, and, of course, the flood narrative.[1] Right in the middle of the primeval history lies the best passage of them all, Gen 6:1–4, that mysterious nugget about the sinfulness of the angels and the daughters of man, emblematic of such wickedness on earth that required destruction in the flood. This is the culmination of a story that begins with the disobedience in the garden and forms the heart of the story that the Creation Museum and the Ark Encounter seek to tell. The AiG focus on the Genesis creation and flood narrative attracts me like a moth to a flame. Add to this the fascinating detail that AiG is a parachurch young-earth creationist organization; then the Creation Museum and the Ark Encounter becomes a veritable playground for a scholar with interests like mine.

In graduate school, perhaps while in the trenches studying Ugaritic and Akkadian, I struggled with the issue of relevance. I was not sure that, at this particular point in the history of biblical studies, further efforts to find cognates for Hebrew terms in the ancient Semitic languages was really telling us anything about how the Bible works in the world. Ultimately, I think this crisis of relevance pushed me toward reception studies of the Bible. I like the weird, I like the

---

1. I follow a rather expansive definition of myth as symbolic narratives; therefore, I do not find the distinction between myth and history in Genesis that useful.

quirky, and I like the creative things people do with the Bible. Exploring these "eddies and undercurrents" tells us about how the Bible impacts people and even shapes culture.[2] Moreover, despite the rise of the "nones" and the "spiritual but not religious," the Bible remains culturally relevant and many of the issues explored in this book continue to shape and inform current cultural debates. Rather than continue parsing verbs, I have thrown my lot in with this kind of Bible study.

According to a recent Gallup poll, 38 percent of Americans hold to a creationist view of human origins, agreeing that God created humans in their present form sometime within the last ten thousand years.[3] Even though Gallup notes that this is a new low, when I read that number I am floored by the fact that approximately ninety-three million American adults are creationists! Young-earth creationists have a spokesperson in the form of Ken Ham, AiG, and two very visible monuments to this belief in the Creation Museum and the Ark Encounter. On the issue of relevance, it should be clear that young-earth creationism, drawn from a particular reading of Genesis, is not a fringe belief. Believers are mobilized at the grassroots level by AiG and are tied to national power brokers through people like the Green family of Hobby Lobby fame and the Museum of the Bible (MotB hereafter).

This is just a brief description of why this is fascinating and why I think it matters. However, there are many things that I have avoided. First among the things avoided are the details of the creationism/intelligent design versus evolution debate. The reader will find a description of creationism and creation science in these pages, including a brief history of creationism, creationism's goals, and creationism's approach to the Bible. As the Creation Museum and the Ark Encounter are young-earth creationist movements and as this theology impacts how they read and present the Bible, then including this material is relevant. Likewise, Ken Ham, the president and CEO of AiG, has an interesting perspective on what science can know about the past that finds treatment in these pages. The reader will not find, however, a complementary description of evolutionary theory and its history or an analysis of the merits of young-earth creationism versus the merits of evolution. It was not my goal in this research to reach conclusions about either (though I do have strong opinions on this topic). Likewise, this book does not explore classroom debates about the teaching of creationism and evolution in public schools. The history of those efforts has been covered elsewhere.[4]

---

2. Yvonne Sherwood, *A Biblical Text and Its Afterlives: The Survival of Jonah in Western Culture* (Cambridge: Cambridge University Press, 2000). Eddies and undercurrents, an image suggested by Yvonne Sherwood, has become my "go-to" description of the work I do. The currents of biblical interpretation, if one is willing to go where the flow leads, can pull you under, spin you about, and deposit you in heretofore unexpected magical places.

3. "In U.S., Belief in Creationist View of Humans at New Low," Gallup Inc., accessed July 24, 2018, https://news.gallup.com/poll/210956/belief-creationist-view-humans-new-low.aspx.

4. Eugenie Carol Scott, *Evolution vs. Creationism: An Introduction*, 2nd ed. (Westport, CT: Greenwood Press, 2009).

Speaking of strong opinions, I believe a brief note on my position on this subject is in order. The reader will find evidence of my personal perspective scattered throughout this book. Having been educated in a milieu influenced of Hayden White and Michel Foucault, I view the concept of impersonal objectivity as an impossible standard. Furthermore, though not the explicit focus of this research, I maintain that many of the initiatives of creationist organizations like AiG are bad for America. Issues like the attempted watering down of public school science education to the subtle (and sometimes not so subtle) perpetuation of racial stereotypes are far too important for neutrality.

This book is about the Bible in a particular subset of American evangelical culture. Though defined as a work on Bible reception history and theory, this work is multidisciplinary and necessarily eclectic in nature. I am an interdisciplinarian, and, as such, I have not colored within the lines of disciplinary boundaries. Though the reader will find biblical studies here, the reader will also find cultural studies, sociology, and even a bit of ethnography. Though I reflect more on this in Chapter 1, many of my colleagues in biblical studies may find this work a bit eclectic, but, as I later argue, I see this as a good thing.

This book can be roughly divided into two parts. The first part takes AiG, the Creation Museum, and the Ark Encounter as its primary focus, looking at AiG Bible readings and how those readings are presented in the Creation Museum and the Ark Encounter. Much of my analysis of these AiG attractions is held in tension with the recently opened MotB in Washington, DC. Though the MotB does things a bit differently than AiG, I maintain that the MotB represents another popular-culture presentation of this evangelical Bible reading. Though the attractions of AiG and the MotB engage in current social and political matters, the MotB does so in a much more subtle manner.

The second part of this book focuses on Creation Museum and Ark Encounter visitors. In these chapters I seek to answer the question of what visitors take away from these attractions and to what degree the AiG presentation influences or changes their understanding of the Bible. My original idea was to gauge changes in visitor perceptions of the Bible by interviewing patrons as they entered the museum and again as they left. That plan, however, hit a roadblock in the form of AiG's refusal to allow interviews of patrons on-site. I was left soliciting interviews with visitors who left reviews of the Creation Museum and the Ark Encounter on TripAdvisor and Facebook and conducting those interviews via Skype or phone. Likewise, I coded hundreds of written reviews left on TripAdvisor and Facebook.

The reader will note that this second part of the book paraphrases quotes from TripAdvisor users. Additionally, quotes pulled from the AiG website are paraphrased throughout. Apparently, my previously held notion of fair use does not always apply to websites. Rather, for many websites use is governed by "Terms of Use" or "Content Use Policies." I will not take TripAdvisor to task on this issue. However, as AiG is a very different company with very different goals, I do have a few comments about their use policy. As the reader will see in the coming pages, AiG, a 501(c)(3) nonprofit, presents itself as an educational entity, with legitimate scientific claims, asking for a fair hearing in the academy, and arguing that their perspective on creation should be taught in schools. AiG websites (here I include the website for the Creation Museum and the Ark Encounter) are among the most important sources of information about AiG perspectives on the issues examined in this book. There you will find technical articles from what AiG calls its peer-reviewed journal, *Answers Research Journal*, to the more accessible materials from *Answers Magazine*. The AiG general content use policy requires permission for use with an exception granted to those whose theological perspectives align with AiG. This audience may copy material from AiG websites for noncommercial Christian educational purposes. The *Answers Research Journal* consents to copy and distribution for noncommercial, non-sale use only. I submit that for an organization that wants to join the academic discussion, and that takes the secular scientific academy to task for working to protect its own interests, these narrow use policies are at odds with stated AiG goals and rhetoric.

Nonetheless, as a whole this book presents a mélange of materials and sources, some of it quirky, some of it funny, and some of it very serious. It is my hope that you find this journey as entertaining as I have.

ACKNOWLEDGMENTS

I am very grateful to Dr. James Bielo for taking the time to share some of his work on the Ark Encounter with me. In many ways this book rests upon the work he has done with the Creation Museum and the Ark Encounter. I hope that, in some way, this work compliments his excellent efforts. It is hard to think and write about AiG without grappling, at some level, with science. Many thanks are owed to Radford University scientists Dr. Jason Davis and Dr. Sarah Foltz for advising me on the idea of "observation science" and "origins science." I would like to thank Alyssa Archer and the staff at McConnell Library for tracking down materials for me—and, I swear, I am bringing those over-due interlibrary loan books back now. Speaking of patience, the members of the Religion and Popular Culture section at the Popular Culture Association have listened to me drone on about this for the last couple years. I have benefited greatly from their questions and comments. The generous support of the College of Humanities and Behavioral Sciences at Radford University funded this research. Where would I be without the help of my intrepid undergraduate research assistants, Lucas Wade Connolly and Katelyn Dobbins? Lucas and I spent many hours discussing horizons of expectation and he made the first trip to the Creation Museum in service of this research. Katelyn got a good dose of coding experience reading through hundreds of online reviews. This work is better for their efforts. Thanks to my friend Brian, who brought me a Daruma doll from Japan. My Daruma doll has watched over me, holding me to account with his one eye, for most of this project. I am proud to say that he now gazes at me with his two lidless eyes. Finally, and this truly is the best for last, this book was made much richer through the attention of Dr. Gabriella Smith. Dr. Smith, with her keen sociological mind, is one of the most insightful people I know. You can see her fingerprints here in obscure Welsh terms and insights on matters related to race. I will never forget the look on her face when my first issue of ICR's *Acts and Facts* arrived at the house. Nor will I ever forget her optimism, encouragement, and support as I worked through this project.

A NOTE ON TEXT/TRANSLATION

Unless otherwise noted, all scripture quotations contained herein are from the New Revised Standard Version Bible, copyright © 1989 by the Division of Christian Education of the National Council of the Churches of Christ in the U.S.A. Used by Permission. All rights reserved.

ABBREVIATIONS

AiG	Answers in Genesis
BDB	Brown Driver Briggs
CSF	Creation Science Foundation
CSM	Creation Science Ministries
Heb.	Hebrew
ICR	Institute for Creation Research
KJV	King James Version
MotB	The Museum of the Bible
NRSV	New Revised Standard Version

Chapter 1

RECEPTION STUDIES: AN INITIATION

"If God used evolution, God came from an ape," declared Ken Ham at a 2016 Vision Conference presentation at the Covington First Baptist Church in Louisiana.[1] Though he had been making similarly provocative statements for decades, prior to 2014 the name Ken Ham had little meaning outside those circles invested in, or critical of, creationist theology. In 2014, however, Ham rocketed to greater public awareness through his highly publicized debate with Bill Nye "The Science Guy" on the question, "Is creation a viable model for origins?" Broadcast live on the internet from the nine-hundred-seat Legacy Hall at the Creation Museum in Petersburg, Kentucky, AiG claims that over three million viewers tuned into the February 4 debate.[2] Predictably, surrogates on both sides declared victory. When the Ark Encounter Theme Park (AiG's second flagship attraction) neared completion in summer 2016, Nye and Ham agreed to meet again for Nye/Ham: The Second Debate. The Ark Encounter Theme Park features a replica of Noah's Ark built according to the specifications described in the Bible (or, at least as closely as modern building codes for a tourist attraction would allow). Different in format from the first debate, Nye/Ham 2 occurred on July 8, 2016. For two hours crowds and cameras followed Nye and Ham around the ark as they engaged in debate.

Both debates are interesting cultural moments—the second even described by Ham as a "clash of worldviews"—that heralded the momentous social and political changes that produced the contentious 2016 presidential race and the eventual election of Donald Trump as president in November. The Nye/Ham debates are a specific example of a larger debate happening in America about the future direction of the country. Consider, for a moment, Ken Ham and his views as represented in AiG, the Creation Museum, and the Ark Encounter. Much more about Ken Ham and his religious perspectives follow but, for now, just know that he believes

---

1. Zach Kopplin, "A Day with Ken Ham," *Slate*, accessed April 25, 2016, https://slate.com/news-and-politics/2016/04/public-schools-are-visiting-ken-hams-creation-museum.html.

2. "Over 3 Million Tuned In for Historic Bill Nye and Ken Ham Debate," Answers in Genesis, accessed May 30, 2019, https://answersingenesis.org/creation-vs-evolution/over-3-million-tuned-in-live-for-historic-bill-nye-and-ken-ham-evolutioncreation-debate/.

Earth is about six thousand years old, that the creation account described in Gen 1 and 2 is scientifically accurate, and that many social and political problems result from a cultural abandonment of the literal truth of Genesis narratives.³ A sense of cultural divide pervades the products of AiG. In fact, University of Cincinnati professor John Lynch has pointed out how even the physical location of the Creation Museum, an isolated rural area on the outskirts of Cincinnati, reflects this cultural gulf. Located just off Interstate 275 a few miles west of the Cincinnati/Northern Kentucky International Airport, there is virtually no other structure in the general vicinity of the Creation Museum. Physical isolation is just as pronounced at the Ark Encounter, which is located off Interstate 75 in Williamstown, Kentucky (pop. 3,952). Technically within the city limits, the Ark Encounter lies in an undeveloped area of Williamstown. In fact, a visitor would hardly know that a small town lies nearby unless they backtracked to the east side of Interstate 75. As Lynch explains, this physical isolation reflects isolation tropes in Christian conversion narratives and reflects the isolation that some Christians feel in modern society.⁴ From Moses leading the Hebrews from Egypt, to the temptation of Jesus by Satan in the wilderness, to Christian monks in desert retreats, there is a long history of Christian narratives depicting the wilderness as a place where a people are reforged and faith is renewed. As places in the wilderness, the Creation Museum and the Ark Encounter perpetuate this tradition, inhabiting the margins of a society that has embraced modernity, creating spaces where like-minded people can gather, create a sense of community, and find renewal in their faith. Interestingly, this stands in rather sharp contrast to the MotB. Located at 400 4th Street SW in Washington, D.C., the MotB sits only two blocks from the National Mall, just to the southwest of the capitol building. Here the Bible is not presented through the isolation trope but rather as situated at the nexus of political power in the United States. With a professed born-again Christian president in Donald Trump, who enjoys wide evangelical support, the opening of the MotB a year after his election lends further symbolic significance to claims that the Bible is surging in political influence. A squared, five-story edifice with 40-foot-tall bronze doors inscribed with the text of Gen 1, the MotB stands as a new temple in the heart of a

---

3. "Do Genesis 1 and 2 Contradict Each Other?" Answers in Genesis, accessed February 17, 2019, https://answersingenesis.org/contradictions-in-the-bible/do-genesis-1-and-2-contradict-each-other/. For those who may be unfamiliar with the Genesis creation narratives, Gen 1 is the seven-day creation story that begins with the creation of light and culminates in the creation of humans and the final day of rest. The concept of day in Gen 1 (Heb. *yom*) is very important for young-earth creationists. Genesis 2 is a second creation story than reverses the order of much of what appears in Gen 1. AiG writers see Gen 1 and 2 as different perspectives on the same event, rather than seeing them as two different creation stories.

4. John Lynch, "'Prepare to Believe': The Creation Museum as Embodied Conversion Narrative," *Rhetoric and Public Affairs* 16, no. 1 (2013): 8, https://doi.org/10.14321/rhetpublaffa.16.1.0001.

new Jerusalem inviting pilgrims from all across the nation to find God within His new home.[5] In the coming pages I suggest that this reflects a contradictory twofold rhetoric evident in evangelical thought in recent years, that of oppression and persecution coupled with real power and influence.

In Christian wilderness narratives the wilderness is not always a place of comfort. Biblical traditions describe how the Hebrews were molded into a renewed community through years of wandering in a wilderness fraught with hardship and danger. Jesus resisted temptation in the desert but faced off against Satan in the process. Early Christian monks found the wilderness to be a place for contemplation on matters of faith and a place of deprivation. In both the Old and the New Testaments, demons and devils inhabit the wilderness. Dangerous indeed, but as the Old Testament hero Samson demonstrates, one can live in a crevice and eat honey scooped from the carcass of a lion; the wilderness is still a place that can be mastered with the right kind of faith.

Many AiG supporters contend they live in a country where the gulf between their religious views and the secular culture continues to widen. These Christians see a country where prayer in public schools is unconstitutional and the pace of social change on issues like LGBTQ rights has been accelerating. As the United States comes to understand marriage differently, and as science continues to redefine our understanding of the world (and our place in it) in secular terms, there has been a growing sense among AiG writers and their supporters that the country has abandoned them. Moreover, in their eyes this separation has been acrimonious. Their cherished cultural and religious values become ridiculed objects piled upon history's trash heap as outdated and irrelevant to "modern" life. In response, evangelical culture has made increasingly strident and authoritative claims about the moral drift of our society and how it should be fixed.

AiG is authoritarian but is suspicious of secular authority. For AiG, as reflected in the Creation Museum and the Ark Encounter, the final authority—the only authority that matters—is God. Moreover, God reveals His authority in His Word. The Creation Museum presents this in the structuring rhetoric of its displays, the contrast between "God's Word" and "man's word." For AiG, fallible human intellect and reason means that secular authority cannot be authoritative. This is seen as especially true of secular, evolutionary science. The Creation Museum fosters a skepticism about secular science that has been part and parcel of the American right for decades.[6] AiG's skepticism about the methods of secular biological and earth sciences echoes the criticisms heard on the right about evolution and, more recently, climate-change science.

---

5. Babylonian Talmud, Yoma 38a. According to Jewish tradition the Nicanor Gates, cast in Corinthian bronze, was one of the seven gates leading into the temple courtyard.

6. Ronald L. Numbers, *The Creationists* (New York: A. A. Knopf: Distributed by Random House, 1992), xiv–xv.

As some have recently argued, authoritarianism, and one's response to authority, is one factor in the fault lines fracturing America.[7] A relationship between "scientific creationism" (the use of science to support the Genesis account of creation) and broader, authoritarian, right-wing movements have already been proposed. Writing in 1987, Alice Kehoe maintained that the creationism/evolution debate is a consequence of the right's larger binary worldview and that this debate "is a means of identifying those who will follow authority in the movement."[8] Kehoe further argued that a willingness to proclaim Bible inerrancy is a "public witness of one's willing submission to authority."[9] This is not submission to just any authority, however. Here the chain of command begins with God and then extends through his interpreters, people like Ken Ham and organizations like AiG and MotB. The challenge for people like Ham and places like MotB is to establish legitimacy as interpreters of this ultimate authority while simultaneously hiding their status as interpreters. Much like the man behind the curtain shaped the presentation of the Great and Powerful Oz, AiG produces a narrative that is meant to demonstrate the awesome nature of the creator but obfuscate the choices made behind the scenes that shape the show. Of course, Ham and other writers at AiG would not describe their role in these terms. In fact, Henry Morris (1918–2006), the father of modern scientific creationism, forcefully argued that the only way to interpret the Bible is not to interpret it at all.[10] Despite their claims to the contrary, it is the role of AiG and MotB as interpreters, and museum visitors as readers of their interpretations, that concerns much of this study.

Reviewing the American cultural divide illustrates that the Creation Museum and the Ark Encounter are much more than cultural curiosities. Indeed, the Creation Museum and the Ark Encounter are very real, and very substantial material responses to the pressures described above. If AiG reports are accurate, by February 2016 the Creation Museum had seen more than 2.5 million visitors since its opening in 2007.[11] Prior to its opening, AiG estimated at least 1.5 million visitors annually would visit the Ark Encounter. If, as Kehoe indicated, there is overlap between scientific creationism and the political right in America, then the Creation Museum and the Ark Encounter provide a unique opportunity to understand how this particular segment of the population understands authority,

---

7. Marc J. Hetherington and Jonathan Daniel Weiler, *Authoritarianism and Polarization in American Politics* (New York: Cambridge University Press, 2009).

8. Alice B. Kehoe, "Scientific Creationism: World View, Not Science," in *Cult Archaeology and Creationism: Understanding Pseudoscientific Beliefs about the Past*, ed. Francis B. Harrold and Raymond A. Eve (Iowa City, IA: University of Iowa Press, 1987), 19.

9. Kehoe, 19.

10. Henry M. Morris, *The Genesis Record: A Scientific and Devotional Commentary on the Book of Beginnings* (Grand Rapids, MI: Baker Book House, 1976), 54.

11. "Creation Museum to Expand as Part of a Three-Year Plan," Answers in Genesis, accessed April 11, 2017, https://answersingenesis.org/blogs/ken-ham/2016/02/04/creation-museum-expand-part-three-year-plan/.

their place in the broader culture, and their hopes for America. All of this is influenced by how AiG, and the audiences of their attractions, understand the Bible.

As demonstrated in the coming pages, Ken Ham and AiG see America as a country in decline, as a country that has strayed from what they view as America's Bible-based moral foundations. The further the country strays from a biblical foundation the further America will slide toward crumbling social structures and families fractured by drug abuse, pornography, and crime. For AiG, the origins of cultural decay lie in the abandonment of biblical authority in all areas, including science. As Americans become increasingly unwilling to accept the worldview of Genesis in its literal, plain sense, the more willing people are to compromise on other parts of the Bible.[12]

Reception Criticism: Where We Have Been

The Bible is a fantastic text, in every sense of the term—fantastic in the sense of embodying some of the world's great literature but also in the sense of its largeness, its fancy, and its fantasy. However, the modern era has pushed society away from embracing the fantastic in favor of the materialistic and scientific ways of explaining the world. Bible interpretation has not been exempt from this process. Yvonne Sherwood points out in her reception study of Jonah that there has been a shift from the primitive to the scientific, "the seemingly unbelievable becomes simply the unknown quantity in an algebraic equation."[13] As enlightenment analytic tools were unleashed upon the Bible, the Bible's enchantments were subjected to rationalization and reduced to literary sources, comparative mythology, history, and various other material processes. The history of these changing approaches to the Bible can be traced in biblical topics published in the *Encyclopedia Britannica*. For instance, the 1771 edition of the encyclopedia accepted the biblical flood narrative as essentially accurate, even claiming that the ark's volume would have been sufficient to hold the necessary animals. However, by the eighth edition the idea of a localized (rather than worldwide) flood appeared in *Britannica* and the ninth edition abandoned all attempts to reconcile the flood narrative with the observable world.[14]

The rationalization process has diminished the reader's appetite for the fantastic. Sherwood writes "In the Mainstream there has been no place for the *fantastic*.... The intolerance for triffid-like plants and monstrous fish is but the most obvious symptom of a distaste for alterity and disruption, and the desire for a text that

---

12. Ken A. Ham and Paul S. Taylor, *The Genesis Solution* (Grand Rapids, MI: Baker Book House, 1988), 10.
13. Sherwood, *A Biblical Text and Its Afterlives*, 46.
14. "Higher Criticism," New World Encyclopedia, accessed November 30, 2018, http://www.newworldencyclopedia.org/entry/Higher_criticism.

is smooth, easily digested, and purged of all that is potentially monstrous or abnormal."[15] Still, those biblical narratives that allow disruption often produce rich reception traditions. Such is the case with the narratives that the Creation Museum and the Ark Encounter are built upon. AiG wants to both re-enchant the Bible while at the same time convincing visitors that stories of a six-day creation, a paradisiac garden, a heaven-scraping tower, and a worldwide flood have rational and scientific explanations. In doing so, AiG produces its own receptions of these biblical narratives and asks its audience to accept these interpretations as authoritative.

The reception study of texts had its genesis in an old debate about where and how meaning is derived from texts. Some maintained that meaning is encapsulated in the author's intent for the text. Thus, to find out what a text really means, one had to learn about the author, his or her biography, and the historical context in which the author lived. Once assembled, these puzzle pieces were thought to illuminate a text's meaning. This approach has dominated higher criticism of the Bible. Implicit in this approach is the idea that learning the languages, cultures, and histories of the Bible's authors and their contemporaries would unlock the true meaning of text. Though AiG quibbles with and rejects many conclusions reached by higher critics, they nonetheless implicitly agree that the Bible's meaning is derived from the authorial intent of God-inspired writers.

Another approach, rooted in the postmodern study of texts, maintains that authorial intent does not matter. Instead, meaning is found in the interaction of readers and the text. Readers are therefore said to receive a text and will derive meaning from a text based upon their own biographies, communities, and historical circumstances. This idea took root in literary studies and from this soil biblical reception studies emerged. Loosely defined, reception studies looks at the manner in which readers create meaning from a text and the rules that govern reading.[16] As we will see in coming pages, AiG writers believe that this approach to the Bible leads to interpretative anarchy.

While this research is a Bible reception study of Creation Museum, Ark Encounter, and MotB readings of the Bible, it is a bit different in that I am working with reception on multiple levels. The first level takes AiG and MotB as its subjects and considers how the Bible is employed at the Creation Museum, the Ark Encounter, and MotB in order to make rhetorical arguments. AiG staff are Bible readers, therefore, I maintain that elements of their textual reception can be discerned in the Bible products on display at the Creation Museum and the Ark Encounter. Additionally, I am interested in the cultural impact of AiG attractions

---

15. Sherwood, *A Biblical Text and Its Afterlives*, 90.

16. Jane Tompkins, *Reader Response Criticism: From Formalism to Post-Structuralism* (Baltimore, MD: Johns Hopkins University Press, 1980). David Parris, *Reception Theory and Biblical Hermeneutics* (Eugene, OR: Pickwick Publications, 2009). Tompkins's is an excellent overview of reader-response criticism. Parris offers a very sophisticated analysis of reception theory.

and cannot help but wonder to what degree patrons of the Creation Museum and the Ark Encounter accept or reject AiG interpretations and to what degree patrons are readers of AiG rather than being readers of the Bible. While it is true that there are sermon-like elements at the Creation Museum and the Ark Encounter, much of the "Bible work" being done at these attractions is communicated through non-textual materials, including physical representations of biblical characters like Adam and Methuselah and biblical objects like the ark. My second level of reception analysis studies show how patrons receive the Bible as mediated to them through the medium of museum and theme park exhibits. Two things of note push this Bible reception in a new direction. The first is the incorporation of material objects in an extended reception analysis. Certainly, there have been Bible reception studies that have focused on art and other non-textual objects; however, the popular culture focus of this study remains relatively unexplored in biblical studies. The methods employed to conduct this research represents another new direction for Bible reception studies. Assessing visitor perceptions of Bible narratives as presented in the Creation Museum and the Ark Encounter meant introducing ethnographic interview methods. Outside of anthropological studies of biblicism, as in the work of James Bielo or Brian Malley, there have been few efforts to employ such methodologies in Bible reception studies.[17] The spirit of this study is partly captured by a statement made by Michel de Certeau in his book *The Practice of Everyday Life*. Though, in this particular instance, he is speaking about television, this statement is nonetheless very apropos for my work: "once the images broadcast by television and the time spent in front of the TV set have been analyzed, it remains to be asked what the consumer makes of these images."[18] Replace TV with Creation Museum, Ark Encounter, and MotB and this statement reflects one facet of the analysis that follows.

Biblical reception studies are indebted to Hans Robert Jauss's (1921–97) landmark work in literary reception titled *Toward an Aesthetic of Reception*[19] and especially the essay "Literary History as a Challenge to Literary Theory."[20] Jauss, in turn, relied upon the work of his teacher, Hans-Georg Gadamer (1900–2002), who wrote about hermeneutics in his work titled *Truth and Method* (1960). Together with his colleague Wolfgang Iser (1926–2007), author of notable works such as *The*

---

17. Brian Malley, "Understanding the Bible's Influence," in *The Social Life of Scriptures: Cross Cultural Perspectives on Biblicism*, ed. James S. Bielo (New Brunswick, NJ: Rutgers University Press, 2006), 194–204; James S. Bielo, *Words upon the Word: An Ethnography of Evangelical Group Bible Study* (New York: New York University Press, 2009).

18. Steve Taylor, "Reading 'Pop-Wise': The Very Fine Art of 'Making Do' When Reading the Bible in Bro' Town," in *The Bible In/And Popular Culture: A Creative Encounter*, ed. Philip Culbertson and Elaine M. Wainwright (Leiden: Brill, 2011), 163.

19. Hans Robert Jauss, *Toward an Aesthetic of Reception*, trans. Timothy Bahti, vol. 2, Theory and History of Literature (Minneapolis: University of Minnesota Press, 1982).

20. Hans Robert Jauss and Elizabeth Benzinger, "Literary History as a Challenge to Literary Theory," *New Literary History* 2, no. 1 (1970): 7–37, https://doi.org/10.2307/468585.

Implied Reader (1974) and the *Act of Reading* (1978), Jauss formed the so-called Constance School of Reception Aesthetics, so named because both worked at the University of Konstanz in Germany. When the reception work of Jauss and Iser reached the United States, it took the form of "reader response criticism," most famously represented in the work of Stanley Fish (1938–).

Reading about Bible reception studies sometimes feels like consuming a word salad. Owing to inconsistently used terms, the technical language used in receptions studies is often unclear. For instance, readers encountering a work in reception might come across the German terms *Wirkungsgeschichte*, *Rezeptionsgeschichte*, and *Rezeptionsasthetik*. These terms get translated, in order, as history of effect, reception history, and reception aesthetics. Moreover, usage of the term "reception history" can variously mean all three of these things or only one of these things.[21] Unraveling these terms will help place the remainder of this work in context.

Wirkungsgeschichte is a term associated with Hans-Georg Gadamer's *Truth and Method*. Gadamer, described as a "decisive figure in the development of twentieth century hermeneutics,"[22] spent most of his career at the University of Heidelberg, purportedly keeping office hours well into his nineties. In *Truth and Method*, his magnum opus on the concept of understanding, Gadamer only spent a few pages discussing *Wirkungsgeschichte*; nonetheless, his analysis would profoundly affect biblical reception studies. *Wirkungsgeschichte*, or the history of effect, describes how understanding a work of art (a text for example) is a historical event precipitated by an amalgamation of horizons.[23] The concept of horizons would become central in later reception theory. In short, horizons represent the expectations of both artists and readers. Social location, historical period, and prior works of art inform these expectations. While an artist's work reflects her own expectations, an audience brings their own expectations to the table and the two sets may not closely align. The term "horizons" captures the gulf that separates these sets of expectations and one goal of reception studies is to examine how that gulf is bridged. The socially and historically situated reader is in dialog with the text and that dialog is constantly in flux. Recognizing the "situatedness" of the reader led Gadamer to argue that there is no objective reading, that prejudice plays a role in reading and that people should "no longer attempt to blind themselves to the influence of history upon interpretation."[24] One consequence of this approach

---

21. Holly Morse, "What's in a Name? Analysing the Appellation 'Reception History' in Biblical Studies," in *Biblical Reception*, vol. 3, ed. J. C. Exum and D. J. C. Clines (Sheffield: Sheffield Phoenix Press, 2014), 246.

22. Jeff Malpas, "Hans-Georg Gadamer," *The Stanford Encyclopedia of Philosophy* (Fall 2018 Edition), ed. Edward N. Zalta, https://plato.stanford.edu/archives/fall2018/entries/gadamer/.

23. Hans-George Gadamer, *Truth and Method*, 2nd ed., trans. Joel Weinsheimer and Donald G. Marshall (New York: The Seabury Press, 1975), 269–70.

24. Morse, "What's in a Name?" 247.

is a move away from the author and her intentions for a text as the sole arbiter of meaning.

Gadamer's elucidation of *Wirkungsgeschichte* laid the foundation for the work of his student, Hans Robert Jauss. Playing with Gadamer's concept of the "fusion of horizons," Jauss formulated a methodology for reception analysis that went beyond *Truth and Method*. While Gadamer allowed some room for authorial intent, Jauss moved even further away from authorial intent as determinate for meaning. For Jauss, the author has no privileged status. Nor do texts stand in isolation upon their own merits, for, as Jauss stated, "a literary work is not an object . . . which offers the same face to each reader in each period."[25] Jauss further expanded upon the idea of the reader's horizon of expectations. This horizon is comprised of works the reader has already read and this horizon is the standard against which the aesthetic value of a new work is determined.[26] The greater the gulf between the new work and the reader's horizon, the greater is the potential artistic merit of the new work. The "great master works," for example, require a "special effort to read them 'against the grain' of accustomed experience."[27] All of this is not to say, however, that the text is completely passive. As Jauss pointed out, texts do not appear in an informational vacuum and texts can suggest types of reception through "covert signals, familiar characteristics or implicit allusions."[28] The text might create expectations and the resultant "direct perception(s)" are describable if one understands the "motivations" and "the signals which set it off."[29]

Wolfgang Iser allowed for some authorial intent in the concept of the "implied reader." The implied reader is the audience that the author of a text imagines for her work. However, the author's intent as it relates to the implied reader does not determine the meaning of the text. Rather, according to Iser, meaning emerges between the reader and the text through the act of reading. More specifically, a reader's expectations of a text will be upset because of twists and turns, gaps and indeterminacies. Readers fill those gaps in varying ways, thus producing the potential for multitudinous interpretations. As readers, we are dissatisfied with ambiguities, contradictions, and vagaries and will attempt to smooth these areas. The impulse to smooth pits and potholes in a narrative provides rich material for Bible reception studies.

In the United States, reader-response criticism came to encompass the reception theory of Gadamer, Iser, and Jauss. The literary theorist Stanley Fish is one of the most influential intellectuals in the formation of reader-response criticism. Often charged with introducing an extreme subjectivism into reception studies, Fish went beyond Jauss and Iser in separating meaning from the authorship of texts. His most famous example is the Jacobs/Rosenbaum list. Appearing in his influential

---

25. Jauss and Benzinger, "Literary History as a Challenge to Literary Theory," 10.
26. Jauss and Benzinger, 8.
27. Jauss and Benzinger, 15.
28. Jauss and Benzinger, 12.
29. Jauss and Benzinger, 12.

work *Is There a Text in This Class?* Fish described how one of his classes derived a poem from a list of names Fish left on the board in a prior class (these names were a reading assignment). In a flurry of interpretative activity, working only with the names on the blackboard—Jacobs-Rosenbaum, Levin, Thorne, Hayes, and Ohman (?)—students interpreted this list as a medieval Christian poem extolling the love and mercy of God.[30] In this form of reader-response criticism, the formal structures of the text, and authorial intention (remembering that Jacobs/Rosembaum was written as a reading list), have no bearing on interpretation. The students who read it as a poem were all members of a medieval poetry class. If there was anything that governed their interpretation of the "list" it was their membership in, and the conventions of, that class. The idea that groups, what Fish called "interpretative communities," govern interpretation is an important contribution relevant to this study. For Fish, readers are imbedded in interpretative communities that govern the reading (and writing) of texts. Fish upholds interpretive communities as an answer to claims of subjectivism. He stated: "This sounds like the rankest subjectivism, but it is qualified almost immediately when the reader is identified not as a free agent, making literature in any old way, but as a member of a community whose assumptions about literature determine the kind of attention he pays and thus the kind of literature 'he' makes."[31]

Having turned toward the audience in literary criticism, reception critics sometimes lose sight of the fact that there are authors and that authors do have an intent, even if the audience reception of a text deviates from the author's vision. In his analysis of encoding/decoding cultural theorist Stuart Hall (1932–2014) reminded us about authors and their intentions. Hall's research focused on the production of television shows, but his argument captures something about the manner in which AiG encodes the Bible in the Creation Museum and Ark Encounter. Hall maintained that mass media products, like television shows, contain messages in the form of sign vehicles. An important concept in semiotics (the study of sign processes and communication), a sign vehicle is a physical manifestation of a sign. A sign, therefore, is a representation of meaning—composed of words, images, and sounds that allow for the communication of ideas—that points to something other than itself. Decoding refers to the meanings that audiences (be they television program viewers, visitors to the Creation Museum, or readers of the Bible) derive from the encoded object. Hall maintained that encoding and decoding both utilize similar processes and that social, political, and economic circumstances inform both production (encoding) and reception (decoding). As it relates to production, Hall asserted that "technical skills, professional ideologies, institutional knowledge, definitions and assumptions" frame the production process.[32]

---

30. Stanley Fish, *Is There a Text in This Class? The Authority of Interpretive Communities* (Cambridge, MA: Harvard University Press, 1980).

31. Fish, 11.

32. Stuart Hall, "Encoding, Decoding," in *The Cultural Studies Reader*, 2nd ed., ed. Simon During (New York: Routledge, 1999), 509.

Hall departed from other reception critics in his willingness to accept that production may constrain reception. He grounded this in the observable fact that communication can happen between the author and the reader. Were it not for some interpretive framework suggested by the encoder, Hall argued, there would be no effective communication at all.[33] The idea that communication occurs between author and audience, suggesting some influence by the encoder on meaning, also informed the work of Norman Holland (1927–), another pivotal thinker in reception studies. Holland, in his study on reader responses to Faulkner's "A Rose for Emily," argued that readers are responding to *something* and while a literary text may only be marks on a paper the text presents a "matrix of psychological possibilities for its readers."[34] Similarly, a television show, or something like the Creation Museum, also suggests possible ways of reading, though the reader is not obligated to accept that suggestion. Holland argued that only some receptions fit the matrix of possibilities presented by a text. Holland asked participants in his study to recall the scene in "A Rose for Emily" where Emily's father stands in an open doorway holding a whip while Emily stands behind him dressed in white. As Holland maintained, a reader who sees an Eskimo in this scene is not "really responding to the story at all—only pursuing some mysterious inner exploration."[35]

Though produced mass communications might encode certain messages intended for the reader, there is no assurance that the reader will accept the intended message. Hall proposed that readers will adopt one of three reading positions. The first is the dominant/hegemonic position. From this position, the reader decodes the message in "terms of the reference code in which it has been encoded."[36] A dominant-hegemonic reader operates inside the dominant code and accepts the worldview that the text presents. This reading position most fully realizes the author's intent. Hall posits that the second reading position is the negotiated position. The negotiated position is of interest because it potentially produces contradictory readings. Adopting this position, the reader allows for some adaptive and oppositional perspectives that run counter to the position of the encoder. As described by Hall, the negotiated position "acknowledges the legitimacy of the hegemonic definitions to make the grand significations (abstract), while, at a more restricted, situational (situated) level, it makes its own ground rules—it operates with exceptions to the rules."[37] By making exceptions to the rules at the individual level, the negotiated position often places itself in tension with the dominant-hegemonic position. Finally, the third position is the oppositional. Hall says the least about this position despite its potential for being

---

33. Hall, 514.
34. Norman N. Holland, *The Nature of Literary Response: Five Readers Reading* (New Brunswick: Transaction Publishers, 2011), 12.
35. Holland, 12.
36. Hall, "Encoding, Decoding," 515.
37. Hall, 516.

the most politically charged. Simply stated, the oppositional position decodes in a manner that is contrary to the dominant-hegemonic position.

Note that the encoded product itself is often less important than the story attached to the product. Hall used several examples to explain what he meant by this. In the abstract, he noted that the rules of televised discourse mediate the transmission of "raw" historical events. Likewise, in this study of the Creation Museum, the Ark Encounter, and MotB, the rules of museum and theme park object production and display mediate the transmission of information about the Bible. Through these mediums these organizations attempt to lend authority to their arguments while creating counter-hegemonic narratives.[38] Hall continued, "The event must become a 'story' before it can become a *communicative event.*"[39] At best then, the encoder is telling a story about an event, be it a television production or a presentation of a biblical narrative, but the story is not the event. For example, representations of violence on TV are not violence but messages about violence. Following this, one might say that AiG is not presenting the Bible, but rather, it is presenting a message about the Bible and in doing so is encoding its own position on the text into Creation Museum displays.

I am not arguing that the Creation Museum's young-earth creationist reading of Gen 1–11 is culturally hegemonic, in the sense that it represents a dominant narrative in American society. According to the PEW research center, 40 percent of Americans identify as creationists. Moreover, the type of creationism espoused at the Creation Museum is an even smaller percentage of this group. However, AiG draws upon narratives that have recently been hegemonic in America. A 2018 PEW survey found that 80 percent of Americans believe in God or a higher power while 56 percent believe in God as described in the Bible.[40] As PEW notes, these numbers have gone down in recent years. So, when AiG writes about biblical authority and God it is employing narratives that are still relevant but are losing influence. Thus, one can view the efforts of AiG and MotB as an effort to prop up a crumbling formerly hegemonic metanarrative. When I talk about the dominant-hegemonic position of the encoder, as it relates to the Creation Museum and the Ark Encounter, I refer to the ideological position of AiG only and the position AiG would like museum visitors to adopt based upon its presentation of the Bible in its tourist attractions.

In the encoding/decoding process, Hall argued that reception is predominant because reception is the "point of departure for the realization" of the message.[41] This point has become axiomatic in reception criticism; once a text leaves the

---

38. Bruce Lincoln, *Discourse and the Construction of Society: Comparative Studies of Myth, Ritual, and Classification* (New York: Oxford University Press, 1989), 8.

39. Hall, "Encoding, Decoding," 508.

40. "Americans' Beliefs about the Nature of God," Pew Forum, accessed April 25, 2018, http://www.pewforum.org/2018/04/25/when-americans-say-they-believe-in-god-what-do-they-mean/.

41. Hall, "Encoding, Decoding," 509.

author's hand, the interaction between reader and text becomes the locus of meaning. Using an example from Roland Barthes (1915–80), Hall maintained that one can understand the message as encoded, often representing the dominant cultural order, as the denotative—the literal meaning of the message the author meant to communicate. An example (still borrowing from Barthes) is that "the sweater always signifies a 'warm garment' and thus the activity/value of 'keeping warm.'"[42] On the other hand, the connotative adds other layers of meaning. The connotative emerges from the reader's interaction with the text, a process that is far beyond the control of the author. For instance, a sweater can also signify the coming of winter or a cold day. If the text "breaches expectations" then the connotative takes on more force as readers work to make sense of the text.[43] The varying levels of the connotative that the reader brings to the text can either enforce the author's message or push the reader toward negotiated or oppositional readings.

Norman Holland's work on the psychology of reading and reception supports the idea that the reader searches for the discursive world in which texts make sense. For Holland, "interpretation is a function of identity."[44] Reading is a process of recreating the self, and the creation of the self through reading occurs in the realization of wishes and the rejection of fears (or pleasure vs. displeasure).[45] The reception of a literary work therefore depends upon the degree to which the reader can recreate a "particular pattern of defense mechanisms and, in a broader sense, the particular system of adaptive strategies that he keeps between himself and the world."[46] This helps explain how different readers can receive texts in contradictory ways. "Each reader, in effect, re-creates the work in terms of his own identity theme. First, he shapes it so it will pass through the network of his adaptive and defensive strategies for coping with the world. Second, he re-creates from it the particular kind of fantasy and gratification he responds to."[47] This "raw" fantasy is further transformed into the reader's moral, intellectual, and social coherence.[48] Holland boils this down to a four-part psychological process of literary response. First, each reader brings highly personal expectations to the work. Second, readers shape texts through wish fulfillment toward some personal fantasy. Third, texts reshaped according to personal fantasy give pleasure and ward off anxiety. Fourth, readers interpret texts in such a manner that they give meaning to the process of identity re-creation.[49]

---

42. Hall, 513.
43. Hall, 513.
44. Norman N. Holland, "Unity Identity Text Self," *PMLA* 90, no. 5 (October 1975): 816, https://doi.org/10.2307/461467.
45. Holland, 817.
46. Holland, 817.
47. Holland, 818.
48. Holland, 818.
49. Holland, *The Nature of Literary Response*, xi.

Gadamer and his students, Jauss and Iser, were largely reacting to formalism in the study of texts. A formalist sees meaning residing in a text, in its structure, and in what the author intended to communicate in the text. A formalist approach demands focused attention on the author and her historical context. Reflecting upon the history of biblical interpretation since the development of higher criticism in the mid-eighteenth century, the impact of formalism on biblical studies is easy to recognize. Until the advent of what are loosely termed "postmodern" methods in biblical studies (reception is often included under this umbrella) the goal of academic biblical scholarship had been to determine the meaning of the text by reconstructing, as closely as possible, the *sitz im leben* of the text. In other words, the key to understanding the meaning of a text lies in the circumstances of its authorship. Though formalism is still the primary mode of interpretation in biblical studies, postmodern methods like reception criticism have made significant inroads by pointing out that these classic methods quarantine the text in a particular time and do little to illuminate the ways later readers use and understand the text.

Reception Criticism: Taking the Cultural Turn

Understanding how readers derive meaning from the text is not advanced through cataloging all the interesting ways the Bible is used. In her digestion of the reception-theory word salad, Holly Morse suggested that the idea of "reception criticism" can help us move past theorizing and cataloging.[50] Reception criticism in biblical studies has often been short on the "criticism" and more focused on collecting interesting and unusual readings of the Bible. Perhaps this is a consequence of emphasizing the "history" in *Rezeptionsgeschichte*, which, as Morse suggests, leads to more description and less analysis.[51] As all readers inhabit communities informed by ideology, it behooves those of us engaged in reception studies to engage in ideological criticism.[52]

This work does not merely highlight just another set of interesting readings of the Bible. George Aichele posits in *The Postmodern Bible* that "hermeneutical power is political power."[53] For that reason I frame this study as a work of reception criticism. The readings examined here are not mere curiosities. Rather, the manner in which the Bible is used by AiG and MotB reflect the ideological position of particular social groups with very real political and social power. The readings examined here reflect real and urgent social debates about the relationship between the Bible and the nation's future.

50. Morse, "What's in a Name?" 252.
51. Morse, 252.
52. Bible and Culture Collective, *The Postmodern Bible* (New Haven: Yale University Press, 1995), 58–59.
53. Bible and Culture Collective, 59.

All this may sound like a further step away from the traditional biblical studies that focus on linguistics and the histories and cultures of the ancient Near East. However, reception critics of the Bible have been telegraphing this necessary move for years. Many perceive these as troubled times for the humanities and the peculiar place biblical studies has had in the humanities is now precarious. If pressures to explain the relevancy of the humanities continue, biblical studies (and indeed, many humanities disciplines) may find themselves sidelined at institutions retooled to train police officers and nurses. Ibrahim Abraham has accused Bible scholars of inhabiting a "privileged interpretative position" supported by methodologies developed for the study of religious texts that do little to illuminate the function of the Bible in modern cultures.[54] It is not enough to analyze popular culture, Abraham says, but the reception scholar must engage in the lives of people consuming popular culture rather than restricting ourselves to authoritative, scholarly, or artistic representations of the Bible. He states: "From the perspective of a scholar of religion and contemporary culture outside the discipline of biblical studies, it is notable that biblical studies can still 'get away' with an Adornoesque approach, marginalizing the interpretive capacities of ordinary consumers of popular culture."[55]

Also working within biblical studies, Timothy Beal issued a challenge for reception critics to push into new areas. In his 2011 article "Reception History and Beyond: Toward the Cultural History of Scriptures" Beal calls for a "harder cultural turn" so that reception critics can engage material, historical, and anthropological methods.[56] As it currently stands, Beal argued, reception studies suffer from limitations that prevent engagement with religious studies writ large. These limitations include a propensity to focus on words in the abstract, failure to consider the material embodied aspects of the Bible, failure to analyze the "economic aspects of scriptural production, marketing, and consumption," and a failure to accept that there is no single, original, biblical text.[57]

I take Abraham and Beal seriously and this work represents my effort to turn Bible reception criticism toward cultural studies. As I am particularly interested in the Creation Museum and the Ark Encounter as material objects, Michael Ryan's description of cultural studies as including "the things we humans make when we

---

54. Ibrahim Abraham, "Would You Adam and Eve It? Social Scientific Contributions to the Study of the Reception of Scripture in Consumer Society," *The Bible and Critical Theory* 10, no. 2 (2015): 32, http://novaojs.newcastle.edu.au/ojsbct/index.php/bct/article/view/602.

55. Abraham, 40.

56. Timothy Beal, "Reception History and Beyond: Toward the Cultural History of Scriptures," *Biblical Interpretation* 19, no. 4 (December 1, 2011): 360, https://doi.org/10.1163/156851511X595530.

57. Beal, 365–67.

translate ideas into objects" is particularly relevant.[58] The subjects of this study are engaged in the process of making meaning, which, as John Storrey writes, has been the stomping ground of cultural studies.[59] Thus, not only is this work about objects but it is also about the intersection of those objects with the Bible and the traditional topics of cultural studies, including race/ethnicity, education, gender, and sexuality. Furthermore, I am less interested in cultural studies from the perspective of "high culture." Instead, in this work I endeavor to examine Bible reception among the average visitors of the Creation Museum and the Ark Encounter. Thus, in this work the reader will find cues taken from students of culture like Jean Baudrillard and Stuart Hall, each of whom provide examples of how culture can be analyzed through popular materials. I found a unique opportunity in this work because, not only could I examine these cultural artifacts but I could also interact with the consumers of those artifacts. To do this I have employed an interview methodology, a type of ethnographic research rarely seen in biblical studies. It is my hope that this approach will illuminate Bible reception in a heretofore-unexplored manner. In addition to interviews (described in more detail later) I have considered other unconventional means of gauging individual responses to the Creation Museum, the Ark Encounter, and the MotB. For instance, thousands of people have posted reviews of each of these attractions on Facebook and TripAdvisor. This material is easily accessible and provides a window into visitors' more spontaneous responses (as opposed to the conditioning of a formal interview) to the Creation Museum and the Ark Encounter. Details on my approach to this material also appear below.

Reception criticism often assumes that text means words on a page and reading is the process of making meaning of those words. However, in this work I extend Bible reception criticism beyond text in the conventional sense and into the realm of other material objects. To date, the reception of biblical texts in other text products has dominated reception criticism in biblical studies. More often than not, those other texts are those widely deemed as literature. Recent works have extended biblical reception criticism into art and music and one need look no further than De Gruyter's *Encyclopedia of the Bible and Its Reception* for an example of a flagship work that attempts to collate all three. In this analysis, I propose that more attention must be paid to non-textual material objects in popular culture contexts. While there is much value in understanding how Shakespeare, Byron, or Blake understood the Bible and how their literature or art reflects these interpretations, it is also just as valuable to understand how "people on the street" understand the text. This is particularly relevant in today's social and political climate as the ideas explored in this study reflect some of the most contentious social debates in America today. Understanding the message that AiG wants to encode in its displays and then examining how AiG audiences receive

---

58. Michael Ryan, *Cultural Studies: A Practical Introduction* (Hoboken, NJ: John Wiley and Sons, 2010), ix.

59. John Storrey, *Cultural Studies and the Study of Popular Culture: An Introduction* (Edinburgh: Edinburgh University Press, 2010), 2.

that message should provide some insight into the influence of biblical texts in social debates that exploit biblical authority, including evolution, creationism, and science education.

Reception Criticism: Let's Just Ask Them

Focusing my analysis on material objects is not the only way in which this work deviates from other Bible reception studies. Again, taking cue from the suggestions of Tim Beal and Ibrahim Abraham, in this study I take seriously the need to get inside the minds of the readers. To realize this, I contacted visitors of the Creation Museum and the Ark Encounter and engaged them in conversation about their visits.

Despite recent developments in Bible reception criticism, Abraham maintains that an adherence to a method designed for the study of sacred texts hampers any additional development.[60] One consequence of this has been a focus on production (of the Bible or its receptions) while paying less attention to consumption. Abraham suggests that one area for potential development would be ethnographic research methods, something rarely done in biblical studies. Such a shift would further distance reception criticism from the analysis of high culture that dominated many studies while embracing popular culture as a location of meaningful analysis.

Analyzing how the great writers, musicians, and artists received and used biblical texts meant analyzing primary and secondary artifacts. If William Blake was still with us we could just ask him questions, thus making our jobs that much easier. Fortunately, for this reception study the subjects are still here, so it seems appropriate to ask them questions about how they experienced the Creation Museum and the Ark Encounter. I have endeavored to do just that. The Creation Museum and the Ark Encounter both have a policy against interviewing patrons on-site. Therefore, in order to locate interview subjects, I approached people who left reviews of these attractions on Facebook and TripAdvisor. Each interview occurred by phone and lasted between thirty and sixty minutes. I also offered an online survey for patrons with modified questions better suited for that format. Written reviews about the Creation Museum and the Ark Encounter posted by travelers on Facebook and TripAdvisor supplement the interviews and the online survey. Regarding the online reviews and the surveys, I cannot guarantee that those comments reflect people who have actually visited those attractions. Nonetheless, any comments on Bible presentation at the Creation Museum or the Ark Encounter are still part of the bricolage that forms this Bible reception study. This work is about perceptions and opinions and it remains true that even non-visitors have perceptions of these attractions. Finally, I have also considered the work of journalists and other writers commenting upon the Creation Museum, especially those who traveled to the museum.

---

60. Abraham, "Would You Adam and Eve It?" 32.

This work is not solely about Creation Museum and Ark Encounter patrons, however. It is also about AiG and MotB and their encoding of the Bible in material objects. Chapter 2 introduces the man, and the organization, behind it all. Here the reader will learn about Ken Ham and AiG. Since Ken Ham is a young-earth creationist, and since understanding the AiG argument requires a working knowledge of young-earth creationism, I introduce the reader to creationism (both young and old earth). Though important, in this research I attempt to avoid the creation science versus evolution debate as much as possible. However, it would be impossible to analyze AiG perspectives on the Bible without understanding its approach to science. Finally, taking Ken Ham as an author and the Creation Museum and the Ark Encounter as his texts, I consider Ham's target audience and the message he is attempting to encode.

Chapter 3 is a narrative walk-through of the Creation Museum and the Ark Encounter. Here the reader will find a detailed description of key displays in the order one would encounter them while visiting these attractions. This chapter introduces the main rhetorical features of the Creation Museum and the Ark Encounter that form the subjects of this analysis.

Chapter 4 considers the Creation Museum and the MotB as museum and the Ark Encounter as a theme park. Here I explore how the Creation Museum's adoption of the museum moniker stacks up against other museums. Likewise, I examine the Ark Encounter as a theme park and consider how the theme park genre governs visitor expectations. Studies of theme parks and museums have focused on both ambiguity and hyperreality. In this chapter, I explore the implication of each as it relates to these attractions and consider all three as storytelling institutions while introducing my concept of *biblical hiraeth*. A Welsh term, *hiraeth* (pronounced like hee-ryth), though difficult to translate into English, captures not only a sense of homesickness but also a certain longing and nostalgia. I found this term particularly helpful as *hiraeth* can describe a longing for a home that never really existed. As I argue in Chapter 4, AiG constructs an idealized image of the Bible and biblical periods that both creates and taps into a *hiraeth* for the Creation Museum and Ark Encounter visitor creating an imagined biblical home and an imagined biblical past.

Chapters 5 through 8 represent a deep dive into the manner in which these attractions present particular biblical narratives. Chapter 5 examines how the Creation Museum and the Ark Encounter flirt with pseudoarcheology and cryptozoology. Chapter 6 considers the Methuselah display at the Creation Museum, seeking to address why such a minor Old Testament figure merits an entire display. I compare the manner in which AiG imagines Methuselah to other recent pop-culture Methuselahs, notably Anthony Hopkins's portrayal in the 2014 film *Noah*. Chapter 7 analyzes a short film shown at the Ark Encounter. Titled *The Noah Interview*, this peculiar and amusing work is a rich source of information about how AiG has imagined Noah and his endeavors. Chapter 8 considers the Ark Encounter's *Fairy Tale Ark* display and considers how this display uses children's books to forward claims about Bible authority.

Chapters 9 and 10 transition to Creation Museum and Ark Encounter patrons and focus on their receptions of Ham's message about the Bible. More specifically, the goal of these chapters is to determine to what degree AiG interpretations of the Bible influence the patrons.

Throughout this work the reader will find a sprinkling of the MotB. Even though MotB opened in the middle of this research, as an important new public presentation of the Bible, it made sense to compare how MotB presents the Bible with the Creation Museum and the Ark Encounter. In Chapter 11 I delve into the ideological motivations of MotB and explore how that ideology is presented in purportedly neutral presentations of the Bible's world influence. In focusing on oppressions of various sorts, the MotB places the Bible within the context of struggles for religious freedoms in America, a narrative that supports many of the arguments made by the Green family in response to the Affordable Care Act.

Chapter 2

HAMMING IT UP WITH ANSWERS IN GENESIS

The AiG website records how Ken Ham, while visiting a secular Australian museum, overheard a father telling his young son that the ape-man exhibit represented his ancestors. Ham describes this moment as heartbreaking and lamented the fact that there was no creation museum to provide the truth.[1] For Ham, that truth is a biblical young-earth creationist worldview that rejects the evolutionist assumptions of the modern natural history museum. Moreover, the abandonment of this biblical perspective can account for many of the problems that plague the modern world. In the years since this encounter Ham would work to shore up the Bible's authority by constructing a young-earth creationist narrative through the institutions of museum and theme park.

Thus began the former Queensland, Australia, public school teacher's tectonic climb to the top of the young-earth creationist heap. While working in the public school system Ham would lecture on creationism during the weekends. Finally, in 1979 he left his teaching position in order to devote more time to promoting creationism and the fledgling Creation Science Foundation (CSF). The CSF emerged from two services run from Ken Ham's home, "Creation Science Supplies" and "Creation Science Education Media Services." Eventually Ham felt called to take his ministry to the United States. *Creation* magazine, originally founded and edited by Australian creationist Dr. Carl Wieland (1950–), was handed over to the CSF in 1979 and Ham formed a corporation to have the magazine distributed in the United States. Ham eventually made his way to the United States and worked for Films for Christ and engaged in some teaching tours sponsored by Master Books. His work led to the production of a film titled *The Genesis Solution* (1987) and over one hundred speaking and radio/TV engagements. Following this, he worked for the Institute for Creation Research and finally moved to the United States in 1987.[2]

---

1. "History of Answers in Genesis," Answers in Genesis, accessed September 9, 2016, https://answersingenesis.org/about/history/.

2. "History of Answers in Genesis." The Institute for Creation Research (ICR) was founded by former Virginia Polytechnical Institute professor Dr. Henry Morris in 1970. Located in Dallas, ICR focuses on research, education, and communication supporting young-earth creationism.

Soon after moving to the United States Ham began exploring ideas for a new creationist organization. By 1993 he determined that the science-oriented ICR needed a complementary organization that would better serve a nonscientific audience. Thus, together with Mark Looy and Mike Zovath, Ken Ham launched the Creation Science Ministries (CSM) in 1994, then a "sisterly" (but independent) ministry to Australia's CSF (with shared board members). In 1994, in order to get the CSM off the ground, Ham left California for Kentucky. Northern Kentucky was chosen because a broad swatch of the American population is within easy driving distance from this location. The name change to Answers in Genesis-US would also occur in this same year. This change was seen as necessary to reflect the idea that the ministry was not solely focused on creation but took as its mission reinforcing the authority of all scripture and promoting a biblical worldview.

By 2004 AiG had nearly one hundred staff members. About the same time cracks were beginning to show in the relationship between AiG-US and AiG-Australia (formerly CSF). These differences were largely over philosophy and operation (not doctrinal issues, as AiG-US points out) and, in 2006, the two organizations separated. In the meantime, Ken Ham had steadily built a radio following with his short, regular, broadcast titled *Answers—with Ken Ham*. Originally airing on forty-five radio stations, by 2006 *Answers—with Ken Ham* was broadcast on eight hundred stations. Ham was also reaching new audiences in print through *Answers Magazine*. Unlike the more science-oriented *Creation* magazine, *Answers* emphasizes a biblical worldview, features practical application of biblical principles, and includes scientific articles aimed at a broader readership. By 2007 AiG worldwide was founded and had translated materials and articles into more than seventy-five languages. Finally, the 75,000-square-foot Creation Museum opened on May 28, 2007, in Petersburg, Kentucky.[3]

Based on attendance numbers alone the Creation Museum has been a success. On February 4, 2016, keeping in mind that attendance figures are self-reported and difficult to verify, Ham wrote that the Creation Museum had surpassed 2.5 million visitors since opening in 2007. Perhaps inspired by this initial success, on December 1, 2010, Ken Ham announced, with Kentucky governor Steve Beshear and Ark Encounter LLC, a planned theme park anchored by a life-sized replica of Noah's Ark. The original press release noted that, in addition to the ark replica, the theme park would include additional exhibits like a walled city, animal shows, a Tower of Babel, a five-hundred-seat special effects theater, and a reproduction of a first-century Middle Eastern village.[4] Originally slated to open in Spring 2014, the Ark Encounter opened on July 7, 2016. At the time of its grand opening only the ark replica and the restaurant were completed, though additional attractions are still planned.

---

3. "History of Answers in Genesis."
4. "News Release: Ark Encounter (12/1/2010)," Answers in Genesis, accessed February 23, 2017, https://answersingenesis.org/ministry-news/ark-encounter/news-release-ark-encounter-12-1-2010/.

The press release announcing the Ark Encounter Theme Park cites a 2009 CBS News survey which found that the recovery of the remains of Noah's Ark would be one of the most important modern archaeological discoveries.[5] This proved inspirational for building a replica of Noah's Ark. Recognizing that Noah's Ark resonates with the popular imagination, Ken Ham saw in it an excellent evangelizing opportunity.[6] A study commissioned by the Ark Encounter and AiG predicted at least 1.5 million visitors annually would visit this ark-themed attraction.

The ark replica at the Ark Encounter aspires to as much authenticity as the function of the attraction, and building codes, would allow. Contrary to what some commentators expected, the Ark Encounter ark is not a sea-worthy vessel, does not sit in water, and there are no live animals on board. It is, instead, a building. Billed as the largest wooden structure in the world, the building façade that faces the arriving visitor is ark shaped, is mostly constructed from wood, and rests upon a series of concrete piers. The wooden beams and frames within the structure are shored up by metal supports and are connected by large bolts. Three concrete towers, housing stairwells, elevators, and restrooms, form most of the building's backside. There are plenty of building materials and methods employed here that would not have been present in Noah's time. However, this ding in authenticity was perhaps countered by employing Amish carpenters on the project, potentially giving it that "old-timey" feel. Nonetheless, any images of blue-shirted craftsmen hand forming and placing each piece of wood should be dispelled. Very modern construction techniques were brought to bear on this project, including *glulams* (laminated wood bends) and very large cranes.

Despite not building a sea-worthy vessel that was capable of floating on a body of water, Ark Encounter designers used other methods to give the ark an aura of authenticity, and consequently, authority. Central to this was matching the size as described in Gen 6 and creating a shape (about which no information is given in the Bible) that would be believable for a vessel this size meant to survive a catastrophic flood. The appearance of the ark is so critical that a February 13, 2011, Ark Encounter blog post addressed this issue by claiming that various portrayals of the ark have a direct effect on the believability of the Genesis flood narrative. According to AiG, for an ark replica to be believable, a realistic size and shape—well suited to surviving worldwide flood—must be presented.[7] Ark Encounter designers used the dimensions listed in Gen 6:15 that specified an ark 300 cubits long by 50 cubits wide by 30 cubits high. To translate cubits into feet, the Ark Encounter chose the long cubit based upon the measuring rod unearthed by Eckhard Unger in 1916 at the ancient Sumerian city of Nippur. Based upon this

---

5. "News Release."
6. "News Release."
7. "Mything the Boat," Ark Encounter, accessed February 23, 2017, https://arkencounter.com/blog/2011/02/23/mything-the-boat/.

standard a long cubit is 20.4 inches which in turn produced an ark replica that measures 510 feet in length, 85 feet wide, and 51 feet high.[8]

The Ark Encounter freely admits that most of the details about exact construction techniques, what Noah and his family looked like, or the type of clothing that they wore, are unknown. However, they also point out that researchers of ancient Near Eastern cultures can make targeted educated guesses (AiG sometimes uses the terms "historical fiction" and "artistic license").[9] Referencing scholarship on ancient Near Eastern history further conveys a sense of authority for Ark Encounter displays. Likewise, the methods employed for creating many of the ark's displays further add to the authenticity. Even the clothes matter as the Ark Encounter desires to portray life during Noah's day as accurately as possible.[10] For instance, tailors hand-stitched the clothing worn by the mannequins depicting Noah and his family from hand-dyed fabrics decorated with designs reminiscent of ancient Near Eastern clothing. Noah is dressed in blue throughout the display and images from biblical stories, including a human heel treading on a serpent (cf. Gen 3:15), have been stitched into his garments.[11] The same principle applies to the jewelry made for the female mannequins populating the ark. Employing educated guesses, the jewelry is based upon historical research and utilized materials that would have been abundant in the ancient Near East, including glass, stone, and seeds.[12]

This desire for historical authenticity is intended to sway the minds of doubting Christians, those who choose to see the Old Testament as metaphorical at best and irrelevant at worst. The display's authenticity is meant to communicate the idea that the Bible's narrative is historical and the Ark Encounter can demonstrate how. The Ark Encounter wants the visitor to understand that Noah could have placed all the necessary animals on the ark and only eight people could have managed the day-to-day tasks of such a venture. However, a lot of creative imagination is required to demonstrate the reliability of AiG claims. For example, regarding the number of animals on the ark, Ken Ham and others at AiG maintain that most people vastly overestimate the number, and size, of the animals taken onto the vessel. In order to make this argument, Ham draws attention to Gen 6:19–21 where Noah is instructed to bring animals according to their "kind" (Heb. *min*). For AiG writers, this hearkens back to the Genesis creation narrative where God made the animals according to their kinds (Gen 1:24). Ham maintains that a "kind" can be

---

8. "Putting the Ark into Perspective," Answers in Genesis, accessed August 15, 2018, https://answersingenesis.org/noahs-ark/putting-the-ark-into-perspective/.

9. "Noah Is Stylin'," Ark Encounter, accessed March 13, 2017, https://arkencounter.com/blog/2016/04/19/noah-is-stylin/.

10. "Noah Is Stylin'."

11. "Noah Is Stylin'."

12. "What Kind of Jewelry Did Noah's Family Wear?" Ark Encounter, accessed March 13, 2017, https://arkencounter.com/blog/2016/06/09/what-kind-jewelry-did-noahs-family-wear/.

loosely understood as a type of "family" in a taxonomic category from which all subfamilies are descendant.[13] One technical term for "kind" in creationist circles is *baramin*. Devised by young-earth creationist Frank Lewis Marsh (1899–1992) *baramin* is a compound comprised of the Hebrew word *bara* (BDB shape, create) and *min* (BDB kind, species). Predictably, the study of *baramins* is *baraminology*.

Several things follow from this. First, AiG argues that Adam named categories of animals rather than each individual animal.[14] This may be imagined as something like Adam saying "this is cat" rather than "this is a lion, and this is a tiger, and this is a panther." In fact, according to AiG, lions, tigers, and panthers would be descendants of whatever it was that Adam named "cat." AiG does not really know what the cat kind would have looked like but asserts that it would have looked something similar to modern cats.

Second, Noah would have needed fewer animals than most imagine on the ark. Take dogs for example. Noah did not take two of every dog breed onto the ark; he took the dog "kind" (or *baramin*). All other dog breeds that exist today evolved from the dog "kind." Therefore, instead of needing space for 339 dog breeds, space was only needed for the *baramin* pair from which all other dog breeds descended. Based upon this idea of *baramins*, AiG and the Ark Encounter estimates that Noah would have required up to eight thousand animals on the ark (and they inflated that number, just in case).

Third, there is room for evolution—of a limited type—in the creation science of AiG. As noted above, all the animals in existence today (and some that are not) are descended from the *baramins* taken aboard the ark. In this limited form of natural selection AiG argues that evolution only occurs within each kind as kinds adapted to nature. AiG absolutely rejects what it calls the "mythical" molecules-to-man evolution and the idea that new kinds can emerge through the evolutionary process.[15] The original kinds were fixed in number when they were created by God.

What Is Creation Science?

Ken Ham and AiG read Gen 1 from the perspective of creation science (sometimes known as scientific creationism). Ronald Numbers, in his effort to concisely define creation science, points to the definition spelled out in the 1981 Arkansas law that mandated equal treatment between evolution and creationism in public schools. The law defined creation science as including

---

13. "How Many Kinds?" Answers in Genesis, accessed August 16, 2018, https://answersingenesis.org/blogs/ken-ham/2012/11/01/how-many-kinds/.
14. "Bara-What?" Answers in Genesis, accessed February 25, 2017, https://answersingenesis.org/creation-science/baraminology/bara-what/.
15. "Evolution Without Molecules-to-Man Evolution," Answers in Genesis, accessed March 15, 2017, https://answersingenesis.org/natural-selection/speciation/evolution-without-molecules-to-man-evolution/.

the scientific evidences and related inferences that indicate: (1) Sudden creation of the universe, energy, and life from nothing; (2) The insufficiency of mutation and natural selection in bringing about development of all living kinds from single cell organism; (3) Changes only within fixed limits of originally created kinds of plants and animals; (4) Separate ancestry from man and apes; (5) Explanation of the earth's geology by catastrophism, including the occurrence of a worldwide flood; and (6) A relatively recent inception of the earth and living kinds.[16]

Even more specifically, AiG adheres to a form of creation science known as young-earth creationism. Creation scientists maintain that the origin of the cosmos as described in Gen 1–2 is scientifically accurate. There are, nonetheless, two prominent positions about the earth's age that are deduced from this stance. Young-earth creationism, a position defended by AiG, holds that the earth is about six thousand years old. This puts young-earth creationists into the most conflict with secular scientific theories that maintain the earth is billions of years old. On the other hand, old-earth creationists still defend the scientific accuracy of Gen 1–2 but argue that the text does not necessitate a young earth. This position allows old-earth creationists to syncretize their biblical beliefs with the conclusions of secular biology and geology on the earth's age.

A response to the widespread teaching of evolution in public schools, young-earth creation science emerged in an organized manner in the 1960s, heralded early in the decade by John C. Whitcomb and Henry M. Morris's text *The Genesis Flood: The Biblical Record and Its Scientific Implications* (1961). Widely lauded as the father of the modern creation science movement, Henry Morris (1918–2006) would continue to publish a number of notable texts on the subject, including the mammoth *The Genesis Record: A Scientific and Devotional Commentary on the Book of Beginnings* (1976). Holding a PhD in hydraulic engineering from the University of Minnesota, Morris served as department chair of civil engineering at Virginia Polytechnic Institute (Virginia Tech) while becoming a leading figure in the creation science movement. His work on creation science became increasingly controversial at Virginia Tech until, in 1969, Morris left the university after seeing "the handwriting on the wall that they didn't want me to stay there too long."[17] In 1970 Morris founded ICR, an organization that Morris led until his retirement in 1996.

The perspectives outlined in *The Genesis Flood* foreshadow many of the arguments made by AiG. For Henry Morris, the lynchpin to young-earth creation science is Noah's flood. Even prior to the work of Morris, early proponents of young-

---

16. Numbers, *The Creationists*, x.

17. Kevin Miller, "Former Virginia Tech Professor Opened Floodgates of Creation Debate," Roanoke Times, accessed January 20, 2017, http://www.roanoke.com/news/former-virginia-tech-professor-opened-floodgates-of-creation-debate/article_c64307bf-5f70-5192-a313-98d1e85782cb.html.

earth creationism recognized that establishing the veracity of the flood was just as important as the creation event described in Gen 1–2. Led by creation science thinkers like George McCready Price (1870–1973), a flood geology emerged in the twentieth century as an alternative way of explaining the geologic column (the series of rock layers in which fossils are embedded). Secular geologists maintain that these layers were laid down sequentially over the course of millions of years by generally slow uniform processes. Counter to this, flood geologists argue that the geologic column is better explained by the action of the biblical flood. Reaching its most influential expression on *The Genesis Flood*, Morris argued that the geologic strata resulted from the hydraulic sorting that occurred during the flood. Hydraulic sorting describes the process whereby water sorts material and causes small, dense particles to sink faster than lighter particles. Morris explains the sequence of fossils in the strata according to this hydraulic process supplemented by his observations that the fossil record, progressing from marine to mammal, could also be explained by the rising flood waters. Those creatures that did not have the option to climb to higher ground (marine life) died first and were stratified first. As the waters rose the land animals drowned and were subsequently stratified. This explanation of the sequence of fossils also serves as an alternative explanation to the evolutionary idea of development from simple marine life to complex land animals.

The manner in which Morris understood science influenced Ham's later writing on the subject. For instance, Morris's "eureka" moment came while observing butterflies. Being an expert in structural design, Morris decided that it was highly improbable that such complex creatures would develop by chance and that special creation was required. In *The Genesis Flood* Morris claims that facts are not in dispute, only interpretations.[18] This later influenced Ken Ham's work on starting points, reflected in the Creation Museum's first display titled *The Dig Site*. *The Dig Site* depicts two paleontologists (each represented by a mannequin). One represents a secular scientist while the other claims to interpret his work from the basis of God's Word. They both use the same data; however, their interpretation of that data is informed by their starting points. In a further blurring of science and religion, Morris also argued that evolution and creation were equally scientific and equally religious. In fact, they are competing scientific hypotheses and both ultimately rest on faith.[19]

Morris's work had a profound impact on Ken Ham, who, on the occasion of Morris's death in 2006, declared Morris to be one of his heroes.[20] Likewise, Morris's *The Genesis Flood* was the first work on creation science that Ken Ham read and

---

18. John C. Whitcomb and Henry M. Morris, *The Genesis Flood: The Biblical Record and Its Scientific Implications* (Philadelphia, PA: The Presbyterian and Reformed Publishing Co., 1961), xxvi.

19. Numbers, *The Creationists*, 244–45.

20. "Dr. Henry Morris Has Died," Answers in Genesis, accessed January 20, 2017, https://answersingenesis.org/blogs/ken-ham/2006/02/25/dr-henry-morris-has-died/.

it had a major impact on the creation science movement in Australia.[21] Indeed, many of the theological positions expressed by Morris on the centrality of the book of Genesis in creation science are echoed in Ham's work, including a reaction against a perceived tendency on the part of modern Christians to dismiss Genesis as mythological or allegorical and thus irrelevant to modern Christian lives. Morris strongly disagreed, stating, "If Genesis were not historically trustworthy, then simple logic showed that neither was the rest of the Bible, including the testimony about Christ"[22] and "if the first Adam is only an allegory, then by all logic, so is the second Adam."[23] This position became the foundation for much of Ham's work with AiG for, as Ham argues, one cannot pick and choose which parts of the Bible are relevant and which are not. In fact, undermining the authority of one part of the Bible undermines the authority of all of the Bible which in turn weakens the Christian theological position and leads, as Ham attempts to demonstrate in the Creation Museum, to the degradation of society. Furthermore, Ham argues that rejecting the literal truth of Genesis makes little theological sense in light of Christian theology about Jesus and the redemption of humankind. If the Genesis narrative is to be taken as allegory (including the Gen 2 narrative of the fall) then for what reason would God have sacrificed the Son?

Science at the Creation Museum

In part, Ham's critique of evolution rests upon his division of science into two types: operational science and historical (origins) science. Ham defines operational science as the science that deals with things that are currently observable.[24] This form of science engages in repeatable experimentation on subjects that can be directly observed by scientists. Historical (origins) science, on the other hand, is an analysis of the past that is not subject to direct observation.[25] According to Ham, conclusions reached through origins science are more fallible because the events and processes being described are not subject to direct observation and experimentation. He finds biblical support for this perspective in Job 38:4 where God asks, "Where were you when I laid the foundations of the earth? Tell Me, if

---

21. "Dr. Henry Morris Has Died."
22. Morris, *The Genesis Record*, xii.
23. Morris, 22.
24. Ken Ham, "What Really Happened to the Dinosaurs?" in *The New Answers Book: 25 Top Questions on Creation/Evolution and the Bible*, ed. Ken Ham (Green Forest, AR: Master Books, 2006), 152. In Ham's debate with Bill Nye he hammered on the distinction between operational and historical science ad nauseam.
25. Ham, 152. Norman L. Geisler and J. Kerby Anderson, in *Origin Science: A Proposal for the Creation-Evolution Controversy* (Grand Rapids, MI: Baker Book House, 1987), also write about this distinction.

you have understanding."²⁶ As this portion of Job rehearses God's creative activity, it makes sense that Ham would turn to these passages in support of his creation science claims. Those familiar with Job 38–42 would also recognize these passages as God's response to Job's charge of injustice. Job is essentially criticized for speaking out on things about which he has little understanding and knowledge. Here, Job's lack of understanding is directly tied to his inability to witness, and ultimately in his inability to comprehend, the making of the cosmos. In Ham's hands these words are used to indict modern secular evolutionary and geological scientists who are also unable to view the processes through which the cosmos, earth, and life were created. For Ham, historical (origins) science is always going to be tentative without some sort of definitive guide that serves as a substitute for the lack of direct observation. That authoritative source comes from the only being present at the creation, and He left us His account of creation in the Bible.

While it is not my goal to wade deeply into the evolution/creationism science divide, it is nonetheless important to point out a few salient facts about how Ham and AiG understand science. For instance, this division between origins science and operational science suggests that natural laws may not be constant through time. While Morris was a bit vague on this issue in *The Genesis Record*, he is quite clear in his short work titled *Evolution and the Modern Christian* where he writes about circumstantial and demonstrative evidence (which is roughly equitable to what Ham calls origins and operational science). Because he views it as unobservable, Morris maintains that the evidence for evolution is circumstantial.²⁷ He goes even further by arguing that the question of origins lies outside the realm of science since it is not subject to scientific experimentation. "Since it is completely impossible to make any actual measurements or experiments on the origins of the universe or life or the various kinds of life, it is therefore also impossible for *science*, as such, to tell us about these things."²⁸ Furthermore, what science says about the past is just as much a faith perspective as what religion says about the past. Therefore, the best use of descriptive science today is to provide "insight into which type of faith is more reasonable."²⁹ There is one crucial young-earth creationist perspective on science; however, that ultimately makes Ham's creationism unscientific. Many would maintain that science builds on a preponderance of evidence without *a priori* assumptions. The presuppositionalism of Ham forces him to argue that all scientific inquiry begins with assumptions. His *a priori* assumption is that God is responsible for creation and he seeks to gather evidence to prove this assumption. This is not science as many secular scientists would understand it. What we have

---

26. Ken Ham, *Six Days: The Age of the Earth and the Decline of the Church* (Green Forest, AR: Master Books, 2013), 49.

27. Henry M. Morris, *Evolution and the Modern Christian* (Philadelphia, PA: The Presbyterian and Reformed Publishing Co., 1967), 18.

28. Morris, 21.

29. Morris, 43.

then, in Ham's young-earth creationism, is an anti-scientific organization adopting the tools and modes of science for its theological purposes.

Reading the Bible at the Creation Museum

When it comes to interpreting Gen 1, Henry Morris stated in *The Genesis Record* that the only way to interpret Genesis is not to interpret it at all.[30] Anybody who views all reading as an act of interpretation might find this a rather peculiar statement. However, on this Morris reflects a long-standing Protestant tradition asserting that the Bible does not need explanation because the Bible is clear and the "authority, meaning, and message of the Bible is self-evident."[31] This negative perception of interpretation rests upon the idea that if interpretation is happening, the reader is bringing his or her own ideas to the text rather than letting God, or the Holy Spirit, speak through and reveal the Bible's meaning.

A quick perusal of nonacademic (and sometimes academic) literature on Christian groups like AiG reveals a tendency to use the term "literalist" in an uncritical manner. As a moniker for describing an approach to Bible reading, at worst it is used in a derogatory manner and often signals unsophisticated and non-nuanced reading. Moreover, to be a literalist is further seen as a sign of an affiliation to fundamentalist religious communities. James Bielo addresses this in his book *Words upon the Word: An Ethnography of Evangelical Group Bible Study* where he suggests that biblical literalism is more about identity than it is a specific approach to reading. Bielo states, "To identify as a literalist is to claim affiliation with certain Christian traditions . . . and separate oneself from others."[32]

Ken Ham has addressed the issue of literalism on many occasions and maintains that there are many different genres of literature represented in the Bible, and he would agree that appropriate readings conform to those genres. For instance, Ham readily admits that there are metaphorical passages in scripture and identifies them as such according to context and genre. Therefore, establishing literary genre determines the reading approach one should take to particular biblical texts. In his discussion of Gen 1, Simon Turpin (general manager and speaker, AiG UK) writes about interpreting Gen 1 according to its literary genre, which he argues is historical narrative, while also accounting for metaphor and other literary styles.[33] To say that Jesus literally fed his body and his blood to his disciples when he said, "Take, this is my body" would make as little sense to Ken Ham as it would to

---

30. Morris, *The Genesis Record*, 54.

31. Candida R. Moss and Joel S. Baden, *Bible Nation: The United States of Hobby Lobby* (Princeton, NJ: Princeton University Press, 2017), 143.

32. Bielo, *Words upon the Word*, 49.

33. "Is Genesis 1 Literal, Literalism, or Literalistic?" Answers in Genesis, accessed March 1, 2017, https://answersingenesis.org/hermeneutics/is-genesis-1-literal-literalism-or-literalistic/.

anybody else. The governing principles for Bible reading are described more fully in the AiG article titled "Unlocking the Truth of Scripture." In this article, author and lecturer Brian H. Edwards lists the literary genres of the Bible, which he identifies as historical narrative, poetry, parable, epistles, and prophecy. Literalist approaches to reading are more likely to result from the readings of historical narratives. As Edwards maintains, if a narrative can be clearly defined as historical then one must assume that the events being described did occur. Poetry, on the other hand, uses figurative language and Edwards maintains that the reader would not take figurative language literally.[34]

What others might call literalism, readers like Brian Edwards would call the text's plain meaning. Properly identifying which literary genre a biblical text belongs to is crucial in determining the plain meaning of the text. Both Ham and Edwards would caution the reader against reading beyond the plain meaning. For this community, the text was meant to be easily understood with little arcane effort. Edwards advocates finding the plain meaning rather than something mysterious or hidden,[35] or, following David Cooper's well-known quip, when the plain sense of scripture makes good sense, seek no other sense.

In light of AiG's young-earth creationist theology, assigning Gen 1 to the genre of historical narrative is crucial because doing so allows AiG to read it literally. Simon Turpin denies the poetic nature of Gen 1 because, in his opinion, it has little figurative language and lacks the parallelisms that characterize ancient Hebrew poetry.[36] He likewise discounts the argument that symmetries in Gen 1 indicate a theological document by pointing out that, even if it were a theological document, this would not preclude the text from containing historical information. He argues the same regarding poetry, which seems to undermine his claim that genre dictates reading conventions. Turbin also maintains that the predominant interpretation of biblical passages—the weight of tradition—also matters greatly. By way of example, Turpin notes that from Augustine to Calvin the predominate understanding of the Hebrew word *yom* (day), was the twenty-four-hour day. Thus, authority should be given to that interpretive tradition and the days of Gen 1 should be understood as standard twenty-four-hour days instead of days of indeterminate length. This is an appeal to authority that leaves little room for advances in our understanding of ancient texts and the cultures from which they emerged. For instance, the period in which interpretations of Gen 1 began to shift away from a young-earth position, the eighteenth and nineteenth centuries (according to Turpin), coincides with the rediscovery of the Bible's lost cultures (ancient Israel's neighbors) and the emergence of higher criticism. With thousands of cuneiform texts coming to light, more information than ever was being shed upon the cultural milieu of the Bible, including how ancient Near Easterners understood creation. Turpin credits

---

34. "Unlocking the Truth of Scripture," Answers in Genesis, accessed March 1, 2017, https://answersingenesis.org/hermeneutics/unlocking-the-truth-of-scripture/.
35. "Unlocking the Truth of Scripture."
36. "Is Genesis 1 Literal, Literalism, or Literalistic?"

people like Augustine and Luther for interpretations based upon the information they had, but it seems shortsighted to adopt a position that does not allow for new readings when new information comes to light.

How meaning is derived from the Bible is an urgent issue for Ken Ham and AiG. At its heart this is an issue of authority, and statements by Ham and his associates clearly imply that no postmodern shenanigans are allowed. Tim Chaffey, current content manager for the Attractions Division of AiG[37] and an author whose essays often appear in Ham's edited volumes, cautions against what he views as postmodern Bible interpretation. In the chapter titled "How Should We Interpret the Bible, Particularly Genesis 1–11?" Chaffey demarcates postmodern approaches to the Bible, whereby the reader can determine what a passage means, and the "author's intended meaning" (AIM).[38] For Chaffey the ideal hermeneutical method is to seek the author's intended meaning rather than forcing meaning into the text from the outside (eisegesis). God worked through people in different contexts using different literary genres; therefore, some work is required to determine God's intended meaning. Chaffey and Ham have developed principles for finding this meaning.[39] First is careful observation of the text. This means asking oneself what the text says and considering tense, speaker, word choice, and repetition, among other things. Second is determining the context of the text. The immediate passages in which the text is embedded, and even the particular book, can clarify the meaning of words, phrases, or sentences. Chaffey even extends this to a consideration of the "flow of history," which means placing the passage in the context of the pre-fall, pre-flood, pre-Mosaic Law, post-exile, Christ's earthly ministry, post-resurrection, or post-Pentecost periods.[40] Third is accepting the clarity of scripture. Chaffey maintains that God wants humans to understand His Word and would thus communicate in a way that humans can understand. This does not mean there are no difficult passages, but rather, the overarching themes of God's Word are clear. Therefore, there is no need to look for hidden meaning in the text. Next one should compare scripture with scripture. This principle rests on the belief that God cannot lie or contradict himself and, therefore, one passage in scripture will never contradict another. Finally, one should assign the proper literary classification to a text (the four categories being history, poetry, prophecy, and epistles) and one should be informed by the church's historical view.

This method is meant to identify the writer's intended meaning and to prevent the "bizarre" interpretations Chaffey associates with postmodern reading. For Chaffey, the hallmark of postmodern reading is the assumed right of readers to

---

37. "Tim Chaffey," Answers in Genesis, accessed October 21, 2016, https://answersingenesis.org/bios/tim-chaffey/.

38. Tim Chaffey, "How Should We Interpret the Bible, Particularly Genesis 1–11?" in *Six Days: The Age of the Earth and the Decline of the Church* (Green Forest, AR: Master Books, 2013), 222.

39. Ham, *Six Days*, 72–74.

40. Chaffey, "How Should We Interpret the Bible?" 227.

decide for themselves what a passage means and deciding truth for herself.[41] In sum, Chaffey would not take kindly to many of the assumptions that underlie reception criticism. We know that reception criticism originated in questions about where meaning in a text is derived, from the author's intent or from the activity of the reader. Clearly Chaffey argues that meaning is derived from the author's intent and to help drive this point home he uses hypothetical examples of "postmodern" reading that amount to little more than exercises in *reduction ad absurdum*. For instance, he asks his readers to imagine a conversation in which one friend says to another that he is going to drive to work the following morning. Chaffey asserts, "If the post-modern approach is accurate and meaning is determined by the recipient of the message, then perhaps your friend is really just telling you that he likes pancakes."[42] Of course, declaring one's love for pancakes is a good message to deliver at every possible opportunity! Chaffey's understanding of what he calls "postmodern" discourse fails to recognize that communication and interpretation still follow rules, be it the mode of interpretation set against Jauss's horizon of expectations or Fish's interpretative communities.

Writing the Creation Museum

Suggesting that the Creation Museum may be read like a text may seem odd in light of the Creation Museum's self-presentation as a museum.[43] Considering that one function of text, image, or object is communicating information, it makes sense to talk about visitors "reading" the Creation Museum. Mieke Bal used the idea of "visual textuality" in her analysis of art reception to capture the idea of "images-as-text."[44] By using non-textual displays and a copious amount of writing, the Creation Museum presents the viewer with both image-as-text and text-as-text.

It would be easy to assume that the purpose of a museum like this would be to "save the lost." Though AiG is happy with that outcome, it was not Ken Ham's primary goal in creating the Creation Museum and the Ark Encounter. Instead, the Creation Museum's primary purpose is to educate the saved. Ham wants believers to understand that the manner in which they understand Gen 1 has implications for how the remainder of the Bible is understood. Additionally, reading the

---

41. Chaffey, 222.
42. Chaffey, 225.
43. Susan L. Trollinger and William Vance Trollinger, in *Righting America at the Creation Museum* (Baltimore, MD: Johns Hopkins University Press, 2016), offer an excellent analysis of the Creation Museum as museum.
44. Caroline Vander Stichele, "The Head of John and Its Reception or How to Conceptualize 'Reception History,'" in *Reception History and Biblical Studies: Theory and Practice*, ed. Emma England and William John Lyons (London: Bloomsbury T&T Clark, 2015), 83.

Bible incorrectly (as defined by AiG) has a negative impact on the health of the larger Christian community. The only correct reading of Gen 1 is a young-earth creationist reading.

Ham argues against the more popular notion that vast amounts of time can be assumed to have accompanied God's creative work. This idea is often expressed in the so-called gap theory and derives from the manner in which theologians understand the Hebrew word *yom*, the word most often translated as "day" in the Gen 1 creation narrative. The gap theory argues that a vast amount of time can be assumed to have passed between Gen 1:1 and Gen 1:2. One form of old-earth creationism, also known as ruin-reconstruction, argues that Gen 1 tells the tale of two creations. The first act of creation rather vaguely notes that God created the heavens and the earth. Following this, a period of millions of years passed during which the cosmos evolved into its current state and the earth assumed the general features familiar to us today. There was then a global catastrophe that left the earth "formless and void" and covered in water, ready for the creation described from Gen 1:2 onward. Some old-earth creationists place the rebellion of Lucifer in this gap and argue that this rebellion lead to the first worldwide flood, known as Lucifer's Flood, that covered the earth with the waters of the deep (Heb. *tehom*).[45]

A second common method of aligning old-earth creationism with Gen 1 is the day-age theory. Genesis 1 describes creation as occurring over a series of days, following the familiar format "there was evening, and there was morning, the first day," proceeding through six days of creation. Some commentators maintain that Hebrew *yom* can be understood as an indeterminate amount of time, thus asserting that a day for God could have been thousands of years. This idea extends the age of the earth in a manner that allows the necessary time for natural geologic and evolutionary processes to occur.

Ken Ham leaves no doubt that he vehemently disagrees with these old-earth perspectives and all of their derivatives. Ham argues that Hebrew *yom* in Gen 1 means a literal twenty-four-hour day and that creation occurred over six literal days.[46] Regarding a gap between verses 1 and 2, Ham maintains that such an interpretation amounts to *eisegesis*, a reading that forces the reader's own preconceived ideas, ideas from outside of scripture, onto the text.[47] To do so violates Ham's hermeneutical principles outlined earlier. Instead, the proper mode of reading is *exegetical*, which Ham describes as "looking at Scripture and attempting to flesh out meaning based on the plain words, the genre, the context, other scriptural references, and so on."[48]

---

45. Numbers, *The Creationists*; Raymond A. Eve and Francis B. Harrold, *The Creationist Movement in Modern America*, Social Movements Past and Present (Boston, MA: Twayne Publishers, 1990).

46. Ham, *Six Days*, 187–88.

47. Ham, 187.

48. Ham, 187.

One important audience that Ham seeks to reach are those Christians who have accepted an old-earth reading of Gen 1 or have accepted secular explanations about the origin of the cosmos.[49] While this is not a matter of salvation for Ham, it does have important cultural implications. First, the authority of the Bible is undermined if Christians reject what ought to be accepted literally. Second, Ham maintains that the crucifixion of Jesus does not make sense if Genesis is not understood as history as it is written. Third, when Bible authority is undermined in this manner, culture is left rudderless, paving the way for the social problems outlined at the Creation Museum.

There is no better substitute for identifying these themes than walking through the Creation Museum and the Ark Encounter. It would be impractical to send all you readers there, which is where I come in as your tour guide. In the next chapter I will guide you through the Creation Museum and the Ark Encounter where we will identify the themes described earlier and examine how AiG is engaged in interpretation despite paradoxically distancing themselves from overt Bible interpretation.

---

49. James S. Bielo, *Ark Encounter: The Making of a Creationist Theme Park* (New York: New York University Press, 2018), 88.

Chapter 3

MOON POOLS AND POOP CHUTES

During an April 2017 interview with an Ark Encounter patron named Charlotte, I asked her how her visit to the Ark Encounter changed how she thought about the biblical flood narrative. She responded, "It made it a lot more real . . . it put it into perspective that this could actually happen, that this boat could actually do what the Bible said it could do."[1] When people talk or write about the Creation Museum or the Ark Encounter there is a strong experiential element that is hard to understand if you have not visited these attractions. As Charlotte demonstrates, what visitors often take away from the visit is tied to the physical presentation of biblical narratives in these spaces. Though AiG promotes presenting the Bible without interpretation, interpretive choices are evident, and the manner in which the Bible story is told at the Creation Museum and the Ark Encounter is not neutral. In the pages that follow I seek to give the reader a sense of what visiting the Creation Museum and the Ark Encounter is like in addition to revealing some of the most important themes evident in the displays.

The Creation Museum

Visiting the Creation Museum felt a bit like lurking in a community that is not one's own. Standing before my open car trunk preparing the tools of my trade (really, just gathering paper and pens) I surreptitiously observed others as they prepared for their journey into the Bible. The tour buses disgorged their excited occupants across the lot. Closer to me families pulled strollers from SUVs and minivans bearing plates from across the nation, some with bold yellow "Don't Tread on Me" tags or displaying Christian-themed bumper stickers—"1 cross + 3 nails = 4gvn"—like badges. I followed chatting families and squirrelly kids into the museum and watched the crowd mill around the portico hallway entrance exhibit known as the *Dragon Legends* display. At this point I began to understand why I felt conspicuous, few people seem to visit the Creation Museum alone. Like many pilgrimage sites, the Creation Museum and the Ark Encounter build

---

1. Charlotte, in discussion with the author, April 2017.

communities and the sense of connection between families and friends and this place was palpable.

Bounded by the exterior glass windows on one side and a faux stone façade on the other, the *Dragon Legends* exhibit funnels people toward the ticket counter and then into the museum's Main Hall and exhibit entrance. Not part of the original museum design, the *Dragon Legends* exhibit was added in 2013 to "up the cool factor" and to introduce Creation Museum visitors to AiG's perspective on dinosaurs.[2] The *Dragon Legends* exhibit suggests that dragons are an ancient name for what we now call dinosaurs. Furthermore, the display posits that in addition to being on Noah's Ark, dragons/dinosaurs survived the flood and continued to exist until recent times. The last poster in the exhibit, titled "Cowboys and Dragons," cites a newspaper article from an 1890 edition of the *Tombstone Epitaph* wherein two cowboys claim to have encountered a dragon-like creature. The relationship between dinosaurs and biblical creation narratives continues in the Main Hall where animatronic figures of children peacefully play alongside dinosaurs. Placing dinosaurs in ancient and contemporary human history has been one of the most sensational claims made by the Creation Museum. It is also a claim that is among the most impactful for museum visitors.

After spending some time in the jazzy new *Dragon Legends* exhibit, I proceeded to the Stargazer's Planetarium for my ticketed viewing of the planetarium show titled *Created Cosmos*. An examination of the vast distances between celestial bodies and the immensity of the bodies within it, *Created Cosmos* is meant to illustrate God's majesty and his "limitless power." During this journey through the cosmos the narrator points out purported problems with secular theories of universe formation and calls nebulae the "artwork of God." It was an interesting show and the description of the universe's immensity was thought provoking not just for me but also for the ladies (let's call them Betty and Tammy) sitting behind me. As I remained seated after the show I caught part of their conversation. What follows is a combination of direct quotes and paraphrase:

> Betty: "Totally mind boggling, the vastness [is] hard to imagine." Nonetheless, there is nothing better than us out there because "He created us to look like him." I just "err on the side of caution." It makes you wonder "who am I?"
> Tammy: I heard that "people become stars when they die," that the soul is energy. "Who knows?"

As I would come to learn in my journey through the Creation Museum and the Ark Encounter, there are those who accept AiG Bible interpretations quite uncritically. However, every once in a while (I later talked to some) there is a Betty and a Tammy applying their own theological spin to the displays and, sometimes, even expressing doubt about the arguments presented therein.

---

2. Bielo, *Ark Encounter*, 75.

Having now traveled the vast distances of the universe, I resumed my terrestrial journey back to the Main Hall and entered the formal exhibits of the Creation Museum. Faced with two paths, the right-hand path, having been designed for kids, seemed more adventurous. Being a big kid myself, I opted for this path. Wide and easy the right-hand path was not as I weaved through narrow sandy walls reminiscent of a slot canyon. Eventually this twisted path deposited me at the *Dig Site* display. Here, two mannequins depict paleontologists working at a mock dig uncovering the fossilized skeleton of the Utahraptor. The figure on the right is dark haired and looks younger than the figure on the left, who is gray and balding. They are surrounded by the implements of their trade, including brushes, pans, and aluminum foil for jacketing fossil remains.

These paleontological tools serve as an early introduction to the scientific rhetoric adopted by the Creation Museum. As exhibit placards explain, the science used by the Creation Museum is the same science used by secular organizations. The reason for differing conclusions has more to do with research starting points than with science. Thus, science leads a researcher who starts with the Bible to very different conclusions compared to a researcher who starts with Darwinian evolution. Despite being a frequent critic of modern secular science, the Creation Museum nonetheless recognizes the cultural authority of science and attempts to legitimate their endeavors with an aura of scientific credibility.

To the right of the dig site is a mock tent wherein sits a large Bible opened to Gen 1 with vv. 24–31 highlighted in yellow. The tools of the trade are not just trowels and aluminum foil after all, they also include the Bible. The yellow highlighting is reminiscent of the manner in which students mark their textbooks, suggesting the Bible as a counter to the textbooks typically used in paleontology classes. Genesis 1:24–31 describes the six-day creation event, starting with the creation of creatures that move about the ground and culminating in the creation of humans. AiG uses this passage to introduce another argument central to both the Creation Museum and the Ark Encounter: that animals were created according to their kinds (Heb. *min*).[3] *Min*, a single word that Richard Hess (writing for Biologos) says is of critical importance, is used by AiG to negate the Darwinian idea that species developed over time.[4]

These highlighted Bible passages serve as a visual reminder of AiG's "starting points" argument that the life sciences must begin with Genesis rather than Darwin's *On the Origin of Species* (1859) or *The Descent of Man* (1871). At this

---

3. BDB "kind" or "species." Originating from an unused root meaning to "portion out."

4. Richard Hess, "The Meaning of Mîn in the Hebrew Old Testament, Part 1," BioLogos, accessed December 7, 2018, /blogs/archive/the-meaning-of-min-part-1. Founded by Francis Collins, former head of the Human Genome Project and current head of the National Institutes of Health, Biologos seeks to demonstrate that the Bible and science mutually support each other. Biologos promotes an evolutionary creationism that asserts that God is the creator of life and that evolution (from an old earth) best describes the diversity of life.

point it becomes evident that the Creation Museum's theology is deeply grounded in presuppositional apologetics. Presuppositionalism is rooted in the neo-Calvinism of Abraham Kuyper (1837–1920) and further elaborated, expanded, and disseminated by the founder of the Westminster Theological Seminary, Cornelius Van Til (1895–97). Presuppositionalism maintains that all of our conclusions are informed by our presuppositions, what AiG here calls "starting points." Thus, the "assumptions that shape a person's worldview" will determine how that individual interprets the Bible.[5] Van Til's presuppositional apologetics maintained that the only rational starting point is God's existence and that God revealed truth through the Bible. Thus, the only rational way to interpret the world is through the Bible for "without faith [the nonbeliever] reasons from the wrong assumptions" leading to false perceptions about the world.[6] It follows that the Enlightenment idea of objective facts is an illusion because all reasoning begins with presuppositions that are not neutral. AiG theology also draws from Gordon Clark's (1902–85) form of presuppositionalism. Like others, Clark viewed the Bible as axiomatic and maintained that the Bible is self-authenticating and without logical contradiction.[7] At the Creation Museum, one finds this dialectic represented as God's Word versus man's word. Man's word is the Enlightenment ideal that the scientific method divorced from divine revelation reveals truth about the world. The God's Word approach is not anti-logic or anti-science but instead argues that proper reasoning must begin with divine revelation.

These heady theological arguments are distilled for the museum patron via a short looped video that introduces the *Dig Site* display. In this video the elder paleontologist (modeled as the older mannequin on the dig site) introduces the Creation Museum's presuppositionalism, the ideas of "same facts but different views" and "starting points." The elder paleontologist introduces his younger colleague, Kim, who then explains that his starting point is an old-earth and Darwinian evolution.[8] This starting point leads him to the conclusion that the Utahraptor at his feet is millions of years old. The elder paleontologist then explains his starting point, which turns out to be the Bible and how he, looking at the same evidence, nonetheless concludes that this dinosaur can be no more than a few thousand years old. Despite being at such extreme intellectual logger heads, the two seem capable of working together without coming to blows.

Additional placards and posters in the *Dig Site* exhibit further emphasize the oppositions between man's word and God's Word. Taking man's word, here equated with "autonomous reasoning," as a starting point leads to evolution and old-earth

---

5. Molly Worthen, *Apostles of Reason: The Crisis of Authority in American Evangelicalism* (New York: Oxford University Press, 2014), 30.

6. Worthen, 30.

7. Gordon Clark and Cornelius Van Til had a famous dispute on the degree to which human knowledge and God's knowledge are the same.

8. Notice the rhetoric of the elder, wiser statesman versus the younger, more rash scholar.

geology.⁹ God's Word starts with the Bible and the Gen 1 creation, which, for the Creation Museum, includes dinosaurs, many of which were buried in Noah's flood.

Following the *Dig Site* are displays that further illustrate the different conclusions derived from man's word and God's Word. As the Bible is the primary source for God's Word, the Creation Museum works to shore up biblical authority by explaining how the Bible has survived numerous discrediting attempts spanning hundreds of years. These have included skeptical probing, attempted destruction, criticism, and replacement. A recent attack, and of primary concern for the Creation Museum, is the secular geological and evolutionary attack on biblical timelines that have undermined a young-earth chronology.

The *Biblical Relevance* display—complete with a Martin Luther mannequin nailing his 95 Thesis to the Wittenburg Church door—introduces the Reformation era concept of *sola scriptura*, the idea that scripture alone is the authoritative source for spiritual matters. The concept of *sola scriptura* is foundational for the Creation Museum's presuppositional apologetics. *Sola scriptura* holds that the Bible is the highest authority on the things about which it speaks. Therefore, for *sola scriptura* to apply, the Creation Museum and AiG must convince the visitor that the Bible does address the scientific matters under consideration at the museum.

Just as soon as *sola scriptura* is introduced, however, museum displays begin to demonstrate the consequences of abandoning scripture. One example is that of Charles Templeton (1915–2001), one-time evangelical superstar turned agnostic and author of *Farewell to God* (1995). Templeton renounced Christianity in 1957. Though his public renunciation occurred nearly a decade after entering Princeton Theological Seminary, the Creation Museum links the two and argues that it was the liberalizing of his Christian faith, through exposure to people and institutions that have compromised on the Bible, that led to his fall and inaugurated a life estranged from Christianity.¹⁰

This suspicion of modern higher education, while at the same time seeking legitimacy in the eyes of these same institutions, is one of the puzzling paradoxes of AiG. On the one hand, AiG reflects the fear of higher education found in many evangelical circles. In my own life, as a professor of religious studies, I have seen this in students who were advised to avoid my classes owing to a fear that I would undermine their faith. Speaking in terms of the so-called culture wars, higher education is perceived as a liberal bastion intentionally designed to produce results that support liberal causes and values. Many evangelicals avoid these institutions through home schooling and parallel Christian-themed organizations. Nonetheless, there remains an envy of secular higher education and a recognition that secular educational institutions, especially in the sciences, are afforded a great deal of authority in American culture. This vast pool of potential authority is too

---

9. Wall text, untitled, Creation Museum, Petersburg, KY.

10. "The Templeton Connection," Answers in Genesis, accessed September 1, 2017, https://answersingenesis.org/blogs/ken-ham/2014/12/06/the-templeton-connection/.

valuable for AiG to reject outright. Thus, they simultaneously tow the evangelical line in criticizing such institutions while also seeking institutional approval.

Templeton's abandonment of scripture prefaces the following *Graffiti Alley* and *Culture in Crisis* displays. Approaching the end of the *Biblical Relevance* display, even before reaching the Templeton poster, one cannot fail to notice the rather ominous glow and unsettling sounds emanating from the entrance to *Graffiti Alley*. The display entry is framed by a gray pillar and lintel design evoking an entryway to a dark underworld, something like Dante's circles of hell. An eerie red light emanates from the entry while the sounds of sirens echo in the distance.

Entering *Graffiti Alley* one first faces graffiti that reads "Modern World Abandons the Bible," setting up an explicit connection between the Bible, cultural decline, and safety. The first half of the display is a walk down narrow, twisted, and dark alleyways that evoke fear and indicate that without the Bible one's path is not safe, straight, clear, or easy.[11] Three different walls are plastered with magazine and newspaper covers, overlapping and peeling like old concert bills pasted to a city wall. A variety of themes and issues are highlighted, including headlines like "What If There's No Hell?," "Up from the Apes," "Is Any Place Safe?," "The War on Christians," "Abortion: The Battle of Life vs. Choice," and "The Mind of a Killer." Other images complete this collage of destruction and decay, including the burning and destruction of the World Trade Center twin towers, fetuses, skulls, and guns.

Rounding the corner from the *Graffiti Alley* one arrives at the *Culture in Crisis*, represented by a model suburban home where various domestic scenes play out in the home's windows. The museum patron adopts the role of peeping tom while peering through mock windows that play video vignettes of a broken family that has abandoned the Bible. In one room a teenage boy looks at porn while trying to convince his younger brother to do the same. Peering through another window the visitor eavesdrops on a phone conversation as a teenage girl worries that she is pregnant and contemplates an abortion. Behind the third window the family matriarch sits at a kitchen table gossiping while disrespecting her husband who lounges in a recliner tending to his own comfort. This final scene is particularly interesting as it perpetuates female gendered stereotypes and seeks to reify a view of gender relations that places the female as subservient to man. The placard that accompanies this video describes the wife as a gossip and as envious, backbiting, and disrespectful.

Across the mock street from this home the museum visitor learns that some churches may be contributing to this family's problems. On the opposite side of the suburban home the museum visitor gets to peep into a church service. Even those who go to church on Sunday engage in the same activities—pornography, premarital sex, gossip, and envy—as the unchurched. A wrecking ball that says "millions of years" has plowed into the foundation of the church, while inside a pastor questions the necessity of reading the Bible literally. The wrecking ball of

---

11. Lynch, "Prepare to Believe," 17.

evolution has left a crack in the church wall that runs across the street and into the suburban home. Evolution has clearly chipped away at the church's foundation and, consequently, is undermining American families. Outside the church the elder paleontologist from the *Dig Site* display (the young-earth creationist) is pushing a wheel barrow filled with bricks that he picked up from the shattered foundation of the church. The implication here is clear: the principles he outlined in the *Dig Site* display are the same principles that will reconstruct this church and save the families who attend.

The *Culture in Crisis* display is both a physically and a mentally uncomfortable vision of society that suggests the only solution to social woes is to start again with God's Word. Thus, it is time for a little time travel. Leaving the *Culture in Crisis* display the museum visitor enters the time tunnel, a rather trippy black tunnel pierced with lights meant to look like stars, leading to the Six Day Theater where a short film on the six days of creation plays. Very grand and uplifting, the film describes God's creative activity on each day of creation. The Six Day Theater introduces another argument central to the creationism wars: the idea that "day" in Genesis (Heb. *yom*) refers to the conventional twenty-four-hour day. This is done to counter the argument that day in Gen 1 was an indeterminate amount of time that could accommodate the views of old-earth creationists.

After being reintroduced to the Genesis creation narrative in the Six Day Theater, the visitor then views the *Wonders of Creation* exhibit. In this large, well-lit room, the wonders of God's created world are on display. This includes videos and posters detailing natural laws; the solar system; and the living world with its bacteria, DNA, and cells. Reflecting a theme that was introduced in the Six Day Theater, the Wonders Room also continues the argument about what constitutes a day in Gen 1. The purpose of the Wonder's Room is to demonstrate the interconnectedness of creation and to assert the necessity of a creator.

From this point onward the museum displays are organized according to what the Creation Museum calls the "7 Cs of History."[12] They are creation, corruption, catastrophe, confusion, Christ, cross, consummation. Following the Wonders Room, the visitor strolls through a re-creation of Gen 2–3 (Creation). Here AiG's creative imagining of biblical narratives begins in earnest. One observes Adam (fully naked, without a single body hair, and obviously missing his genitals) in the garden naming the animals. Adam and Eve (with her hair modestly arrayed over her breasts), lounge in a pool, recline among the ferns and forest wildflowers, and enjoy a cool swim—all under the watchful eye of a serpent hanging above their heads in a tree branch. The serpent is a harbinger of things to come as the following displays are about to take a very dark turn. The visitor again enters dark, twisted hallways, before encountering a display of Gen 3:6 in which Eve offers Adam fruit from the Tree of Knowledge. Eschewing the traditional apple (a nod toward textual fidelity), in Eve's outstretched hand museum designers placed red and white berries that look like large currants.

---

12. "The Wonders Room," Creation Museum, accessed September 7, 2017, https://creationmuseum.org/blog/2006/10/02/the-wonders-room/.

Most telling of all, and perhaps foreshadowing what appears in the next display, red stains coat the fingers of Eve's left hand, presumably fruit juice but looking very much like blood. Adam's hands are unstained, leaving Eve with blood on her hands and presumably the greater share of the guilt. This blood is a precursor to much more to come, including reproduction and pain in childbirth (Gen 3:16), animal sacrifice (according to AiG, initiated in Gen 3:21), and Abel's blood crying out from the ground (Gen 4:8).

According the Creation Museum's storyline, the world has now fallen and blood and death will be humanity's fate from this point forward. Following the Gen 3:6 display a couple more dark twists in the hallway lead to the *Cave of Sorrows*. Representing corruption (the second of the 7 Cs of History), the *Cave of Sorrows* is one of the most disturbing exhibits in the Creation Museum. The *Cave of Sorrows* takes the relatively small and local disturbances in the *Culture in Crisis* (which focuses on one anonymous family and one anonymous church) and expands them to a global scale. Just prior to entering the *Cave of Sorrows*, the museum patron is faced with a door, barred by multitudinous locks, upon which has been scratched "The World's Not Safe Anymore." Turning left at this door one enters a long narrow room with stark gray concrete walls. Large sepia tinted photographs of skulls, agonizing childbirth, tornados, drug addiction, starvation, and mushroom clouds adorn the walls. Above these images, a text, in large letters, reads, "All of creation suffers from the effects of God's judgment because of sin, anxiously awaiting the day when God's curse will be removed" with an explanatory note to see Rom 8:20–22.[13] There is a cacophony of sounds that include those of storms, crying babies, sirens, gunfire, breaking glass, and, to the perceptive listener, audio of Adolf Hitler. Deeper in the *Cave of Sorrows* projectors cycle through stark black and white images displayed on the concrete walls. Here again the visitor sees images of Hitler and the Third Reich, mushroom clouds, tornados, and drug abuse. Another placard declares, "This is not how it was meant to be!"[14] All of the calamity on display in the *Cave of Sorrows* is the result of sin. I noticed that few people linger in this display.

As a display prominently featuring death, the *Cave of Sorrows* recalls the biblical use of caves as burial places. From the earliest biblical narratives to the last, caves feature prominently. For instance, Gen 23:17–20 describes how Abraham secured a cave at Machpelah as a burial place for himself and Sarah. Of course, the most famous burial of them all, that of Jesus, was in a tomb hewn in rock (Matt 27:60). Despite being a place associated with death, caves are also places of sanctuary, hope, revelation, and rebirth. Thus in the Hebrew Bible David escapes Saul by fleeing to a cave (1 Sam 22:1) and there formed his guerrilla force from the aggrieved who sought him out. In a later episode, David hides in an Ein Gedi cave where he passes on an opportunity to ambush Saul

---

13. According to Rom 8:22, the "whole creation has been groaning in labor pains." AiG views Rom 8:18–22 as representing the results of God's cursing creation, that the earth had fundamentally changed, and that death had been introduced to the world as a consequence of Adam and Eve's sin.

14. Wall text, untitled, Creation Museum, Petersburg, KY.

within its confines (1 Sam 24:1–7). Furthermore, Ps 142 purports to be David's prayer for deliverance while hiding in a cave. In 1 Kings God's prophets hide in caves during Jezebel's prophet-killing rampage (1 Kgs 18:3–4). Also, in 1 Kings, Elijah, while hiding in a cave on Mt. Horeb, receives the word of God and is told to return to the wilderness of Damascus (1 Kgs 19:8–15). Caves as places of rebirth are well represented in world mythology, and the Bible is no exception. From the Japanese story of Izanagi's escape from the underworld to the resurrection of Jesus, the entrance into, and emergence from, caves are narratives about the conquest of death and rebirth. Therefore, as bleak as the Creation Museum's *Cave of Sorrows* is, it is not meant to represent the end. Exiting the *Cave of Sorrows*, the visitor encounters displays that explain the world's history as a result of corruption. With newly opened eyes the visitor comes to understand how human history can be accounted for through the sin of Adam, a story that culminates in a rebirth through the death and resurrection of Jesus.

Leaving the *Cave of Sorrows*, the corruption theme continues with a display of Adam and Eve presiding over the first blood sacrifice, animals killing for flesh, a sexy Adam toiling in the soil, and Cain killing Abel. Finally, entering Methuselah's tent one receives a warning that "something terrible is coming." Corruption had increased to the point that catastrophe was imminent (we deduce, in the form of Noah's flood). That Methuselah was chosen to deliver this message is a decision that is explored in a later chapter.

An exhibit featuring the building of Noah's Ark represents the third C of History (catastrophe). One of the largest, most detailed, and most popular displays in the Creation Museum, the portion of the ark on display is built to scale according to the size described in the Bible (though only 1 percent of the ark is represented here). An animatronic Noah supervises workers, most of whom appear not be Noah's family members. This is perhaps surprising given that the only people mentioned in Gen 6–9 are Noah with his wife and his sons, Shem, Ham, and Japheth, and their wives. Skeptics often point to the difficulty of building a structure of this size with just the eight people mentioned in the flood narrative. AiG counters that there is no reason to assume that Noah did not hire workers. Assumptions such as these, which come to be described as "artistic license" and "educated guesses" at the Ark Encounter, are used by AiG to expand the biblical narrative. Some of those among Noah's hired help are skeptical of the work they have been asked to complete, scoffing at Noah's seemingly foolhardy mission. Meanwhile, Noah continues to warn them of the coming judgment.

In many ways the Creation Museum's Ark display is the lynchpin to the museum's argument. As we earlier learned about young-earth creationism, since Whitcomb and Morris's *The Genesis Flood*, the only way to explain the earth's geological features is the hydraulic action of a worldwide flood. It is therefore imperative that AiG present a flood event that is, for the visitor, historically and scientifically plausible.[15] This is why Noah's Ark and the flood displays receive some of the most expansive and speculative interpretations. Here the visitor learns much about how

---

15. Bielo, *Ark Encounter*, 95. In his analysis, Bielo links plausibility and authenticity with the possibility of a conversion experience.

the Creation Museum imagines ark construction, including displays of workers boiling pitch and a description of the planking methods possibly used.

Many skeptics question how so many animals could have been adequately cared for on a vessel of this size for the time period(s) described in the Genesis narrative. Thus, the next display describes how Noah could have handled day-to-day operations on the ark. As we will later see at the Ark Encounter, AiG does not sugarcoat the flood event. Therefore, the *Voyage of the Ark* display includes a diorama of the ark rising on flood waters while a few remaining people cling in desperation to the last remaining mountaintops jutting above a new, vast, ocean. Rendered in miniature, the flood diorama shows people struggling to climb the last peaks, people fighting one another on top (one appears to be strangling another), others being stalked by tigers, while others lie about presumably dead. In this same room model cages demonstrate how animals were kept, watered, fed, and cleaned, while an animatronic Noah sits in his study (which suggests that Noah was no uneducated yokel and that, as an educated man, he may have had some knowledge of shipbuilding) answering questions about how the ark functioned.

After pausing for a moment to refute evolution and ancient earth theories, the Creation Museum resumes its tour of the 7 Cs of History with "confusion." Using the Tower of Babel incident (Gen 11) this display explains the origins of the various languages, cultures, and races. The confusion of tongues occurs because, once again, humans have disobeyed God and instead of going forth and filling the earth they have gathered together in Babel. The confusion of tongues forces people to disperse. Confusion offers the Creation Museum's solution to racism by noting that all humans are in fact one race, all descended from Noah, and ultimately from Adam. Thus, they argue, the modern notion of "race" is inaccurate. Displayed artifacts like slave shackles and Nazi memorabilia emphasize the evils perpetuated by this inaccurate notion of race. The Creation Museum, the Ark Encounter, and the MotB try to present themselves as progressive on race. AiG attempts this by disputing the notion of race. MotB, on the other hand, raises issues of racial oppression. In a later chapter both are explored as examples of a problematic color-blind racial discourse.

The final three Cs of history—Christ, cross, and consummation—are very briefly represented with a single poster for each. This might strike the visitor as being rather odd considering the centrality of Jesus in Christianity. However, it is important to remember that the Creation Museum's argument is that the literal truth of Genesis is the reason for the salvation offered through Jesus. Genesis is the first, and most important, starting place for a group like AiG that wants to uphold biblical authority and emphasize the consequences of abandoning even part of the Bible.

An Encounter with the Ark Encounter

Regardless of one's opinion on the events the Ark Encounter purports to portray, there is no doubt that the Ark Encounter's ark replica is a magnificent piece of architecture. Billed as the world's largest timber-frame structure (which is not the same as being the world's largest wooden structure),[16] exclamations of wonder fill the shuttle bus from the parking lot (one mile distant from the ark) as the ark comes into view. Sitting on a hill in the rural Kentucky countryside, one cannot help but relate the Ark Encounter's geographic isolation to the cultural isolation of the Christian organization who built the ark and many of the believers who visit. Time contracts and the visitor can take comfort in sharing Noah's isolation as he struggled with a project, held in disdain by his neighbors (despite the fact that Gen 6–9 does not mention Noah's neighbors, mockery, or any sense of isolation that Noah may have felt).

The parking lot shuttle deposits visitors quite a distance from the ark itself. On a cloudy day the timbers of Kentucky's new Noah's Ark are as gray as the sky—fitting, for the glowering clouds threaten to unleash rain as we rush to the safety of the ark's interior, sort of an accidental object lesson for the message being conveyed here by AiG. The distance creates a good opportunity, aided by the pond that sits near the shuttle drop off, for a selfie with the full length of the ark in the background. Those who are not prone to walking, or who cannot for health reasons, appreciate this selfie opportunity less.

On July 7, 2016, phase one of the Ark Encounter theme park opened in Williamstown, Kentucky. Described as a sister attraction to the Creation Museum, the Ark Encounter theme park was another project of AiG. Phase one of the Ark Encounter theme park included the opening of a full-size, according to biblical dimensions, wooden replica of Noah's Ark. Billed as the largest timber-frame structure in the world, this ark is 510 feet long by 85 feet wide by 51 feet high. Inside the ark are 132 bays with exhibits that educate the visitor on what life was like before the ark, construction of the ark, information about the flood, how animals were kept on the ark, and other information about the practical day-to-day operations of the vessel, as imagined by AiG.

The years preceding the opening of the Ark Encounter were fraught with controversy surrounding the project. These ranged from tax incentives offered by the commonwealth of Kentucky to criticisms that the amount of money and materials used to build the ark diverted resources away from different kinds of outreach. AiG faced many of the same criticisms while building the Creation Museum as well. In answering these criticisms, Ken Ham insists that the Ark Encounter was not built because of pride, idolatry, or greed (as a money-making venture). Instead, Ham envisions the Ark Encounter to be a message of hope delivered to a lost world.[17] Following Mark 16:15 and Matt 28:19, the Ark Encounter is a gospel meant to make disciples. The larger message embodied in

---

16. "More False Accusations Against the Ark Refuted!" Answers in Genesis, accessed March 29, 2017, https://answersingenesis.org/blogs/ken-ham/2016/01/26/more-false-accusations-against-ark-refuted/.

17. "Our Real Motive for Building Ark Encounter," Answers in Genesis, accessed February 22, 2017, https://answersingenesis.org/ministry-news/ark-encounter/our-real-motive-for-building-ark-encounter/.

the ark is that even though rebellion is in the hearts of humans, God still provided the gift of salvation.[18]

In reading Ham's thoughts on these issues, one gets a sense of how he places himself in Christian history, which he describes as being marked by people drifting away from God's Word, followed by God raising up people to call others back to the Word.[19] Ham describes how this spiritual battle has continued for six thousand years and how those six thousand years have been punctuated by moments when the Godly rise up to lead the people back to God. The reformation is one of those periods and Ham believes we are in the midst of a similar period today. For instance, Ham declared the opening of the Creation Museum and the Ark Encounter as historical moments of Christian outreach.[20] This is a time, Ham maintains, that God is choosing people to spread his message in unique venues, including Christian-themed tourist attractions.[21] Though he does not explicitly state so, it is hard to escape the conclusion, based upon the context of these statements, that Ham views himself as one of these special people chosen by God.

The ark sits on a series of concrete piers that raise the structure above the ground. On busier days people wait for entrance in long, snaking lines underneath the ark. The concrete piers and the bottom entrance into the ark demonstrate that, as critics gleefully point out, this structure is not built as a functioning ocean-going vessel. It is, as Ken Ham and Ark Encounter LLC admit, a building meant to house tourists and thus meets all the building code requirements for such a structure. Anybody who expects a sea-worthy vessel, perhaps floating in water, is bound to be disappointed.

Entry into the ark and access to its three display levels (the fourth-level restaurant is not yet open to the public) is gained via a series of centrally located ramps. Watching the flow of people up the ramps I was left with the impression of a modern reenactment of Noah boarding the boat, though in this case it is people rather than animals being gathered. If the first ark was meant to save all the animals, the mission of this new ark is to save all the people. The interior of the ark exudes a warm yellow/brown glow and the structure's largely unfinished wood looks like a Rocky Mountain lodge one might find in Montana. Modern building techniques appear in places with steel plates and bolts joining massive pieces of wood together. The central supporting timbers are of such a girth that no individual could wrap his or her arms around one. Standing in the middle of the ark one can look four stories up to the skylights placed in the roof.

Touring the Ark Encounter is a physically different experience compared to that of the Creation Museum. Much like the Bible itself, the Creation Museum

---

18. "Our Real Motive."

19. "Era of Christian Attractions Is Calling People Back to Christ," Answers in Genesis, accessed February 22, 2017, https://answersingenesis.org/ministry-news/ark-encounter/era-of-christian-attractions-calling-people-back-to-christ/.

20. "Era of Christian Attractions."

21. "Era of Christian Attractions."

has a linear story to tell and forces the visitor to experience that story from beginning to end along a narrow and predetermined path. Not so in the Ark Encounter. Incorporating a more modern approach to museum design the visitor has complete freedom in how they explore the exhibits placed therein. Once can start at the bottom and climb to the top, or the reverse, and walk completely from one side of the ark to the other. Displays are placed in separate bays that line the exterior walls of the ark, leaving the large central walkway clear.

The "same facts but different views" rhetoric of the Creation Museum gets a slight makeover at the Ark Encounter where it becomes "one world, two views." This slight reframing makes this rhetoric both more binary and more cosmological in nature. "Different views" implies a multiplicity of different perspectives while "two views" more clearly reduces the argument to God's Word versus man's word, a rhetorical device that is used at the Creation Museum to represent the biblical creation model versus the secular evolutionary model. "Same facts" becomes "one world" which suggests that in the proper interpretation of Genesis the very nature of the world is at stake.

The first level exhibits are rather sparse. There is a mannequin diorama of Noah and his family offering sacrifice on an altar. Following this are a series of cages from which emanate the sounds of various animals. On this floor, ark designers present the types of cages, and the feeding and watering systems that they imagine Noah could have devised. Many of the cages contain models of animals and introduce the visitor to the idea of "kinds" referenced in the Genesis creation narrative (Gen 1:21). In the Ark Encounter, "kinds" represent the same idea that "family" represents in mainstream biology. If the animals are not exactly recognizable, that is because they are the imagined ancestors of the animals that exist today.[22]

In addition to details on how the number and kind of animals were chosen for the Ark Encounter displays, the first deck also provides an overview of the seven days of creation as interpreted at the Ark Encounter. As with the Creation Museum, it is important that Ark Encounter designers define "day" from Gen 1 as the standard twenty-four-hour period, a concern that is central to young-earth creationist theology. Following the seven days of creation a series of posters emphasize the perfection of creation (it should be noted that this image of perfection reflected in Adam and Eve is very Caucasian). Flawless marriage, perfect authority, and perfect humanity are issues that arise again in later displays as the intellectual capabilities of ancient humans is explored vis-à-vis the possibility of ancient people constructing a vessel like the ark.

A prominent part of the Ark Encounter discourse is an insider/outsider debate wherein the criticisms of skeptics are addressed in various ways. For instance, there is a display that addresses the possibility of unicorns on the ark. The idea that the ancient authors of the Bible believed in unicorns derives from the KJV translation of the Hebrew word *reem* (BDB, wild ox) in a handful of animal-related passages

---

22. See above, page 49.

in the Hebrew Bible.[23] For example, this may be found in Job 39:9, which, in the KJV, reads, "Will the unicorn be willing to serve thee?" Bible critics are sometimes amused by these verses and use them to support the argument that the Bible is a book of fairy tales. Following a common exegetical technique related to these passages, the Ark Encounter historicizes these verses by arguing that unicorns are a reference to the rhinoceros or some other now extinct animal.[24]

We see here an impulse toward historicity and a downplaying of the mythological. One of the primary functions of the Ark Encounter is to encourage the visitor to understand the flood narrative as a historical event, not as a metaphor or a story. Therefore, it becomes imperative to remove every trace of the fantastic from the story so that the visitor comes away with a sense that this really could have happened. As we will see in the coming paragraphs, the Ark Encounter has to engage in a great deal of speculation in order to create this sense of historical plausibility.

The mechanics of operating an ark full of animals is the subject of the ark's second floor. Ark designers admit to a certain amount of speculation here, what designers call "educated guesses," "artistic license," and "plausible models." Educated guesses are an important part of my analysis in later chapters as this artistic license impacts how Ark Encounter patrons understand the Bible. Nonetheless, a series of exhibits demonstrate ways that eight people could have cared for thousands of animals. These exhibits include watering systems that could keep each animal watered for days at a time, refillable feeders that do not require filling on a daily basis, waste removal systems that require animals on treadmills, moon pools for waste disposal, and ventilation systems that rely on wave action in moon pools to push fresh air through the ark.[25]

There are some admittedly ingenious proposals here, and, as with the Creation Museum, the Ark Encounter wants the visitor to understand that Noah and his contemporaries were intelligent enough and had an appropriate level of technology to accomplish this engineering. Thus, a display of the pre-flood world disputes the idea that ancient peoples were knuckle-dragging cave dwellers. Displays maintain that humans were "intelligent and creative from the start" (perhaps even more intelligent than modern humans) and that pre-flood cultures had written language.[26] Indeed, going far beyond the details provided in Gen 6–9, the *Noah's Library* display is a testament to literacy and sophistication, with multiple shelves and baskets of scrolls, ink pots, pens, and Noah himself sitting at a desk grasping a pen above a partially written document. The ark itself is presented as evidence of ancient engineering acumen and the Ark Encounter

---

23. Cf. Num 23:22, Ps 92:11, Job 39:9–10, Isa 34:7.

24. "Unicorns in the Bible?" Answers in Genesis, accessed December 27, 2018, https://answersingenesis.org/extinct-animals/unicorns-in-the-bible/.

25. All of which are explored in more detail below.

26. Wall text, *Education,* Ark Encounter, Williamstown, KY.

maintains that the ancient pyramids are evidence of the type of engineering technology handed down from Noah (implying that Egypt's pyramids were built by Noah's descendants). Though there is a caveat that such narratives are derived from artistic license, the Ark Encounter even provides a backstory that explains how Noah could have acquired his knowledge of engineering, blacksmithing, and woodworking.

Strolling along the second floor the visitor eventually arrives at a rather peculiar display façade. Having so far experienced heady and serious displays about ancient peoples and their engineering capabilities, suddenly the visitor faces a display entrance framed by cartoon animals. The faux wood entrance to the *Fairy Tale Ark* display is topped by a lintel upon which crouch cartoon versions of animals, including a cow, elephant, and monkey (among others) against a rainbow backdrop. This display's purpose is to warn visitors about the dangers of so-called fairy-tale arks found in many Noah's flood depictions targeted at children. These images often include a small boat overflowing with cute and cheery animals flanking a smiling and waving Noah. After stepping through the display entry, the risks of fairy-tale ark imagery are made clear on a large wall placard, framed by a large serpent, which reads, "If I can convince you that the flood was not real, then I can convince you that Heaven and Hell are not real."[27] According to the Ark Encounter, fairy-tale arks are misleading because they downplay the reality of the biblical flood and place the ark on the same footing as other mythical and legendary narratives. To illustrate this, the Ark Encounter uses the 7 Ds of Deception (a companion to the 7 Cs of History found at the Creation Museum). Examined in more detail in chapter 8, the 7 Ds of Deception focus on how these images are deceptive, disorienting, and destructive.

AiG does not shy away from the fierce image of God implied by His worldwide flood. A much photographed display simply called *The Door* follows the *Fairy-Tale Ark* display. This door in the side of the ark, mentioned in Gen 6:16, is unadorned except for the subtle image of a cross projected onto the side facing the visitor. As one might expect, God sealing Noah and his family behind this door (derived from Gen 7:16) while those living outside faced certain doom raises many tough questions. Informational placards at *The Door* address if God is cruel, why death is a punishment for sin, and why God was compelled to judge the whole world. Playing off this door theology, the display quotes John 10:9 which reads, "I am the door. Whoever enters through Me shall be saved," thus illustrating the Ark Encounter's argument that the literal truth of Genesis is necessary to accept New Testament truth while linking the salvation offered to Noah to that offered by Jesus.

The popular third-floor displays depict family living quarters and the effects of the flood upon world geology. In Noah's living quarters the visitor views how the ark occupants lived rather comfortably. Living quarters are well appointed

---

27. Wall text, untitled, Ark Encounter, Williamstown, KY.

with furniture, beds, linens, rugs, wall hangings, and decorations. Ark designers must have imagined fielding questions about the sumptuous living quarters and addressed this in a display placard titled "Why Are the Living Quarters So Nice?" Again, as this display readily admits, a great deal of artistic license and educated guesses are employed while attempting to avoid contradicting the Bible. In the living quarters the visitor meets Noah's family and learns about, via the creative re-imaginings of the Ark Encounter, the personalities and the potential responsibilities of each while living on the ark.

Following this are the geological mechanics and global effects of the flood. As with many Ark Encounter displays, the *After the Flood* exhibits offer information about flood geology that is not strictly biblical. For instance, one proposal states that magma meeting seawater created massive geysers that spouted water high into the atmosphere that fell again as a global rainstorm. The earth's supercontinent eroded and the land shifted toward the continents that are visible today. Animals that look like pterosaurs soar above the ark as other animals leave the boat, thus suggesting that such creatures survived the flood and possibly lived among humans for quite some time.

As with the Creation Museum, the Ark Encounter devotes space to countering the idea that the Bible promotes racism. Though different in presentation, the Ark Encounter argument is quite similar to that put forward at the Creation Museum. The modern races descended from Noah's family members. The mannequins representing Noah's family feature skin tones and other physical features that would later represent the dominant racial traits of their descendants in the areas where each family group settled. Thus, Ham's wife Kezia is depicted with dark skin suggesting the origins of the dark-skinned peoples of Africa, the region where Ham's descendants are thought to have lived. According to the Ark Encounter, Noah's descendants gathered at Babel in defiance of God's command to spread across the earth, necessitating the confusion of tongues in order to disperse the people. Like the Creation Museum, to counter claims that the Bible supports racism, Ark Encounter displays argue that all people are descendants of Adam, made in God's image, are loved equally by God, and were all made as one race.

In contrast to the Creation Museum, the Ark Encounter does more to emphasize the technological acumen of ancient humans. Visitors learn that ancient humans had the technology to build a tower of Babel. The fact that similar ziggurat and pyramidal structures occur in diverse cultures after the dispersion of Noah's descendants is taken as evidence of direct historical descent from the Tower of Babel. The Ark Encounter even addresses popular pseudoscientific and pseudoarcheological speculation about the origins of the ancient technologies used to build towers and pyramids. In case you were wondering, the Ark Encounter argues against aliens introducing this technology.

Of course, explaining pre-flood technological potential serves to support the idea that Noah had the knowledge and the technology to build a structure the size of the ark. As in other AiG materials, the Ark Encounter maintains that we just do not know how advanced the pre-flood cultures were, though proficiency with metal and stone is assumed. Indeed, it is even argued that the Tower of Babel event was a technological setback as the nation scattering surely slowed the pace of technological innovation.

The Ark Encounter turns its perspective on the intelligence of ancient humans against evolutionists. A "One World, Two Views" poster maintains that humans, as created beings, were created from the beginning to be highly intelligent and "capable of remarkable achievements."[28] In contrast the Ark Encounter portrays the secular evolutionary perspective as depicting human ancestors as "unintelligent grunting brutes."[29] The Ark Encounter admits that ancient cultures did not have technology equivalent to modern levels. However, frequently both the Ark Encounter and the Creation Museum dangle tantalizing hints about "sophisticated technologies" while remaining vague enough to avoid committing to "educated guesses" on what those technologies might have been. As will be demonstrated in a later chapter, AiG has a flirtatious relationship with pseudoarcheology and cryptozoology.

Walking through the Creation Museum and the Ark Encounter one is left with the impression that the Bible alone is not a sufficient source upon which to build this museum and theme park. The gaps in the biblical narrative, the places where visitors will likely have questions, become the places where AiG engages in its most creative interpretive activities. AiG, as an interpretive community, is governed by the reading conventions of the young-earth creationist movement. So, while they fill the gaps in the biblical narrative with their own "eddies and undercurrents" it is still a reading governed by the conventions of this interpretative community. It is this interpretive community that is the subject on the next chapter.

---

28. Wall text, *One World Two Views*, Ark Encounter, Williamstown, KY.
29. Wall text, *One World Two Views*.

Chapter 4

BIBLICAL HIRAETH AND STORIES OF HOME

On my bookshelf there sits a deluxe Jesus action figure, complete with plastic fishes and loaves, mini amphorae of wine, and featuring, most notably, glow in the dark hands. I have a second Jesus action figure that has a wind up "walk on water action" that allows him to glide across a tabletop. In some sense the form and functions of these items are governed by the genre expectations of toys. Though the concept of genre is often associated with literature and art, it is true that other physical objects conform to genre standards. For example, the meaning of an object displayed in a museum will be informed by the conceptions associated with museums. In contrast, an object labeled as a toy will be understood and handled according to the standards of toys. For example, many toys, like bobble heads for instance, tend to toward exaggeration. My Jesus toys, based as they are upon biblical narratives, tend to exaggerate those features of the narrative that are already outstanding. In this way they function like a caricature wherein an outstanding facial feature, like a big mustache, gets exaggerated to comedic proportions. Thus, in the translation to material object we find that complex images and narratives can become, if not exaggerated, at least emphasized. To some degree this is similar to what AiG has done with the Creation Museum and the Ark Encounter. These attractions function much like caricatures of the Bible wherein certain features of the text become exaggerated at the expense of other portions of the text.

As physical places, the Creation Museum, the Ark Encounter, and MotB conform to particular genre expectations. As self-proclaimed museums (Creation Museum and MotB) and a theme park (Ark Encounter) these attractions tap into specific genres of physical space that frame how people encounter these objects. Moreover, each of these attractions is a storytelling institution and, thus, the story they are trying to tell is partly governed by the genre expectations of the museum and theme park. As the concept of the museum carries a great deal of prestige and authority in America, both the Creation Museum and the MotB, as storytelling institutions, are able to use these genre expectations to further obfuscate their role as storytellers and Bible interpreters. Furthermore, the manner in which these biblical narratives are constructed both supports and creates a certain longing, homesickness, and nostalgia—what I will call *biblical hiraeth*—in the visitor.

Storytelling Institutions

To label something as a museum creates a whole host of expectations. In this it is useful to compare the Creation Museum with the MotB. Both label themselves as museums, but they each approach the concept of the museum differently. Despite presenting itself as a museum, without an accessioned collection the Creation Museum does not conform to the commonly understood definition of a museum.[1] What one finds at the Creation Museum are many animatronics, mannequins, reproductions, and placards. On the other hand, the MotB does have a cataloged collection of artifacts which brings it closer to the conventional definition of a museum. While, at some level, it is important to point out what really is and is not a museum, spending too much time on this misses the larger point. The fact remains that AiG adopted the museum label for rhetorical effect in order to foster credibility and a sense of authority.[2] Despite the fact that the Creation Museum is not a museum according to authoritative definitions, that the Creation Museum defines itself thusly will have real consequences in the minds of patrons.

By naming itself a museum, the Creation Museum taps into a long-established authoritative rhetoric that encourages the visitor into a certain mind-set before entering the doors of the facility. Though the idea of the natural history museum is rather modern, museums of all stripes are among the most trusted institutions in the United States. In fact, Americans tend to trust museums more than they trust books. Accord to a 2001 poll by the American Association of Museums, 87 percent of Americans "find museums to be one of the most trustworthy or a trustworthy source of information among a wide range of choices."[3] A more recent poll commissioned by the Institute for Museum and Library Services found that museum visitors rated museums at 4.62 on a 5-point scale of trustworthiness.[4] The book is at a distant second place with 61 percent of Americans citing books as the most trustworthy sources of information.[5] Popular trust in museums is bolstered by an erroneous perception that museums are places that present just the facts. People trust museums to be interpretation-free zones where visitors can escape bias and are free to form their own opinions about the materials presented therein. It is not widely recognized, however, that museums, even those most venerable and learned institutions like the Smithsonian or the Louvre, are places that engage in interpretation. Visitors to these institutions are receiving displays that have been

---

1. Casey R. Kelly and Kristen Hoerl, "Genesis in Hyperreality: Legitimizing Disingenuous Controversy at the Creation Museum," *Argumentation and Advocacy* (Winter 2012): 125.

2. Kelly and Hoerl, 125.

3. Elizabeth Merritt, "Trust Me, I'm a Museum," *American Alliance of Museums*, February 3, 2015, https://www.aam-us.org/2015/02/03/trust-me-im-a-museum/.

4. Merritt, "Trust Me, I'm a Museum."

5. Jill Stevenson, "Embodying Sacred History," *TDR/The Drama Review* 56, no. 1 (2012): 96.

curated, selected, and have been placed in a particular context to tell a story. As storytelling institutions, the Creation Museum and the MotB each seek to tell a story about the Bible and they seek to use the format of the museum, and all the authority that comes with it, to lend credibility to that story.[6] As Jill Stevenson points out, people already have feelings of awe about museums and the museum experience further enhances this.[7] The Creation Museum's God's Word/man's word heuristic, and letting the visitor decide, employs museum expectations to great effect. Likewise, in order to garner authority, the MotB's attempt at a value-free Bible presentation also relies on museum expectations.

Even Better than the Smithsonian[8]

The Creation Museum uses this inherent trust for museums to effectively present itself as a place free from interpretation—just presenting facts—to a public free to make up their own minds. One means by which the Creation Museum seeks to accomplish this is their "God's Word/man's word" heuristic. The Creation Museum displays begin by introducing the visitor to the concept of same facts, different interpretations. Then, throughout the museum, placards will present a "fact" followed by a compare and contrast on how that fact is understood according to God's Word and man's word. By way of example, an early display presents the fact that fossils exist. The display then lays out how those fossils formed according to God's Word (they were rapidly buried in the sediment resulting from Noah's flood) and how fossils formed according to man's word (slowly buried in the sediments over long spans of geologic time). Through this device, coupled with the authority that comes with the museum label, the Creation Museum enables the perception that it presents both sides of the argument, is fair, is open-minded, and encourages people to decide for themselves.[9]

The concepts of fairness and open-mindedness are critical to how the Creation Museum positions itself. The idea of just presenting the facts, letting all sides have a fair hearing, has been an important element in creationist strategies to get creationism into secular science education. Many creationist organizations and spokespeople play upon people's inherent sense of fairness by arguing that all sides should get to present their case. They further maintain that creationism has not had this opportunity because creationism has been oppressed by a secular scientific community seeking to protect its interests. The Creation Museum

---

6. Bielo, *Ark Encounter*, 43.
7. Stevenson, "Embodying Sacred History," 96.
8. Momofall12, "Better Than the Smithsonian!" TripAdvisor, September 8, 2014, https ://www.tripadvisor.com/ShowUserReviews-g39743-d619562-r227824637-Creation_M useum-Petersburg_KentucKY.html.
9. Note that this is a rhetorical technique employed by Fox News and other right-wing organizations in their attempts to create counter-hegemonic discourses.

positions itself within this discourse as providing a corrective to this perceived effort to marginalize creationism in the scientific community.[10] By presenting both sides of the argument (God's Word versus man's word) the Creation Museum even creates the additional perception that they act with more fairness and integrity than the secular scientific community because they are willing to give secular science a voice in the Creation Museum. Though explored in more detail later, the concept of open-mindedness appears frequently in patron reviews and comments on the Creation Museum and the Ark Encounter. For patrons, open-mindedness is used to both describe the museum and is a recommended mind-set for people visiting the museum. For example, cms777 notes that the Creation Museum setup appeals to the open-minded and allows people to reach their own conclusions.[11] Skbranson says that the Creation Museum gently presents its point of view in a comfortable manner at a comfortable pace.[12] Appeals to open-mindedness must be understood against the rhetoric fostered by creationists that secular science is a closed community unwilling to give alternative perspectives a fair hearing. Thus, appeals to approach the Creation Museum and the Ark Encounter with an open mind furthers the impression that AiG, its attractions, supporters, and patrons are the true defenders of free inquiry against the dogma of secular science.

Utilizing the museum label also allows the Creation Museum to instill in its visitors the expectation that the displays held within reflect the same level of authority expected in displays in other museums. Some museum visitors afford this level of authority to the Creation Museum. For instance, Diana B says of the Creation Museum that it transports people back in time and presents history in a manner comparable to other museums. For Diana, this is the essence of what it means to be a museum.[13] The museum label encourages the visitor to assume that the Creation Museum materials have met "the rigorous standards of scientific review and can be accepted as demonstrated fact."[14] The very act of displaying items in a museum setting is an exercise in definition and control. Moreover, since the nineteenth century museums have provided the interface between the general public and scientists making the museum "the public face of the scientific

10. This rhetoric is explored in more detail in Chapter 5.

11. cms777, "Great for Those Willing to Honestly Research," TripAdvisor, April 30, 2010, https://www.tripadvisor.com/ShowUserReviews-g39743-d619562-r62902766-Creation_Museum-Petersburg_KentucKY.html.

12. skbranson, "Fun and Educational," TripAdvisor, February 18, 2017, https://www.tripadvisor.com/ShowUserReviews-g39743-d619562-r461010627-Creation_Museum-Petersburg_KentucKY.html.

13. Diana B., "A Place for Families," TripAdvisor, December 6, 2014, https://www.tripadvisor.com/ShowUserReviews-g39743-d619562-r243185178-Creation_Museum-Petersburg_KentucKY.html.

14. Brent Hege, "Contesting Faith, Truth, and Religious Language at the Creation Museum: A Historical-Theological Reflection," *Theology and Science* 12, no. 2 (April 3, 2014): 142–63, https://doi.org/10.1080/14746700.2014.894730.

endeavor."[15] By presenting itself as a museum, the Creation Museum links itself to the modern practice of doing and presenting science.

The Creation Museum's central message is the notion that the world is coming apart because we have rejected biblical authority in our lives. Thus, the Creation Museum presents itself as an alternative refuge to this chaos. This works because of the authority given to museum objects, objects that have "exalted status in a museum" while the "physicality suggests a stable, unambiguous world."[16] However, the Creation Museum is rather peculiar in that it does not house an accessioned collection. Except for items on loan for special display, the visitor is not going to find valuable artifacts, works of art, or cultural objects. The true value of the Creation Museum does not lie in the objects contained inside, but in what AiG would describe as a priceless and potentially soul-saving message. Likewise, the MotB seeks to deliver a similar message, even if the MotB places more emphasis on functioning and looking more like a typical museum. After all, the MotB visitor will find rare and ancient objects and artifacts often associated with a typical museum.

There are other significant ways in which the Creation Museum and the MotB overlap. One goal that both the Creation Museum and the MotB share is delivering a message that the Bible is indestructible. One large display at the Creation Museum describes how the Bible has survived various attacks. These attacks on God's Word began in the Garden of Eden with the serpent questioning God's commandment not to eat the fruit from the tree in the middle of the garden (Gen 3:3). Questioning God's Word, according to AiG, leads to humans abandoning God's Word. Further attacks on God's Word included attempts to destroy, discredit, criticize, poison, replace, and, most recent, attacks on the biblical time line. Of course, this last is a commentary on calculating the age of the earth. According to the Creation Museum, the church once believed God's Word on the earth's age,[17] then the church questioned God's Word by proposing that six thousand years is not enough time to account for the earth's geology, and finally the church abandoned God's Word by accepting that earth is millions of years old. Despite these attacks, the Bible has proven indestructible and it cannot be destroyed because it is God's supernatural Word. Likewise, the MotB seeks to demonstrate the resilience and the pervasiveness of the Bible. The original 2010 mission statement of the MotB reads thus: "To bring to life the living word of God, to tell its compelling story of preservation, and to inspire confidence in the absolute authority and reliability of the Bible."[18] The collection of bibles and Bible fragments that have survived hundreds of years through a variety of calamities becomes evidence of the text's indestructability.

---

15. John M. MacKenzie, *Museums and Empire: Natural History, Human Cultures and Colonial Identities* (Manchester: Manchester University Press, 2010), 1.
16. Kelly and Hoerl, "Genesis in Hyperreality," 132.
17. Using the Bible, Bishop Ussher calculated that creation occurred on 4004 BC.
18. Moss and Baden, *Bible Nation*, 53.

Like the Creation Museum, the MotB also seeks the scientific legitimacy that has been associated with museums. Also, like the Creation Museum, the MotB seeks to present itself as a place free of interpretation, where people can explore and make their own determinations about the items on display. This attempted veneer of neutrality is evident in the 2012 rewriting of the MotB mission statement, which reads, "We exist to invite people to engage with the Bible through our four primary activities: traveling exhibits, scholarship, building of a permanent museum, and developing elective high school curriculum."[19] Steve Green, whose collection (commonly known as the Green Family Collection) forms the basis of the MotB, emphasizes the nonsectarian nature of MotB as evidence of its impartiality.[20] However, nonsectarian does not mean religiously neutral, it does not mean nonreligious, and it does not mean non-Christian. AiG is a nonsectarian organization as well but that does not prevent their presentation of a very particular message based on a particular reading of the Bible. Thus, MotB's attempt at using nonsectarianism as a substitute for neutrality rings hollow.

The veneer of neutrality is further supported by MotB's efforts to recruit credentialed scholars, experts in analyzing and dating ancient manuscripts. This reflects a peculiar tension not just at MotB but at the Creation Museum as well. Much of Protestant history, and this has become particularly evident in the past few years, not only emphasized a suspicion of experts and science but also maintained that experts are not needed to interpret the Bible. This was, in fact, the heart and soul of the Protestant reformation and its rejection of Catholic authority. Moss and Baden cite Richard Hofstader's seminal work on anti-intellectualism in describing the evangelical "dismissal of 'expert' opinion in favor of the 'knowledge' of the layperson" that "has found its modern evangelical counterpart in, for example, the rejection of scientific discoveries regarding evolution in favor of a creationist biblical model of human origins."[21] As an anti-evolutionist pointed out in a recent Texas science curriculum controversy, "Somebody's gotta stand up to the experts!"[22] In another example, the BBC published a conversation between Georgia Purdom, PhD, a molecular biologist employed by AiG, and William Crawley. The online discussion comments in response to the interview sparked a lively debate about the nature of science, in which a discussant called Casur1 responded, "If you're asking if I'm contemptuous of the scientific establishment, the answer is yes. They have no credibility at all as far as I'm concerned, mainly because their chief concern at any given moment is their 'standing,' not the truth or otherwise of a given theory."[23]

19. Moss and Baden, 53.
20. Moss and Baden, 27–28.
21. Moss and Baden, 87.
22. Moss and Baden, 29.
23. "Bbc—Will & Testament: A Creationist with a Phd," accessed August 2, 2018, http://www.bbc.co.uk/blogs/ni/2012/08/a_creationist_with_a_phd.html.

The AiG suspicion of secular scientists is clearly on display at the Creation Museum with barely disguised contempt. In fact, it is secular science, particularly evolutionary science, that is blamed for the moral bankruptcy and decay in modern American society.[24] However, the Creation Museum does not claim to be anti-science and many museum patrons also support science, provided it is the right kind of science. For some visitors, secular science is not real science at all. Mark B proclaims that, as opposed to secular museums, the Creation Museum does authentic science and answers the real questions being neglected by secular scientists.[25] Others claim that the science presented at other museums is biased in a manner that the Creation Museum is not. For instance, eerb claims that the Creation Museum offers the only perspective on science that is free of religious bias. To truly understand this statement, one must note that many creationists view evolution, and the atheism they believe it to be founded upon, as religious perspectives on the world.[26] AiG claims to love science and claims to be better at science than secular scientists. A July 21, 2016, article published on the Creation Museum website proudly proclaims that creationist science is better science. The article maintains that science was created by God and that the Creation Museum loves science.[27] Despite being part of this evangelical milieu fostering suspicion of experts, the Creation Museum goes to great lengths to emphasize the credentials of their staff scientists. "Creationists Do Better Science" notes that visitors can learn about the science of the human body, cells, and biology from highly credentialed scientists. Among the scientists on staff are Dr. David Menton (PhD, biology, Brown University),[28] Dr. Andrew Snelling (PhD, geology, University of Sydney),[29] and the previously mentioned Dr. Georgia Purdom (PhD, molecular genetics, the Ohio State University).[30] AiG clearly walks a line between disdain for science

---

24. According to Ken Ham, this is true because evolutionists have taught America that humans are not special, that humans are products of random events, and that humans are animals. Thus, Americans have lost a moral compass because we no longer have a sense of being created beings with a purpose.

25. Mark B., "A Must Visit!!!" TripAdvisor, October 27, 2016, https://www.tripadvisor.com/ShowUserReviews-g39743-d619562-r432167417-Creation_Museum-Petersburg_KentucKY.html.

26. eerb, "An Important Display of Science," TripAdvisor, January 13, 2012, https://www.tripadvisor.com/ShowUserReviews-g39743-d619562-r123021922-Creation_Museum-Petersburg_KentucKY.html.

27. "Creationists Do Better Science," Creation Museum, accessed August 2, 2018, https://creationmuseum.org/blog/2016/07/21/creationists-do-better-science/.

28. "Dr. David Menton," Answers in Genesis, accessed August 2, 2018, https://answersingenesis.org/bios/david-menton/.

29. "Dr. Andrew Snelling," Answers in Genesis, accessed August 2, 2018, https://answersingenesis.org/bios/andrew-snelling/.

30. "Dr. Georgia Purdom," Answers in Genesis, accessed August 2, 2018, https://answersingenesis.org/bios/georgia-purdom/.

while at the same time using the prestige and respect for science to shore up its creationist claims.

Academic credentials are also important at the MotB. Moss and Baden point to the scholars engaged in consulting work for the MotB which allows the MotB to claim that their projects have "received input from leading academic minds."[31] Called the Scholars Initiative, the academic research branch of the MotB is designed to foster Bible research in a wide variety of institutions and supports projects that examine both the language and the material culture of the Bible.[32] However, as Moss and Baden discovered, the scholars employed by the Scholar's Initiative are not always the best qualified. In some cases, scholars and students have worked on manuscripts and fragments with little prior experience in the study of the languages required or the techniques and methods used to study and handle ancient texts.[33] However, the employment of people of questionable expertise actually meshes better with the suspicion of academic authority described above.[34] People associated with the creationism of AiG and with the MotB have expressed the opinion that the Bible does not need interpretation. Following the Protestant principle of interpretation-free Bible reading, "personal judgment outweighs the accumulated generations of expertise, be it clerical or scholarly," and following Dwight Moody, a "common sense rationalism" reveals the truth of scripture.[35] Nonetheless, the world's top museums have highly credentialed staff and advisory boards who lend exhibits legitimacy owing to their authority. This places the Creation Museum and the MotB in the position of needing to shore up staff credentials in spite of this underlying suspicion of experts.

As a storytelling institution, the MotB is telling a story similar to that of the Creation Museum. Clearly the MotB seeks to highlight the Bible's role in America, its impact on American history, and to bolster the Bible's authority. The MotB's second floor houses an exhibit called *The Impact of the Bible* that describes the impact of the Bible in American history and across the world. Here the Bible is credited with helping develop democracy and fostering religious liberty. The MotB's Bible presentation is a bit more uplifting than the story told at the Creation Museum. At the Creation Museum, abandonment of the Bible has led to a culture in decay, depicted in displays like *Culture in Crisis* and the *Cave of Sorrows*. Both of those displays blames the ills of society, things like drug use, pornography, war, famine, and genocide, on a broad abandonment of the Bible.

---

31. Moss and Baden, *Bible Nation*, 76.

32. "Scholars Initiative," accessed August 2, 2018, http://www.museumofthebible.org/research/scholars-initiative.

33. Moss and Baden tell the story of Jennifer Larson, a professor of classics at Kent State, who was approached by Scott Carroll to study a Greek papyrus with her students. Larson pointed out that she was not a papyrologist and that the students working on the project had not had elementary Greek. Moss and Baden, *Bible Nation*, 62–63.

34. Moss and Baden, *Bible Nation*, 87.

35. Moss and Baden, 124.

The MotB does include controversies related to the Bible, for example, how both sides in the Civil War used the Bible to justify their positions, but the overarching narrative is not as bleak and grim as that of the Creation Museum.

As a museum, the layout of the Creation Museum is out of step with best practices of modern museum design. Natural history museums have their origins in early modern privately owned in-home collections known as cabinets of curiosities. Eventually these collections came to be housed in what we might recognize today as a natural history museum. However, early natural history museums did not allow the patrons random access to the displays. In fact, visitors were required to follow a prescribed path through the museum and divergence from that path was discouraged. The purpose, according to Trollinger and Trollinger, was to place the patron on a particular trajectory and to instill in the viewer a sense of being subject to the laws being described in the museum.[36] In other words, the museum walked the patron along a particular narrative. Modern museums have abandoned this design model in favor of open floor plans. The open floor plan no longer forces the patron along a particular path thus leaving the patron free to consume the displays in whatever order she wishes.

That the Creation Museum was designed in the mid-2000s and opened in 2007 would indicate that museum designers were aware of the open floor plan concept and consciously chose to reject it. Rather than offering an open floor plan, the Creation Museum forces visitors through the display along a prescribed path. This design choice is necessitated by AiG's theology and its efforts to create a walk-through sermon. AiG is telling one story in two chapters at the Creation Museum and to grasp the significance of this story museum patrons must understand the linear cause and effect of the various story elements. As John Lynch describes it, the Creation Museum display is a "spatial sermon" and the Creation Museum presentation is a physical embodiment of that sermon.[37]

The first part of the Creation Museum sermon is about American culture in decay and the path through this portion of the museum is itself a theological statement.[38] The culture in decay narrative focuses on biblical authority and the social and political consequences of abandoning the Bible. As the viewer proceeds along this path, the ceiling drops and the path becomes increasingly maze like. Lynch suggests that the purpose of such a layout is to create a sense of tension, fear, and dissonance in the patron, the feeling that something is wrong.[39] This sense of wrongness is heightened by the images on the displays.

From the *Culture in Crisis* display the visitor passes through the time tunnel and into a Six Day Theater where the Genesis creation narrative is introduced. Lynch describes this transition between these displays as a symbolic death and rebirth. The increasingly dark displays and twisted walkways of the *Graffiti Alley*

---

36. Trollinger and Trollinger, *Righting America at the Creation Museum*, 23–24.
37. Lynch, "Prepare to Believe," 7.
38. Lynch, 15.
39. Lynch, 7.

and *Culture in Crisis* exhibits can only end in death and the only salvation from death is a rebirth through the truth of the Bible.[40] He writes: "This spatial sermon aims to create tension and dissonance in visitors that can be resolved only by a symbolic death that leads to redemption in a new identity."[41] It is important to note, however, that it is not just the Bible alone but also AiG's particular interpretation of the Bible that offers rebirth.

The efficacy of this effort relies on the implicit trust Americans place in museums. It is ironic that the Creation Museum taps into this implicit trust in order to push its ideology while, at the same time, arguing that most secular natural history museums are not trustworthy. For AiG, secular natural history museums are not trustworthy because they force upon the patron a vision of history filtered through an evolutionary lens. On this topic AiG employs the language of deception. For instance, Dr. Terry Mortenson, researcher and writer for AiG, accuses evolutionists of misleading the public with deceptive and dogmatic claims that fail to stand up to examination.[42] Gordon Lanz and Mark Looy, writing for AiG, described the Darwin display at the American Museum of Natural History in New York as dogmatic and propagandistic. The authors assert that intelligent design and creationism were deliberately cast as religious and, thus, nonscientific. Lanz and Looy describe this situation as condescending and lament what they see as the indoctrination of hapless museum patrons.[43]

The Creation Museum adopts the form of the natural history museum while simultaneously serving as a challenge to those same museums.[44] While AiG hopes to tap into the authority of the museum, writ large, the Creation Museum also stands as a challenge to the secular natural history museum and inverts many of the tropes found in such museums. Consider, for example, the *Dig Site* display featuring two paleontologists. Here the young-earth creationist is depicted as self-assured, curious, and knowledge-seeking while the evolutionist is, in the words of Stevenson, depicted as the "person who cannot engage in a reasonable and thoughtful debate about the facts and instead blindly follows a 'theory' as if it were the unquestioned truth."[45] This display flips the script by depicting what many would have viewed as the dogmatic religionist as a fighter for free inquiry and fair play. Both paleontologists address the museum patron. The narrative attributed to the evolutionist lacks confidence and employs verbiage

---

40. Lynch, 14.

41. Lynch, 7.

42. "Adam, Morality, the Gospel, and the Authority of Scripture," Answers in Genesis, accessed March 2, 2017, https://answersingenesis.org/bible-characters/adam-and-eve/adam-morality-gospel-and-authority-of-scripture/.

43. "Darwin Exhibit at the American Museum of Natural History," Answers in Genesis, accessed March 6, 2017, https://answersingenesis.org/reviews/darwin-exhibit-at-american-museum-of-natural-history/.

44. Stevenson, "Embodying Sacred History," 99.

45. Stevenson, 100.

that indicates uncertainty and hesitancy. This furthers the inversion of what would commonly be expected from two such figures. One would expect that the evolutionist, as a scientist, would be depicted as confident and curious about the natural world and open to correction and disconfirmation. One the other hand, as a religious figure the creationist would be dogmatic and rigid. The inherent stumbling blocks many people experience while contemplating evolutionary theory is one of the reasons that the Creation Museum can effectively employ this strategy. Many are skeptical about evolution because it is perceived, rightly or wrongly, as something that is difficult to observe and is hard to understand and trust. The Creation Museum capitalizes on this conceptual difficulty by emphasizing the visible.[46] AiG does this through its framing of operational science against origins science. Since scientists cannot directly observe the past, then without an authoritative guide like the Bible, much of what constitutes science about the past is merely secular speculation.

The manner in which the Creation Museum is simultaneously able to use, but also subvert, what it views as secular science emerges from both a Protestant suspicion of expertise that extends all the way back to the Reformation further fueled by the recent postmodern skepticism about truth claims. Emerging as a response to the failure of modernism to solve social ills, and to prevent devastating world wars, postmodernism, also forged against a background of colonialism, argued that grand narratives (metanarratives) are not objective and are always self-interested. Even science was unable to escape a decades-long re-examination of "truth" as evidenced in Thomas Kuhn's *The Structure of Scientific Revolutions* (1962). In this seminal work, Kuhn argued that scientists inhabit paradigms and that each paradigm is identified by its own procedures and ideas that govern how scientists think and work. Moreover, these paradigms shift in sudden moves that Kuhn calls revolutions. New paradigms are often incomprehensible to those working in the old paradigm and staid scientists will often never resolve the differences between the old and the new.[47] Without belaboring the point regarding Kuhn's position in postmodern thought (and Thomas Kuhn does believe that he has been significantly misunderstood), for our purposes it is sufficient to point out that Kuhn's contribution was pointing out that science and scientific knowledge are socially constructed.[48] One axiomatic proposal of postmodern thought is the idea that all knowledge is socially constructed and is situated according to economic, political, and social situations. Consequently, there is no possible access to absolute truth that exists independently of these filters.

Even though AiG does not use the terminology of Kuhn or of postmodernism, the *Dig Site* display is predicated upon the idea that scientific

---

46. Stevenson, 105.

47. John Horgan, "What Thomas Kuhn Really Thought about Scientific 'Truth,'" Scientific American Blog Network, accessed March 8, 2017, https://blogs.scientificamerican.com/cross-check/what-thomas-kuhn-really-thought-about-scientific-truth/.

48. Horgan, "What Thomas Kuhn Really Thought about Scientific 'Truth.'"

facts are socially constructed. This allows the museum to propose that the secular paleontologist's claims rest on no objective reality independent of the scientific community in which he is embedded. This particular scientific community is governed by the socially constructed narrative known as Darwinism. By framing Darwinism as a socially constructed narrative the Creation Museum is able to dismiss the scientific claims based on Darwin's work.[49] The main point of the *Dig Site* display is that science is always informed by the starting place of the scientist, a rhetoric that "draws on a discourse very close to social constructionist science studies."[50] Ham argues that AiG's starting point is superior "because 'all the Scripture is God-breathed' (2 Timothy 3:16), we can trust that what these men wrote is the inspired, inerrant, and infallible word of God."[51]

The Creation Museum uses the museum genre to tell a story about the Bible, but it also uses the museum genre to tell stories about the AiG community and the people drawn to this attraction. In other words, as a museum and tourist destination, AiG is creating a sense of culture and community while creating and reinforcing an us-versus-them discourse. The Creation Museum both creates and reflects the culture in which it is embedded. According to its own rhetoric, the Creation Museum defines itself against mainstream thought on many cultural (not just scientific) issues. Running against the grain of secular society helps foster a sense of social and cultural isolation. Seeing themselves as participants in the culture wars, AiG and its supporters view themselves as fighters on the margins of a culture gone astray.

This sense of separation and isolation is reflected in the relatively remote and isolated locations of both the Creation Museum and the Ark Encounter. Turning off the highways, being surrounded by little more than trees and farmland, visiting the Creation Museum and the Ark Encounter is like visiting places out of time separated from the rest of the workaday world. The MotB, on the other hand, employs this sense of space differently. While the Creation Museum plays with an isolation and wilderness trope, reflecting a sense of marginality in modern society, the MotB places itself in the middle of American power structures. In doing so, the MotB gives truth to the lie being fostered by AiG. Steps from the US Capitol, the MotB is an undeniable physical reminder of the social influence and the political power exercised by people, like the Green family, who support these institutions. The sense of persecution and oppression fostered by the Creation Museum and the Ark Encounter fires up the base while the MotB funnels that energy into real political influence.

---

49. Ella Butler, "God Is in the Data: Epistemologies of Knowledge at the Creation Museum," *Ethnos* 75, no. 3 (September 2010): 299, https://doi.org/10.1080/00141844.2010.507907.

50. Butler, 231.

51. Ham, *Six Days*, 71.

Hiraeth and Longing for the Imagined Home

AiG has given us, in both of its attractions, an example of what Tim Beal called "geopiety."[52] Borrowed from John Kirtland Wright, geopiety represents an image of the Holy Land that is based upon romantic notions and imagination paired with a deep reverence for physical space.[53] Beal catalogs several examples of geopiety from roadside attractions like Bedford, Virginia's Holy Land USA, a family-created replica of significant Holy Land sites, to major tourist attractions like Orlando's Holy Land Experience where visitors engage with actors dressed in period garb. Geopiety is therefore deeply ingrained in the American religious imagination.

Aside from touching in some way upon the Bible and the Holy Land, one thing all these sites, the Creation Museum and the Ark Encounter included, share is a desire to create sacred space and sacred time. Participating in this allows the visitor to place themselves in contact with a perceived purer time and to imagine themselves living with people, like Noah, who embody all the best values they imagine in themselves and see as missing from secularized American culture. As Bielo describes it, the Ark Encounter focuses on immersion in order to generate "affective attachments to the past"[54] to overcome one central problem faced by Christians, the temporal and geographic separation from the origins of their faith.[55] That the Creation Museum and the Ark Encounter succeed in transporting people back in time is evident in the manner in which visitors describe their experiences. The experiences that visitors describe are closely tied to the perceived authenticity of these attractions. Beal coins the phrase "religious recreation" to describe such places. Moreover, Beal argues that religious recreation rests upon a profound sense of nostalgia, a homesickness, "a longing to have our everyday lives set within the horizon of a sacred story."[56]

As Beal's description suggests, no single word in English captures the complex feelings, moods, and longings that places like the Creation Museum and the Ark Encounter reflect. What I am seeking to describe is better captured in the Welsh word *hiraeth*. Not easily translatable, *hiraeth* captures that sense of homesickness, longing, nostalgia, and yearning as it particularly relates to a lost home or perhaps even to a home that never existed.[57] It is also "a longing to be where your spirit lives" which can include both physical places or a place in the past or a place that

---

52. Timothy K. Beal, *Roadside Religion: In Search of the Sacred, the Strange, and the Substance of Faith* (Boston, MA: Beacon Press, 2005), 28.

53. Beal, 28.

54. Bielo, *Ark Encounter*, 25.

55. Bielo, 36.

56. Beal, *Roadside Religion*, 27.

57. Pamela Petro, "Dreaming in Welsh," *The Paris Review*, September 18, 2012, https://www.theparisreview.org/blog/2012/09/18/dreaming-in-welsh/.

never was.[58] Be it a museum like the MotB or the Creation Museum, or a theme park like the Ark Encounter, they each serve as remedies for what I call *biblical hiraeth*. When patrons enter these places and describe being transported back in time, they are, in a sense, returning home. It is a sense of longing for a better time, when the Word of God was taken seriously and governed society, and a sense of nostalgia that draw people to these places. Moreover, as *biblical hiraeth* would seem to suggest, it does not matter if this idealized time and place ever really existed. For the visitor it is real and is the place where the spirit lives. As a longing for a time or a place set apart, *biblical hiraeth* complements the concept of sacred space. Sacred space represents the places where the divine comes into contact with the world, where one can commune with the divine and renew a connection that is "always being worn away by the pressures of everyday life."[59]

In the history of religion sacred spaces have been marked by a sense of ambivalence, places of both danger and refuge. The function of the ark in biblical narrative is one of salvation for those with the right beliefs and AiG's ark offers the same for visitors today. The Creation Museum and the Ark Encounter are places of cultural refuge, a characteristic common to many religiously themed attractions. For instance, studies demonstrated that Heritage USA, the South Carolina theme park founded by Jim and Tammy Faye Bakker of PTL fame, found that the theme park functioned as a refuge for "certain types of Christians" where they could collectively and privately engage in a culture that included prayer and laying on of hands without exposing themselves to public ridicule.[60] Likewise, visitors to the Creation Museum and the Ark Encounter appreciate these attractions as places where young-earth creationists, evangelicals, and biblical literalists are able to find their people. As here5 exclaimed about the Creation Museum, there was a palpable sense of being home that was enhanced by the freedom to revel in one's Christian identity without attracting negative attention.[61] In this way, the Creation Museum (like all museums) serves as a "material vehicle" for "shared memory" and a shared culture.[62] As is typical of "memory places," visitors make special arrangements to visit. As a shared memory place the Creation Museum commands attention, represents, inspires, instructs, reminds, admonishes, exemplifies, offers affiliation, and serves as a place of public identification of that affiliation.[63]

---

58. "Hiraeth: Word of the Week," accessed May 21, 2019, https://sites.psu.edu/kielarpassionblog2/2016/04/02/hiraeth/.

59. Beal, *Roadside Religion*, 27.

60. Michael Stausberg, *Religion and Tourism: Crossroads, Destinations, and Encounters* (New York: Routledge, 2011), 114.

61. here5, "Family Vacation," TripAdvisor, August 26, 2016, https://www.tripadvisor.com/ShowUserReviews-g39743-d619562-r411246892-Creation_Museum-Petersburg_KentucKY.html.

62. Kelly and Hoerl, "Genesis in Hyperreality," 128.

63. Kelly and Hoerl, 128.

Biblical Hiraeth *and the Theme Park*

Even though the Creation Museum labels itself as a museum, it still incorporates some theme park sensibilities. In a May 27, 2007, article on the opening of the Creation Museum, the *Seattle Times* quoted Eugenie Scott, director of the National Center for Science Education, who called the Creation Museum "the creationist Disneyland."[64] Scott was correct because, in form and function, it appears that AiG was attempting to intentionally foster a Disney-like vibe.[65] Indeed, among the most important Creation Museum display designers was Patrick Marsh, the art director for the "Jaws" and "King Kong" displays at Universal Studios in Florida—and himself a creationist.[66] In a 2002 interview, shortly after he was added to the Creation Museum design team, Marsh stated that the Creation Museum would incorporate the best technological advances in theme park design.[67] As central as the museum identity is to the rhetoric of the Creation Museum, it is interesting to note that the appellation of "museum" was not chosen for the Ark Encounter. Instead, the Ark Encounter is described as a theme park in AiG blogs, articles, and newsletters. As a theme park, not only does the Ark Encounter include the Noah's Ark replica but it also has zip lining, the Ararat Ridge Zoo, and the West Village with a performance stage and shops. Future expansion plans include a Tower of Babel and a 10-Plagues-of-Egypt Thrill Ride.[68]

The Creation Museum takes as its concern biblical authority and it seeks to shore up the Bible's authority with visual depictions of biblical narratives. These include dioramas with mannequins and complex animatronics depicting scenes from the Bible, including Adam and Eve in the garden, the first animal sacrifice, Methuselah, and Noah building the ark. Though labeled a theme park rather than a museum, the Ark Encounter does much of the same, including proposals about how animals were caged and fed, and what life was like for Noah and his family on the ark. This includes a lavishly decorated model of the family living quarters presented in painstaking detail. That the Bible can only come alive and achieve realism through material displays suggests an inadequacy of the biblical text and

---

64. Peter Slevin, "Genesis on Display," *The Seattle Times*, May 27, 2007, http://www.seattletimes.com/nation-world/genesis-on-display-at-creationist-disneyland/.

65. Bielo, *Ark Encounter*, 22.

66. "Creative Designer Honors the Creator," Answers in Genesis, accessed January 31, 2017, https://answersingenesis.org/ministry-news/creation-museum/creative-designer-honors-the-creator/.

67. "Creative Designer Honors the Creator."

68. Karen Heller, "A Giant Ark Is Just the Start: These Creationists Have a Bigger Plan for Recruiting New Believers," *Washington Post*, May 24, 2017, sec. Style, https://www.washingtonpost.com/lifestyle/style/a-giant-ark-is-just-the-start-these-creationists-have-a-bigger-plan-for-recruiting-new-believers/2017/05/24/b497bd14-2920-11e7-be51-b3fc6ff7faee_story.html.

its ability to engage readers.[69] In this regard, AiG assumes that its patrons are from Missouri, the "Show-Me state." Based upon patron comments about the Creation Museum and the Ark Encounter, presenting the Bible in these material objects has efficacy. As will be explored in more detail below, seeing material representations of biblical narratives makes the story more real. This was the case for Charlotte who told me that one effect of seeing the ark replica at the Ark Encounter was that it became "a lot more real"[70] and for ninjasgf who spoke of the Creation Museum as a time machine to the days of Genesis.[71] Others note that seeing the Ark Encounter ark replica helped them really understand the dimensions of the vessel as described in Genesis.[72] Creation Museum and Ark Encounter patrons speak about the Bible coming alive because of these material displays.[73]

Biblical hiraeth—the longing for an idealized biblical home that may have never existed—intersects with authenticity and the hyperreality of the theme park. An intense focus on authenticity is important to the perceived veracity of the displays at both attractions. After all, AiG's message about the Bible's truth could be undermined if visitors deemed the displays to be shoddy or inauthentic. At the Ark Encounter AiG spared little expense in creating as much realism as possible. The Ark Encounter is a simulacrum, or copy of a particular story and time described in the Bible. There comes a point, as Baudrillard taught us, when the realism of simulacra approaches "hyperreality." The Creation Museum and the Ark Encounter are no exceptions. As defined by Umberto Eco, hyperreality is "fantasy structures and virtual worlds promulgated by media and visual technologies [that] become indistinguishable from the materiality of the real."[74] In hyperreal cultures, the real and the copy become disconnected to such a degree that the copy becomes the real. To use a non-biblical example, the whole premise of reality television works because the audience has accepted the reality represented by such shows despite the fact that these shows do not reflect any reality at all. To use Baudrillard's terms, the reality show is a "copy with no original." On one hand, as the opening chapters of Genesis are a collection of narratives with very little material or historical support, then the Creation Museum and the Ark Encounter depictions of Genesis narratives are quite literally copies with no original. Regarding realism, following Eco, "the fact that it seems so real is real, and the thing is real even if, like Alice in Wonderland, it never existed."[75] This is why a replica of Noah's Ark, or an animatronic Methuselah, serves such important

---

69. Stevenson, "Embodying Sacred History," 97.
70. Charlotte, discussion.
71. ninjasgf, "What an Experience!" TripAdvisor, October 30, 2015, https://www.tripadvisor.com/ShowUserReviews-g39743-d619562-r323229935-Creation_Museum-Petersburg_KentucKY.html.
72. Charlotte, discussion.
73. Isabella, in discussion with the author, April 2017.
74. Kelly and Hoerl, "Genesis in Hyperreality," 134.
75. Kelly and Hoerl, 135.

functions for the Creation Museum and the Ark Encounter. A simple painting of the ark, or a portrait of Methuselah, would not convey the same sense of authority and lacks the hyperrealistic verisimilitude. At the Creation Museum, Methuselah's hands were sculpted from a model whose hands reflected a rough-and-tumble lifetime of manual labor.[76] At the Ark Encounter, individual hairs were crafted for the ark's animals and, in some cases, scales were hand carved from epoxy putty.[77] Embracing extreme authenticity, pushing toward hyperreality, is liberating for curators and designers of attractions like the Creation Museum or the Ark Encounter. As Kelly and Hoerl point out, "Hyperreality frees curators from the imperative to prove their object's authenticity and enables them to destabilize the metonymic relationship between the traditional display object or natural history and the distant past."[78]

It is one of the contentions of this work that the Creation Museum and the Ark Encounter function as hyperreal simulacra that take on a reality that is more real than the biblical texts from which these images are drawn. This conclusion is supported, in part, by frequent visitor exclamations that the Creation Museum and the Ark Encounter seem so realistic and bring the Bible to life. It is, however, a reality that is also fantasy. Analysts like Baudrillard have noted that theme parks like Disneyland sell a fantastic past and peddle in an idealized fantastic reality that is more desirable than the world outside the theme park gates.

Biblical hiraeth is a symptom of Fredric Jameson's "nostalgia for the present" which finds expression in the Ark Encounter as theme park. For Jameson, part of the postmodern condition is to "think the present historically" because culture, owing to a capitalist reformulation of time, has forgotten how to think about history.[79] Or, as described by Svetlana Boym, there is a "dislocation in space but also [a] changing conception of time."[80] Thus, modern understandings of history are governed by a modern pastiche that "presents the past as a glimmering mirage." *Biblical hiraeth* encompasses nostalgia but is also something more than nostalgia. Nostalgia is a longing for and a possibility of returning home, to an "enchanted world with clear borders and values."[81] It is therefore easy to understand the appeal of the Creation Museum or the Ark Encounter as this home for, indeed, the man's word/God's Word heuristic supports that sense of clear borders and

---

76. "Methuselah's Hands . . . Found!" Answers in Genesis, accessed September 16, 2016, https://answersingenesis.org/ministry-news/creation-museum/methuselahs-hands-found/.

77. "Making the Ark Encounter Animals," Ark Encounter, accessed August 14, 2018, https://arkencounter.com/blog/2016/11/01/making-ark-encounter-animals/.

78. Kelly and Hoerl, "Genesis in Hyperreality," 135.

79. Fredric Jameson, *Postmodernism, or, the Cultural Logic of Late Capitalism* (Durham, NC: Duke University Press, 2005), ix, 284.

80. Svetlana Boym, "The Future of Nostalgia," in *The Svetlana Boym Reader*, ed. Cristina Vatulescu et al. (New York: Bloomsbury Academic, 2018), 221.

81. Boym, 223.

values. *Hiraeth*, however, extends this idea to a longing for a home that may have never existed. Or, in Jameson's terms, this is a longing for the glimmering mirage. Hyperreality is liberating for the visitor inflicted with *biblical hiraeth*. The efforts of the Ark Encounter to create that place that is *more* real, a copy with no original, becomes an outlet for *biblical hiraeth*. Thus, the hyperreality of the theme park and *biblical hiraeth* become mutually supporting. *Biblical hiraeth* pulls people to the Ark Encounter while the Ark Encounter provides the fuel for *biblical hiraeth*.

At the Creation Museum, the MotB, and the Ark Encounter the genres of museum and theme park work together to lend authority to the seemingly realistic stories that AiG and the MotB want to tell. As storytelling institutions these places give form and structure to the longing, homesickness, and nostalgia—what I termed *biblical hiraeth*—for a time and place governed by biblical principles, even if that idealized time and place, as imagined by both patrons and attraction designers, never really existed. In light of changing cultural values, things like the rise of the religious "nones," shifting evangelical demographics, and the diminishing influence of the Bible in culture, these "prefabricated images of home offer an escape from anxiety of loss."[82] In the coming chapters on Methuselah, Noah, and fairy-tale arks we delve into very specific examples of the biblical worlds being created at the Creation Museum and the Ark Encounter and how patrons are receiving these narratives.

82. Boym, 252.

Chapter 5

DRAGONS, DINOS, AND TECH

Pseudoarcheology

In recent years Rob Skiba, a nondenominational theologian and Bible researcher, has slowly been building a following based upon his theories about the Nephilim (Gen 6:4), ancient technology, and Noah's flood.[1] His ideas are disseminated via books like *Archon Invasion: The Rise, Fall, and Return of the Nephilim* and via YouTube where he currently has 177,941 subscribers and his videos have been viewed 23,595,853 times. In *Archon Invasion*, Skiba argues that the Genesis 6 Experiment led to the creation of the giant Nephilim, who themselves engaged in genetic experimentation to produce monstrous hybrids like satyrs, centaurs, and minotaurs. Furthermore, he argues that the genetic code of the giant Nephilim may have survived the flood through the wives of Noah's sons and that there are forces on earth today who are trying to use genetic engineering to bring these genetic monsters back.[2] To illustrate these concepts, in his blog Skiba includes an illustration of a monster with the body of a horse, the torso of a man, and the head of a tiger.[3] When we see such things we will know that things are as they were in the days of Noah and that the end is surely nigh. All of this is inspired by an obscure reference in Gen 6:1-4, a passage that Gerhard von Rad called a "cracked erratic boulder," a fragment of what must have once been a longer story.[4]

Skiba is a recent example of an interpretative tradition that finds ancient technologies and alternative histories in the Bible. Being interested with such readings, I was fascinated to find that AiG, at both the Creation Museum and the Ark Encounter, flirts with this interpretative community. While visiting the

---

1. "Who Is Rob Skiba?" accessed April 7, 2019, http://www.babylonrisingblog.com/FAQ.html.
2. Rob Skiba, "Archon Invasion, Robs Channel," accessed May 23, 2019, http://robschannel.com/archon-invasion.
3. "God vs God—The Days of Noah," accessed April 7, 2019, http://www.babylonrisingblog.com/Godvsgod1.html.
4. Gerhard von Rad, *Genesis: A Commentary* (Louisville, KY: Westminster John Knox Press, 1973), 113.

Creation Museum it was an unexpected treat to encounter the idea that dragons/dinosaurs may have lived in America as recently as the late nineteenth century. Over the years I have delighted in Bible readings that have found space aliens, genetic engineering, and army-destroying batteries in the Bible. That these readings are possible speaks to the textual ambiguities that have produced such rich reception histories. While AiG does not dive as deep into ancient technologies and alt-histories as people like Graham Hancock (1950–) or Erich von Däniken (1935–), there is, nonetheless, a fascinating engagement with the worlds of pseudoarcheology and cryptozoology.[5] Moreover, in many ways the rhetorical methods used by pseudoarcheology and ancient mysteries writers are quite similar to the methods used by creation science advocates like Ken Ham and AiG. Central to this rhetoric is the claim that pseudoarcheological, cryptozoological, and creation science arguments are scientific and as science they should be taken seriously by the mainstream scientific community.

For AiG, faith seems to be an insufficient explanation for why people should accept the historical reality of Noah's Ark and the flood. The manner in which AiG presents its argument reveals a tacit assumption that visitors require the narrative to be rationalized, tempered by reason, supported by material evidence, and placed within a scientific framework. This is why much of the Ark Encounter is devoted to the technical aspects of Noah's Ark and the flood event. If these events can be proven in a naturalistic sense, then faith becomes less of a stumbling block.

In reading through the Ark Encounter's blog entries, it becomes evident that project leaders were fielding many questions, and addressing doubts, about the technology Noah had available to him for such an undertaking. This particular issue appears many times in separate blog entries, and AiG's answer, in part, has some similarities to the work of Erich von Däniken and Zecharia Sitchin (1920–2010), both of whom made rather remarkable proposals about the advanced technology of ancient civilizations.[6] The Ark Encounter argues that the antediluvians possessed an intelligence more advanced than commonly assigned to ancient peoples. Based upon God's original creation being "very good" the Ark Encounter assumes that Adam had a fully and perfectly functioning brain unclouded by the effects of sin and the fall. Furthermore, the taint of sin accumulated over time, and thus, the generations that were closer to Adam possessed intellects less affected by sin. Because they possessed minds that were freer from the taint of sin, the Ark Encounter claims that ancient peoples possessed a level of technological development heretofore unrecognized. Who could know, then, what tools and technological wonders were available to Noah? The Ark Encounter website maintains that antediluvian people were more advanced than many people

---

5. Erich von Däniken, *Chariots of the Gods? Unsolved Mysteries of the Past*, trans. Michael Heron (New York: G.P. Putnam's Sons, 1970); and Graham Hancock, *Fingerprints of the Gods* (New York: Crown Publishers, 1995).

6. Von Däniken, *Chariot of the Gods* and Sitchin's *The Earth Chronicles Series*. They also propose that the origins of this technology were extraterrestrial.

realize.⁷ Predictably, evolutionary theory is fingered as the reason scholars have failed to recognize the intellectual and technological development of ancient humans. According to AiG and the Ark Encounter, in adopting an evolutionary understanding of human development as a ladder of progress scholars have no choice but to see ancient humans as more primitive and less advanced.⁸

The Ark Encounter is generally careful to avoid speculation about what specific technologies were available to Noah. However, in a blog entry titled "When Is a Window Not a Window?" the Ark Encounter hints at how the three decks of Noah's Ark may have been lit. Genesis offers little information: "Make a window for the ark, and finish it to a cubit above; and put the door of the ark in its side; and make it with lower, second, and third decks" (6:16). The Hebrew word translated as "window" in this verse (and sometimes as "roof") is the word *tsohar*. However, ark designers had a difficult time imagining how a window at the top of the ark would have illuminated the lower two decks. Ark designers further note the window appears again in Gen 8:6 when Noah "opened the window of the ark that he had made." Here, however, AiG points out that "window" in Gen 8:6 is a translation of the Hebrew word *challon* and not *tsohar*. Thus, *challon* and *tsohar* must refer to different things. They therefore recall an ancient Rabbinic tradition whereby *tsohar* in Gen 6:16 was imagined as a large shimmering pearl or gem that hung from the ark's rafters. While noting that this is very speculative (but flirting with it nonetheless), the blog entry cites Rene Noorbergen's *Secrets of the Lost Races* (1978) as a source.⁹

Secrets of the Lost Races belongs to a genre of literature sometimes known as pseudoarchaeology. Other better-known examples in this genre include Erich von Däniken's *Chariots of the Gods?* (1968), Zecharia Sitchin's multivolume Earth Chronicles series (1976–2007), and Graham Hancock's *Fingerprints of the Gods* (1995). Works of pseudoarchaeology commonly argue that the ancients were far more technologically advanced than mainstream scholars recognize. Other authors writing in this genre maintain that the great works of the ancients, like the pyramids of Egypt, were impossible with the level of technological development achieved by the ancients alone. Explanations for the origin of such technologies vary, but many suggest the intervention of other forces, like space aliens. These authors further maintain that evidence for this can be found in the material artifacts of ancient civilizations. Thus, the horned cap (a Mesopotamian symbol of divinity) often depicted on figurines of the Mesopotamian goddess Inanna/Ishtar gets reinterpreted as a space helmet.¹⁰ Others propose that the geoglyphs known

---

7. "Man's Pre-Flood Potential," Ark Encounter, accessed February 23, 2017, https://arkencounter.com/blog/2012/01/06/mans-pre-flood-potential/.

8. Failing to recognize, however, that the ladder of progress view of evolution is a misrepresentation.

9. "When Is a Window Not a Window?" Ark Encounter, accessed February 23, 2017, https://arkencounter.com/blog/2012/09/07/when-is-a-window-not-a-window/.

10. Von Däniken, *Chariots of the Gods?* 62.

as the Nazca lines in southern Peru was an "airport" for flying saucers—a landing spot for ancient aliens.[11] Nobody writing for AiG is that specific about the types of technologies Noah used and certainly nobody suggests the intervention of aliens in the construction of Noah's Ark. Likewise, there are no specific references to things like electricity and engines or the other advanced technological features sometimes referenced in pseudoarcheology literature. While inviting patrons to wonder about the type of technology was available to Noah, AiG stops just shy of explicitly stating that Noah had access to technology that rivals our own.

Though Ken Ham's speculative approach to ancient technology is rather subtle, other pseudoarcheological speculations about the Bible have made more dramatic claims. Numerous examples can be found in *Atlantis Rising Magazine*, founded in 1994 and now a major clearing house for pseudoarcheological and speculative articles about the past. *Atlantis Rising* describes itself as "providing a serious forum for alternative ideas of pre-history, science and culture."[12] Not surprisingly, the publication has become the magazine of record on ancient mysteries, alternative science and unexplained anomalies."[13] In a 2008 *Atlantis Rising* article, author Joseph Frank argued that the ark of the Covenant was a highly advanced technological device, an "ultra-sensitive capacitor able to receive, store, magnify and discharge various forms of energy directed at it."[14] Functioning like a "sonic cannon," manipulating these energies allowed the Israelites to destroy the walls of Jericho.[15] This explains why, as poor Uzzah learned (2 Sam 6:6–7), the ark was very dangerous to work around. In his book *The Bible and Flying Saucers*, Barry Downing asks the reader to entertain the notion that, among other things, the Hebrews were led from Egypt by a UFO.[16]

This literature introduces some of the rhetorical similarities between alt-history writers and some young-earth creationist literature. Writers in both areas argue that there is a conspiracy afoot, by those who support the dominant scientific paradigms, to keep alternative views away from the public. The "About Us" page of the *Atlantis Rising* website states:

> While many scientifically oriented publications are content simply to pass on the latest pronouncements of the established research community, *Atlantis Rising Magazine* regularly reports on news and developments which challenge the very

---

11. Von Däniken, 16.

12. "About Us," Atlantis Rising Magazine Library, accessed April 10, 2010, https://atlantisrisingmagazine.com/about/. *Atlantis Rising Magazine* has since ceased publication.

13. "About Us."

14. Frank Joseph, "Ancient High Tech and the Ark of the Covenant," Atlantis Rising Magazine Library, January 1, 2008, https://atlantisrisingmagazine.com/article/ancient-high-tech-and-the-ark-of-the-covenant/.

15. Joseph, "Ancient High Tech and the Ark of the Covenant."

16. Barry Downing, *The Bible and Flying Saucers* (New York: Marlowe and Company, 1997), 78.

foundations of orthodox thinking. *Atlantis Rising* offers you what many in the mainstream press and the tabloids don't—the hard-to-find-out truth.[17]

Appealing to a conspiracy is one of the bedrock strategies used by creation science advocates who argue in favor of teaching creationism in public schools. Creation science advocates have viewed themselves as a persecuted minority who blame their failure to get a public hearing, and recognition from the mainstream scientific community, not on faulty science but on the efforts of mainstream scientists who refuse to allow any challenge to the dominant evolutionary theory. Consequently, creation science proponents appeal to the concept of fair play to argue that all perspectives on the question of origins should be presented. By asking schools to "teach the controversy" these efforts are meant to create the false perception of a lack of consensus on evolutionary theory in the scientific community. The teach the controversy approach suggests that there are multiple perspectives on creation and that different perspectives should receive equal consideration. Moreover, underdog stories play well with the general public and the David (creation science) versus Goliath (evolutionary theory) trope that frames these narratives often elicits sympathy. This David-versus-Goliath rhetoric features prominently in the work of ancient mysteries authors who present themselves as tireless heroes selflessly fighting a system that seeks to protect its own interests while silencing the opposition.

Though changing somewhat in recent years, for much of its history creation science advocates were largely amateur and armchair biologists and geologists. Many creation science thinkers had very little to no formal training in either discipline, but they nonetheless insisted on a hearing in academic outlets. Many early creationist proponents, like George McCready Price (1870–1963), Harry Rimmer (1890–1952), and Bernard Ramm (1916–92), had no advanced credentials in the relevant sciences (Price), held honorary degrees (Rimmer), earned advanced degrees in unrelated fields (Ramm) or, as in the case of the ICR's Harold Slusher (1934–), secured advanced degrees from questionable institutions or diploma mills.[18] When these individuals (both creationists and ancient mysteries writers) fail to get the hearing they think they deserve, they are quick to cry foul and point to unfairness and bias. Continued rejection by mainstream science eventually led to bitterness and disdain. In the case of pseudoarcheologists, professional archeologists are described as "rigid and timid dogmatists conspiring to suppress important truths about humanity's past."[19] Bernard Heuvelmans, the father of cryptozoology (the study of cryptids, animals whose existence is unsupported or

17. "About Us."
18. Numbers, *The Creationists*, 288.
19. Jeb J. Card, "Steampunk Inquiry: A Comparative Vivisection of Discovery Pseudosciences," in *Lost City, Found Pyramid: Understanding Alternative Archaeological and Pseudoscientific Practices*, ed. Jeb J. Card and David S. Anderson (Tuscaloosa: University of Alabama Press, 2016), 20.

disputed), declared that mainstream scientists were the "high priests of this new religion."[20] Many pseudoarcheologists romanticize the early days of archeology and geology, when, prior to the formal establishment of those disciplines as sciences, all work was done by nonexperts.[21] Romanticizing this period, and attempting to emulate its results, puts pseudoscientists even further behind these scientific fields as theory and method have clearly advanced far beyond this perceived golden era. Similarly, young-earth creationists like Ken Ham fixate on Darwin and the weaknesses of evolutionary theory as it existed in the late nineteenth century while ignoring the fact that evolutionary theory has advanced far beyond Darwin's foundational work.

Ancient mysteries writers, publishing on topics like the biblical flood, exhibit many of these attitudes. Peter Bros, author of "The Case for the Flood: Exposing the Scientific Myth of the Ice Age," rails against the boundary policing of mainstream science. He writes that mainstream science imposed its view against prehistoric civilizations by

> enforcing the eighteenth-century rule of reason which stipulated that God could not be used as an explanation for physical reality, thereby rejecting out of hand the possible validity of all biblical accounts and, in the case of a worldwide prehistoric society, the possibility that a flood of biblical proportions destroyed all but the megalithic evidence for that civilization.[22]

For Bros, it is hypocritical that mainstream science criticizes the nonrational and the mythical in what they call the pseudosciences when mainstream science has been guilty of disguising its own mythology. He describes mainstream science as "an enterprise that turns beliefs into facts, and it accomplishes this feat so well that its myths become more real than the actual facts."[23] Michael Cremo, author of *Forbidden Archaeology*, writes about the mainstream science "knowledge filter." Cremo has no formal training in science and is particularly bombastic when it comes to describing "academic elites" as bigoted, arrogant, and more interested in preserving their "own prerogatives and authority than the truth."[24] Like Heuvelmans, Cremo describes the modern, mainstream, academic science

---

20. Card, 24.
21. Card, 20–21.
22. Peter Bros, "The Case for the Flood: Exposing the Scientific Myth of the Ice Age," in *Forbidden History: Prehistoric Technologies, Extraterrestrial Intervention, and the Suppressed Origins of Civilization*, ed. J. Douglas Kenyon (Rochester, VT: Bear & Co., 2005), 44.
23. Bros, 46.
24. J. Douglas Kenyon, "Exposing a Scientific Cover-Up: Forbidden Archaeology Coauthor Michael Cremo Talks about the 'Knowledge Filter' and Other Means for Cooking the Academic Books," in *Forbidden History: Prehistoric Technologies, Extraterrestrial Intervention, and the Suppressed Origins of Civilization*, ed. J. Douglas Kenyon (Rochester, VT: Bear & Co., 2005), 24.

community as a priesthood that functioned much like the "entrenched religious establishment" just prior to the scientific revolution.[25] For Cremo, modern scientists function like a religious bureaucracy and work to protect their own power, which they use to guide society.

Anthropologist James Bielo, borrowing from Pierre Bourdieu, points out that this discourse functions in the context of power struggles defined by the doxic, orthodox, and the heterodox. The doxic represents an unchallenged dominant position, generally taken for granted. Recent PEW surveys have demonstrated that while 62 percent of Americans believe humans have evolved over time, only 33 percent believe that humans evolved by natural processes alone. Therefore, in the context of the general American population, evolutionary theory clearly does not hold the doxic social position. Rather, Bielo maintains, the struggle between the orthodox and the heterodox better describes the relative positions of evolution and creationism. Evolutionary science occupies the orthodox position and largely does so because of the accepted authority and "high social status" of modern science.[26] Creationism occupies the heterodox position because it is "a socially real intrusion on the 'universe of possible discourse.'"[27] What creationists and other pseudoscientists attempt to do, however, is harness the social capital of science in order to enhance the authority of their own arguments. This is why creation scientists utilize a seemingly scientific methodology and why they insist on admittance into the formal academic apparatus of secular science.

A comparison of the rhetoric of Cremo, Bros, and creationists like those at AiG is revealing. For example, a Creation Ministries International article from February 2008 addresses the lack of creationist publication in mainstream peer-reviewed journals by asserting that the role of peer review has been to protect the secularist and evolutionary agenda.[28] An April 9, 2008, AiG website article downplays the effectiveness of peer review as being poorly understood and of limited usefulness because peer review cannot guarantee accuracy and quality.[29] Undoubtedly there are problems with the peer-review system; however, the most important implication of this comment is to explain creation science's rejection in mainstream secular science outlets as a function of a faulty peer-review system rather than as resulting from the merits of its work. In a March 6, 2016, article

---

25. Kenyon, 26.

26. James S. Bielo, "Creationist History-Making: Producing a Heterodox Past," in *Lost City, Found Pyramid: Understanding Alternative Archaeological and Pseudoscientific Practices*, ed. Jeb J. Card and David S. Anderson (Tuscaloosa: University of Alabama Press, 2016), 86.

27. Bielo, 86.

28. "Creationism, Science and Peer Review," accessed September 28, 2018, http://creation.com/creationism-science-and-peer-review.

29. "Toward a Practical Theology of Peer Review," Answers in Genesis, accessed May 23, 2019, https://answersingenesis.org/creation-science/toward-a-practical-theology-of-peer-review/.

Ken Ham derided intolerance against Christian authors by secular academic gatekeepers.[30] In the same article Ham claims that many creationist articles are rejected in secular outlets because of the creationist content rather than the soundness and the quality of the article's argument.[31] This notion of a vast conspiracy to deny creationists a venue reflects the rhetoric found in the work of Bros, Cremo, and others who work in the pseudosciences.

These secularists, as Ham terms them, fill the biblical role of the scoffer. In his online article "Answering Claims about the Ark Project" Ham regrets having to respond to skeptics and, in the body of this article, uses the term scoffers no less than six times.[32] A keyword search for the term "scoffers" on the AiG homepage (answersingenesis.org) returns 204 results. The term scoffers in AiG literature performs an important rhetorical function that points to the mainstream rejection of young-earth creationist ideas. In addition, employing the term scoffers places AiG within a deep interpretive tradition about the flood narrative that places hecklers and scoffers in the story. Placing hecklers in the narrative makes the flood story one of vindication. Noah becomes an exemplar of a man who was steadfast in his belief and was eventually vindicated via the drowning deaths of those who mocked his efforts. Thus, young-earth creationists can hold onto the hope, by modeling Noah, that they will not only be proven right but that those who mock their efforts will also be punished.

Cryptozoology

While the Creation Museum and the Ark Encounter are flirting with pseudoarcheology, coquettishly whispering pseudoarcheological rhetoric, they are each fully in bed with cryptozoology. Cryptozoology, a pseudoscience originating in the work of Bernard Heuvelmans (1916–2001), is the search for evidence of creatures whose existence remains unproven according to Western scientific standards. Heuvelmans defined cryptozoology as "the scientific study of hidden animals, i.e., of still unknown animal forms about which only testimonial and circumstantial evidence is available, or material evidence considered insufficient by some!"[33] As described by Heuvelmans, cryptozoology is multidisciplinary in nature, basing investigations not just in physical anthropology and biology but also in folklore,

---

30. "Secularist Intolerance against Scientific Paper," Answers in Genesis, accessed May 10, 2019, https://answersingenesis.org/who-is-god/creator-god/secularist-intolerance-against-scientific-paper-briefly-mentions-creator/.

31. "Secularist Intolerance against Scientific Paper."

32. "Answering Claims about the Ark Project," Answers in Genesis, accessed April 18, 2017, https://answersingenesis.org/ministry-news/ark-encounter/answering-claims-about-the-ark-project/.

33. Samantha Hurn, "Introduction," in *Anthropology and Cryptozoology: Exploring Encounters with Mysterious Creatures* (New York: Routledge, 2017), 1.

myth, linguistics, archeology, and history.[34] The subjects of cryptozoological research are called cryptids and some of the most widely discussed include superstars like Sasquatch, the Loch Ness Monster, Mothman, and Chupacabra.

Young-earth creationists and cryptozoology make natural bedfellows. As with pseudoarcheology, both young-earth creationists and cryptozoologists bristle at the rejection of mainstream secular science and lament a seeming conspiracy to prevent serious consideration of their claims. For young-earth creationists, the pursuit of cryptids, especially dinosaurs and dragons, is important because of their potential to undermine evolutionary theory. If it can be demonstrated that humans and dinosaurs co-existed (or still do), as writers like Dave Woetzel assert, then the ancient earth chronologies required by evolutionists and geologists would be seriously called into question.[35] AiG and other young-earth creationist writers argue that humans and dinosaurs lived together and that both the Bible and the presence of dragons in ancient folklore supports this.

The Bible is a rich source for cryptozoological speculation because many strange creatures inhabit its pages. Many young-earth creationists point to the biblical creatures Leviathan and Behemoth, both famously appearing in Job 40–41, as evidence of dinosaurs in the Bible. In Job 41 Leviathan sounds remarkably like a dragon. Following the NRSV, Leviathan has skin like mail and a back covered in close-fitting shields arranged in rows. A flame emerges from its mouth and smoke belches forth from its nostrils and no sword, spear, or arrow can harm it (Job 41). Isaiah 27:1 describes Leviathan as a monstrous coiling sea serpent. Behemoth is equally mysterious, being described as grass eating and having a tail stiff as a cedar and bones that are tubes of bronze and limbs like bars of iron (Job 40:15–18). Many translations choose to naturalize these monsters by suggesting that Leviathan is a crocodile and Behemoth is a hippopotamus (both of which are offered by BDB as translations of the Hebrew terms).

However, young-earth creationists eschew the crocodile and hippo identification in favor of viewing Leviathan and Behemoth as dinosaurs. For example, a 2001 *Creation Journal* article titled "Behemoth or Bust" describes a three-week research expedition to Cameroon in search of a mythical creature called the *mokele-mbembe*, a creature that the article describes as being similar to the biblical Behemoth.[36] The article concludes that the best explanation for the biblical description of Behemoth is to accept it as a dinosaur. Going one step further, the article argues that creatures like the *mokele-mbembe*, or the *li'kela mbembe*, are modern living dinosaurs.[37] If it can be demonstrated that dinosaurs still inhabit the earth, serious questions about the evolutionary timeline would follow.

---

34. Hurn, 1–2.

35. Dave Woetzel, "Cryptozoology & Creation Apologetics," accessed March 21, 2017, http://www.genesispark.com/essays/cryptozoology-creation/.

36. "Behemoth or Bust," Genesis Park, accessed September 28, 2018, https://www.genesispark.com/essays/behemoth-or-bust/.

37. "Behemoth or Bust."

Leviathan is not the only dinosaur young-earth creationists find in the Bible. A 2006 article in the *Creation Research Society Quarterly* titled "The Fiery Flying Serpent" speculates about the creature mentioned in Isa 14:29. This passage mentions a fiery flying serpent (Heb. *saraph*) in the context of a prophecy about the Philistines, "for from the root of the snake will come forth an adder, and its fruit will be a flying fiery serpent." According to "The Fiery Flying Serpent," the flying reptile described in Isaiah is likely a pterosaur.[38]

The fiery flying serpent suggests something more akin to a dragon than a dinosaur. Indeed, many young-earth creationists argue that the creatures known as dragons are either misidentified dinosaurs or are dimly remembered dinosaurs. Such is the case at the Creation Museum's *Dragon Legends* exhibit. The *Dragon Legends* exhibit is floored with stone pavers, dark brown and reddish in color, framed by an interior wall modeled to look like exposed granite, as though one were facing a sheer mountainside, or cliff, or perhaps even a cave—mimicking the type of wild place one might expect to find a dragon. Hanging on the walls are poster displays that recount select legends about dragons or dragon-like creatures, including brief descriptions of encounters with dragon-like creatures in *Beowulf* and the histories of Herodotus. This exhibit argues two things. First, AiG maintains that dragon legends could have been embellished descriptions of living dinosaurs, and second, the disappearance of dinosaurs may have occurred more recently than commonly recognized.

The final poster in the *Dragon Legends* exhibit, before entering the Main Hall, is titled "Cowboys and Dragons." The "Cowboys and Dragons" poster reprints a short article from the April 26, 1890, edition of the Tombstone, Arizona, paper titled the *Tombstone Epitaph*. The excerpt describes how two ranchers came across a "winged monster" that resembled an alligator with wings, had an 8-foot-long head, sharp teeth, and eyes as large as dinner plates. The ranchers estimated that the monster had a wingspan of 160 feet. Following this excerpt, the Creation Museum display asks if it is possible that the ranchers encountered the "legendary Thunderbird or Piasa of Native American lore, a creature whose descriptions remind one of a pterosaur."[39]

The Creation Museum proposes that the widespread nature of dragon myths, and the similarities in the stories, can be taken as evidence of the existence of dinosaurs in recorded human history.[40] Indeed, as the term "dinosaur" was introduced in 1841 by Sir Richard Owen one would expect a different term applied to such creatures in ancient history. AiG maintains that prior to 1841 all large reptiles were called dragons. Furthermore, the term dinosaur refers to a specific type of dragon whose legs were directly beneath their bodies and whose hip

---

38. "The Fiery Flying Serpent," Genesis Park, accessed September 28, 2018, https://www.genesispark.com/essays/fiery-serpent/.

39. Wall text, *Cowboys and Dragons*, Creation Museum, Petersburg, KY.

40. "Dragons: Fact or Fable?" Answers in Genesis, accessed March 23, 2017, https://answersingenesis.org/dinosaurs/dragon-legends/dragons-fact-or-fable/.

structure raised them from the ground.[41] Thus, dinosaurs are a subtype of dragon, as reflected in the Creation Museum poster display that states "not all dragons could be called dinosaurs. But all dinosaurs could have been dragons."

To support this idea biblically, AiG points to the fifth day of the Gen 1 creation narrative and the creation of the great sea creatures (Heb. *tanninim*). Starting with the BDB definition of *tannin* as serpent, dragon, or sea monster, AiG further argues that, depending on context, *tannin* can refer to both a dragon and a dinosaur (since all dinosaurs are dragons).[42] Two *tannin* discussed at some length in articles by AiG include the Behemoth (Job 40), considered a sauropod, and the Leviathan (Job 41), considered a kronosaurus.[43]

The language used to connect dragons and dinosaurs at the Creation Museum is much more tentative than language used on this topic on the AiG website. The AiG article "Dragons: Fact or Fable?" exhibits more certainty and unambiguously states that dinosaurs are dragons.[44] By way of contrast, a poster display in the *Dragon Legends* exhibit notes that dragons "could have been" dinosaurs. This waffling language helps keep this discourse in the realm of speculation without fully committing to such an outlandish claim. It is, in other words, about plausible deniability. The "Cowboys and Dragons" poster cited above also uses contingent language: "Is it *possible* that these cowboys encountered the legendary Thunderbird [emphasis mine]?"[45] The Creation Museum website suggests that ancient artistic depictions of dragons *could* reflect creatures the artists were seeing.[46] This contingent language, what James Bielo calls the "suggestive register," is prevalent throughout the *Dragon Legends* exhibit.[47] Bielo, who interviewed and observed Creation Museum design teams, notes that the *Dragon Legends* exhibit designers claimed to simply be asking "what-if?" Bielo quotes a Creation Museum artist named Jon who states, "We're not showing any reality and we're not saying [legends] are proof [of dinosaurs]. It's more, we're asking 'Could it be?'" Bielo rightly points out that this "just askin'" rhetoric is common in pseudoscientific work and furthers the agenda of disrupting mainstream science.[48] On the other hand, it is a rather strange approach for an organization whose authority rests upon presenting realistic, certain, and authoritative statements about the past.

As we have seen, young-earth creationists like Ken Ham paradoxically foster a sense of being persecuted by the mainstream scientific community whose sanction they very much desire. Unable to accept that their rejection by secular

41. "Dragons."
42. "Dragons."
43. "Dragons."
44. "Dragons."
45. Wall text, *Cowboys and Dragons*.
46. "Dragon Legends," Creation Museum, accessed March 23, 2017, https://creationmuseum.org/dinosaurs-dragons/legends/.
47. Bielo, "Creationist History-Making," 82.
48. Bielo, 93.

science is grounded in how modern science is understood and practiced, and unable to accept that the merits of creation science do not meet the standards of modern secular scientists, they turn instead to stories of oppression, conspiracy, and persecution. They become, therefore, modern Noah's working on their ark, facing rejection and ridicule by mainstream society but soothing themselves with assurances that their vindication will come. While the flood narrative is important to AiG as foundational for explaining the earth's geologic features, it is also a story that governs and explains their relationship to a largely unbelieving culture. In the next chapter we turn more specifically to the manner in which the flood narrative is presented at the Creation Museum, through the character of Methuselah, who assures us that "something terrible is coming."

Chapter 6

SOMETHING TERRIBLE IS COMING

The Creation Museum's animatronic Methuselah is a rather peculiar figure, described by some as creepy, in that *unheimlich* way of the automaton.[1] He sits in a mock striped tent through which the museum visitor passes prior to entering the *Noah's Ark* exhibit. He is modeled in a sitting position, simultaneously leaning on and cradling a large staff, wearing rather conventional Middle Eastern style white robes and keffiyeh. Methuselah talks to the visitor and begins his monologue with a joke whereby he assumes the museum patron would guess him to be a mere six hundred years old (insert chuckle). Following this, Methuselah reveals that he knew Adam and he discusses Adam's son Cain and the arrival of industry, metalworking, music, and art through Cain's descendants. Sadly, Methuselah opines that Cain's descendants forgot about God and just chose "to live their own way." Methuselah then reveals that God warned his grandson Noah about the impending flood and instructed him to build the ark. He opines that with each passing day judgment draws nearer, that "something terrible is coming," and that nobody believes Noah. Methuselah assures the listener, however, that what God says is true.

One of the things that makes Bible reception studies so interesting is the variety of novel interpretations people bring to the text, especially in those areas that are ripe for creative reading. Often these are stories that are tantalizingly vague, like Gen 6:1–4, or are about individuals about whom we just want a little more information. When I first visited the Kentucky Creation Museum, I was simultaneously puzzled and intrigued that museum designers devoted an entire display to Methuselah. At 75,000 square feet, the Creation Museum only has so much space to cover a story that spans thousands of pages. Nonetheless, they chose to give a considerable amount of space to a seemingly minor Hebrew Bible figure.

This chapter is the first of several that explores the presentation of biblical characters and events at the Creation Museum and the Ark Encounter. As part of my multilevel reception study of these attractions, these chapters focus on the significance of these displays for AiG and how AiG's Bible reading is represented

---

1. MidwestMuseumfan, "Not Worth the Money," TripAdvisor, August 10, 2009, https://www.tripadvisor.com/ShowUserReviews-g39743-d619562-r37299728-Creation_Museum-Petersburg_KentucKY.html.

in their material objects. This particular chapter focuses on the Creation Museum's animatronic Methuselah as a case study of AiG's use of the Bible. Recognizing that the Bible readings produced by AiG are not done in isolation, this chapter also compares the Creation Museum Methuselah with that presented in Darren Aronofsky's 2014 film *Noah*. This comparison further illuminates AiG's understanding of Methuselah as well as illustrating how two different interpretative communities approach the same text. Despite the different interpretative communities, it turns out that both AiG and *Noah* present Methuselah as an apocalyptic figure.

Methuselah: The Do-Nothing Patriarch

A staple of Bible trivia, Methuselah has the distinction of being the Bible's oldest person. However, aside from his incredible age of 969, the Bible actually says very little about him. Genesis 5:21 introduces Methuselah as the son of the still young (according to antediluvian standards) sixty-five-year-old Enoch. Prior to his translation into heaven three hundred years later (Gen 5:24), Enoch gave Methuselah other (unnamed) brothers and sisters. While still a youngster, at the spry age of 187, Methuselah fathered Lamech and in later years fathered other unnamed sons and daughters before dying at the bone-creaking age of 969. Methuselah appears one other time in the Hebrew Bible in the lineage of Saul (1 Chr 1:3). Methuselah's sole appearance in the New Testament (Luke 3:37) is in the genealogy of Jesus.

While he may have been the longest lived of the antediluvians, he did not outlive others by much. For instance, according to Gen 5:20 Methuselah's grandfather Jared lived for 962 years, just a mere seven years shy of Methuselah's record-setting age. Aside from outliving Jared by seven years, Methuselah just did not do much. With his age as his primary claim to fame, it is curious that Methuselah receives an entire Creation Museum exhibit.

Sometimes naming conventions can reveal information about the literary role of biblical characters. Various translations of the name Methuselah periodically appear but the most widely accepted is "man of the dart,"[2] though "when he is dead it shall be sent" has been proposed.[3] Despite the popularity of "when he is dead it shall be sent" in some theological circles (for its clear prophetic import), "man of

---

2. Strong's 4968.

3. John Gill, *An Exposition of the Old Testament*, Vol. 1. London: printed for the author; and sold by George Keith, at the Bible and Crown in Grace-Church-Street, M.DCC.LXIII. [1763]-65. *Eighteenth Century Collections Online* (accessed May 23, 2019). http://find.gal egroup.com/ecco/infomark.do?&source=gale&docLevel=FASCIMILE&prodId=ECC O&userGroupName=viva_radford&tabID=T001&docId=CW3319103522&type=multip age&contentSet=ECCOArticles&version=1.0. 40. Gill proposed "When he dies there shall be an emission."

the dart" is favored by AiG.⁴ These translations derive from the two component parts of Methuselah's name (Heb. *math* and *shelach*). The first component, *math*, means "man." The second part of Methuselah's name, *shelach*, when derived from the Hebrew verb *shalach*, denotes some type of thrown or missile weapon, like a spear. Analyzed thus, Methuselah becomes "man of the dart." However, the basic meaning of the Hebrew verb *shalach* is "to send." In addition, rather than translating the first part of Methuselah as "man," some chose the Hebrew verb *mut*, which means to die or to kill. When translated in this manner Methuselah becomes "when he is dead it shall be sent."⁵ Without any additional context Methuselah as "man of the dart" seems to add little to the narrative. However, the translation "when he dies it shall be sent," when placed in the context of the flood narrative and Methuselah's death in the proposed year of the flood, can be read as prophetic.

In the article "When Did Methuselah Die?" AiG's Bodie Hodge supports translating Methuselah as "man of the dart," or "man of the sword."⁶ Moreover, following John Gill, Hodge points out that some have argued that the name Methuselah incorporates the Hebrew word for death and various alternative translations of the name have ranged from "when he dies there shall be an emission" to "He dieth, and the sending forth."⁷ This further led, Hodge maintains, to translations like "when he dies it shall come" or "upon his death there will be a major change." Despite the clearer prophetic import, Hodge concludes (based upon the opinion of Dr. Ben Shaw at Greenville Presbyterian Theological Seminary) that the translation "when he dies it shall come" (and its variations) is likely inaccurate, despite the fact that Methuselah appears to have died the same year as the flood.⁸ Nonetheless, Hodge concludes that since Enoch was a prophet, then it may be reasonable to expect something prophetic about Methuselah's name.⁹ While rejecting the prophetic import of Methuselah's name, the Creation Museum nonetheless places him in a prophetic context as the herald of the flood apocalypse.

The decision to place Methuselah in the role of introducing the flood was no whim or matter of convenience. Rather, museum designers agreed that Methuselah was the ideal figure to serve as a bridge between Adam and Noah. AiG points out that Methuselah would have known Adam and would have passed down information about him.¹⁰ If knowing Adam was the sole criteria for this role, however, then having an animatronic Enoch introduce the flood would have

---

4. "When Did Methuselah Die?" Answers in Genesis, accessed September 16, 2016, https://answersingenesis.org/bible-timeline/genealogy/when-did-methuselah-die/.

5. Richard S. Hess "Methuselah," in *Anchor Bible Dictionary, Volume 4, K-N*, ed. David Noel et al. (New York: Doubleday, 1992), 801. Hess translates Methuselah as "man of Shalah" with Shalah being "god of the infernal river."

6. "When Did Methuselah Die?"

7. "When Did Methuselah Die?"

8. "When Did Methuselah Die?"

9. "When Did Methuselah Die?"

10. "Methuselah's Hands . . . Found!"

been sensible, and perhaps would have been even more authoritative. After all, according to Gen 5:25 Enoch was so righteous that he walked with God and was bodily taken into heaven. Likewise, according to AiG's timeline, Noah's father Lamech could also have known Adam and could have been placed in this role. Indeed, an animatronic Noah could have made the best introduction to the flood considering he had God's favor and received the message from God to build the ark (Gen 6:8). Not to cast aspersions on Methuselah's character, but when God considered the inhabitants of the earth it was Noah who found favor in God's eyes (Gen 6:8), not Methuselah, and not Lamech. One wonders what Noah's father and grandfather did, or did not do, that prevented God from turning his favorable eyes upon them.

Justifying the choice of Methuselah as flood provocateur can be further supported by reading beyond the biblical text and considering the role Methuselah played in the book of Enoch (1 Enoch) and other non-biblical Jewish legends. 1 Enoch, a collection of intertestamental Jewish texts—the oldest portions of which were written in the late fourth century BCE[11]—records a collection of apocalyptic visions given to Enoch. For posterity's sake, Enoch writes down his visions and charges Methuselah with preserving and passing them on (*1 En.* 82.1–3).[12] Methuselah becomes a messenger in 1 Enoch, which foreshadows Methuselah as messenger at the Creation Museum. Moreover, it is clear that Mike Matthews and others at AiG are familiar with the 1 Enoch narrative even though AiG does not view 1 Enoch as authoritative. In an article on the AiG website, the authority of extra biblical texts is rejected when none of the New Testament authors cite them.[13] There is at least one exception to this rule. The New Testament Epistle of Jude references the Genesis flood narrative and reproduces a prophecy that appears to be drawn from 1 Enoch. Jude 1:14–15 quotes *1 En.* 1.9 saying: "See, the Lord is coming with tens of thousands of his holy ones, to execute judgement on all, and to convict everyone of all the deeds of ungodliness that they have committed in such an ungodly way, and of all the harsh things that ungodly sinners have spoken against him."[14] Bodie Hodge explains the implications of this quote in Jude as it relates to the AiG perspective on the apocrypha. Hodge cautions the reader not to assume that a single quote from Enoch appearing in Jude is enough to make all of 1 Enoch canon. Rather, he claims that it is better to understand only this single Enochian prophecy as inspired and its inclusion in Jude stands as evidence of such.[15]

---

11. George W. E. Nickelsburg and James C. VanderKam, *1 Enoch: A New Translation Based on the Hermeneia Commentary* (Minneapolis, MN: Fortress, 2004), vii.
12. Nickelsburg and VanderKam, 113.
13. "Is the Bible Enough?" Answers in Genesis, accessed November 4, 2016, https://answersingenesis.org/bible-questions/is-the-bible-enough/.
14. Nickelsburg and VanderKam, *1 Enoch*, 20.
15. "When Did Methuselah Die?"

Methuselah Hands Things Off to Noah

The existence of an animatronic Methuselah, and indeed, the very existence of the Creation Museum, suggests something about the intertwined nature of religion and material culture. Despite the ubiquity of material things in religious culture, until recently the general arc of biblical reception criticism has overlooked the relationship between popular material culture, the Bible, and reception. Thus, analyses of material displays of the Bible—like those presented in the Creation Museum—have generally missed analysis by reception critics. This has been true despite W. J. T. Mitchell's declaration of the pictorial turn, the idea that images and pictures have replaced words as the "dominant mode of expression in our time."[16] To quote William Keenan and Elisabeth Arweck, "When dealing with the things of the spirit, matter matters inordinately."[17] In the case of the animatronic Methuselah, the form and function of the object reflects very little from biblical narratives but rather invents, imagines, and expands the story. The only obvious biblical physical fact about Methuselah is his extreme age, thus, unsurprisingly, the Creation Museum presents the visitor with an automata that appears very old. Aside from age, there is little about Methuselah from Gen 5 that would suggest the manner in which he is presented in the Creation Museum.

As with many things associated with the Creation Museum and the Ark Encounter, Methuselah is a reflection of the hyperreal. In the article "Methuselah's Hands . . . Found!" Mike Matthews explains that it was important to model Methuselah's hands as the calloused hands of a farmer.[18] This concern for Methuselah's hands and feet (a concern seemingly important enough to have prompted an entire blog entry) represents the overarching quest for authenticity exhibited by AiG at the Creation Museum. Hands and feet, being difficult to sculpt, are a particular area of concern as it relates to the realism of the animatronic Methuselah. The final solution was to create a mold of the hands and feet of a church acquaintance of Mike Matthews.[19]

In the Hebrew Bible God's hand (Heb. *yad*) is among the most frequently mentioned parts of His body. The hand of God (Heb. *yad ha'Elohim*) is a symbol of God's power and the salvific acts he takes on behalf of his people. Not only does God create from his hand but he also redeems his people with his hand. For instance, God's hand stretched out against Egypt ultimately allows the Hebrews to go free (Exod 3:19–20). The hand of God shelters his people. Thus, according to Exod 33:22–23 "while my glory passes by I will put you in a cleft of the rock, and I

---

16. W. J. T. Mitchell, *What Do Pictures Want? The Lives and Loves of Images* (Chicago, IL: University of Chicago Press, 2005), 5.

17. William J. F. Keenan and Elisabeth Arweck, "Introduction: Material Varieties of Religious Expression," in *Materializing Religion: Expression, Performance, Ritual* (Hampshire: Ashgate, 2006), 1.

18. "Methuselah's Hands . . . Found!"

19. "Methuselah's Hands . . . Found!"

will cover you with my hand until I have passed by; then I will take away my hand, and you shall see my back; but my face shall not be seen." God's hand is also the hand of judgment, particularly relevant for the Methuselah display as a warning of a coming apocalypse. Thus, Jer 25:15 states: "For thus the Lord, the God of Israel, said to me: 'Take from my hand this cup of the wine of wrath, and make all the nations to whom I send you drink it. They shall drink and stagger and go out of their minds because of the sword that I am sending among them.'" Isaiah 51:17 also describes the hand of God offering the cup of His wrath. Sometimes God's hand holds the cup of wrath but in other instances God's hand strikes directly. Jeremiah 15:6 warns: "'You have rejected me,' says the Lord, 'you are going backward; so I have stretched out my hand against you and destroyed you.'" By taking an Old Testament figure about whom little is said (or known) and drawing particular attention to his hands, Creation Museum designers were able to tap into the theological importance of hands in the Bible as both instruments of punishment and salvation to make Methuselah a signifier of the apocalypse.

The fact that hands are more difficult to sculpt and draw also plays into the creationist message of the Creation Museum. For creationists, the human hand is viewed as evidence of design rather than of evolution. An August 27, 2015, AiG article describes the human hand as having ideal proportions and that the human hand, with its opposable thumb, is unique, implying that it has no basis in evolution.[20] In an article titled "Our Index Finger: Pointing to the Creator" author Jonathan Jones argues that the hand is far too complex to have emerged from an evolutionary process. That every part of the hand must work together to function properly points to a creator.[21] Therefore, the hand's complexity for both artists and sculptors recalls the creationist argument that complexity is evidence of creation.

Some Sort of Witch Doctor

The Creation Museum is not the only place that has recently put significant effort into imagining Methuselah. The 2014 Darren Aronofsky film *Noah* depicts Methuselah (Anthony Hopkins) in a prominent role as a hermit-like, berry-loving mystic, with miraculous healing abilities. For the purposes of this study, it was illuminating to compare how two different organizations handled Methuselah at roughly the same time. For both AiG and Darren Aronofsky, this particular cultural moment seemed to call for an apocalyptic Methuselah.

Aronofsky's Methuselah resulted from an unconventional reading of the biblical text. He retains his role as Noah's grandfather, and, meeting expectations,

---

20. "Are Human Hands More Primitive Than Chimps?" Answers in Genesis, accessed October 19, 2018, https://answersingenesis.org/human-evolution/human-hands-primitive-chimps/.

21. "Our Index Finger—Pointing to the Creator," Answers in Genesis, accessed October 19, 2018, https://answersingenesis.org/human-body/our-index-finger/.

he is depicted as a greatly aged man. His hair is a long white mullet descending from a balding crown (colloquially known as a "skullet"). His skin is heavily aged and wrinkled and his left eye appears to droop. Despite his advanced age, this Methuselah is rather spry and appears to have few problems moving around. As with the Creation Museum, Aronofsky uses Methuselah as a link between the past (Adam) and the present (Noah) by placing within his possession a seed from the Garden of Eden. This seed later sprouts into a forest that provides the wood for Noah's Ark.

Methuselah's backstory is presented early in the film and filmmakers clearly utilized non-biblical Jewish legends about Methuselah in forming his character. In doing so, Aronofsky was able to create a Methuselah richer in character than that of the Creation Museum. In *Noah* Methuselah was the champion of creatures known as the Watchers. Described in 1 Enoch, the Watchers are the angels who left heaven in order to pursue their lust for human women.[22] Aronofsky's Watchers are creatures of light created by the Creator on the second day, the day he made the Heavens. Originally watching over Adam and Eve, the Watchers pitied the humans after their fall and descended to earth in order to help them. In doing so they disobeyed the Creator who caused them to become encased in stone and mud when they arrived on earth. The Watchers endeavored to share what they knew about Creation, but humans eventually turned against them and began hunting and killing them. Despite this, the Watchers are later convinced to help Noah build the ark.

When Methuselah, as the Watchers' guardian, appears on screen he is arrayed in armor, a helm obscures all but his eyes and nose, and he carries a large sword. In battle he draws the sword and it glimmers with a fiery yellow and orange glow. He thrusts the sword into the ground at his feet causing the ground to erupt into flame. The resulting fire rushes forth before him igniting the enemy. This is the Methuselah of Jewish legend, a demon-slaying warrior with a super sword that allows him to "slay 94 myriads of the demons in a minute."

Nature and environmental destruction frame Aronofsky's *Noah*. Indeed, Methuselah shares with Noah a prophecy from Enoch that men are to be punished for what they have done to the earth. (Methuselah was surprised, however, to learn that the annihilation would be by water rather than fire.) The spread of Cain's cities over the land created an exploited postapocalyptic ruin. Noah and his family walk a desolate landscape of parched land, ash, and blackened tree stumps.

Methuselah lives in a cave on a green mountain set in the midst of a blackened landscape. When Noah locates Methuselah the viewer learns that—in addition to possessing a miraculous sword of remarkable power—Methuselah has other mysterious abilities. He puts Shem into a deep sleep by placing his hand on the boy's face and hissing "shh." He is skilled with mysterious herbs and berries, brewing for Noah a tea with hallucinogenic properties through which Noah receives the

---

22. Nickelsburg and VanderKam, *1 Enoch*, 23–24.

command to build the ark. The fact that Methuselah is peculiarly obsessed with berries just further enhances his connection to nature.

Unlike the position adopted by AiG, Aronofsky's Methuselah dies in the flood. Recall that only Noah found favor is God's sight. Does this mean that Methuselah suffered from the same flaws that doomed the rest of the world? AiG materials suggest otherwise. As a godly person, the son of Enoch, fulfilling his part of the divine plan, AiG's Methuselah is a righteous man for whom death in the flood would have been undeserved. This is why AiG goes to great lengths to emphasize that Methuselah died in the year of the flood, but before the flood actually started.[23] For Aronofsky, even the nature-loving Methuselah cannot escape the apocalyptic wrath of Mother Nature.

Looking past Methuselah and into the broader context of this story it is clear that Ken Ham and Darren Aronofsky each imagine God's orientation toward humans in different ways. For instance, at the Creation Museum the visitor listens to Methuselah discuss how the descendants of Cain have forgotten God. This, of course, plays into a typically Christian theology of sin and free will suggesting to the visitor that the blessings of God are there for those who remember God. Indeed, one premise of the Creation Museum is that as people forget God and God's teaching (as embodied in the Bible) conditions in society continue to deteriorate.

In *Noah*, this orientation is reversed and the viewer is left with the impression that God (the Creator) has forgotten humans rather than humans forgetting God. By way of example, Tubal-Cain, king and leader of the people attacking the ark, elicits sympathy when he expresses his anguish that the Creator no longer talks to him. When Tubal-Cain confronts Noah about his ark, he states: "The Creator does not care what happens in this world. Nobody has heard from Him since He marked Cain. We are alone. Orphaned children, cursed to struggle by the sweat of our brow to survive. Damned if I don't do everything it takes to do just that."

If both Methuselahs met in a cage match, it seems clear that Aronofsky's Methuselah would win the fight. Anthony Hopkin's Methuselah is a hale and powerful figure compared to the frail and old figure that appears at the Creation Museum. They both possess wisdom, but that wisdom appears to emerge from different fountainheads. Being able to manipulate and preserve the materials of nature, Aronofsky's Methuselah exercises a wisdom based upon a close relationship with the natural world. The wisdom of the Creation Museum's Methuselah is more abstract and seems related to the close relationship he and his family maintain with God. The Aronofsky presentation of Methuselah certainly makes sense in light of the larger environmental theme of the film. Ultimately, as the last seed from the first garden produces the timber for the ark, it is clear that nature is salvific. In both, humans are the reason for the flood; however, in the biblical narrative the annihilation occurs within the context of multiple rebellions, including the fall of Adam and Eve, the angelic rebellion of Gen 6:1–4, and the subsequent corruption

---

23. "When Did Methuselah Die?"

of humans. At the Creation Museum, the correct relationship to God seems to be the measuring rod, while in Aronofsky's film humanity's relationship to nature determines the outcome.

Storytelling Methuselah

The historical consciousness of any given period does not exist "as a set of openly stated or recorded propositions" but exists, according to Jauss, as a horizon of expectation."[24] As Paul de Mann notes in his introduction to Jauss, there are collective expectations (preconscious and subconscious) that are themselves a result of reception as an individual's work is amalgamated into the broader landscape "against which new works will, in turn, be silhouetted."[25] A related concept is the so-called horizon of change. The horizon of change is the degree to which a text invalidates an old perspective and creates a new perspective. In short, the horizon of expectation is the criteria (preconscious and subconscious) against which a reader interprets a text. The distance between the horizon of expectation and the horizon of change is called the aesthetic distance. Readings that results in little or no change in perspective would presumably have a very short aesthetic distance while those readings that promote profound change have a great aesthetic distance.

This does not mean, however, that interpretation is the Wild West where anything is possible and few rules govern reading. Instead, interpretation is governed by the historical context and the social codes and mores in which people are situated. It is here that Jauss could be faulted for not going far enough. Generally Jauss assumes, as Martyn Thompson points out, only one horizon of expectation when, in fact, several horizons "socially differentiated" exist against which reading occurs.[26] In the prior paragraphs two readings of Methuselah, each emerging from different horizons, are described. Of those two, I would propose that it is Aronofsky's Methuselah that has the greatest aesthetic distance and thus represents the best opportunity for a change in horizon of expectation.

As described in *Christianity Today*, Darren Aronofsky "is known for dark, edgy independent films that center on characters with obsessive and self-destructive personalities."[27] Raised culturally Jewish, Peter T. Chattaway described Aronofsky's film *Noah* as "midrash for the big screen," a description of *Noah* that Aronofsky

---

24. Paul de Man, Introduction to *Toward an Aesthetic of Reception* (Minneapolis, MN: University of Minnesota Press, 1982), xii.

25. de Man, viii.

26. Martyn P. Thompson, "Reception Theory and the Interpretation of Historical Meaning," *History and Theory* 32, no. 3 (1993): 263, doi:10.2307/2505525.

27. Interview by Peter T. Chattaway, "Darren Aronofsky Talks to CT about 'Noah,'" ChristianityToday.com, accessed February 8, 2017, http://www.christianitytoday.com/ct/2014/march-web-only/darren-aronofsky-interview-noah.html.

embraces even to the point of describing his Noah as a continuation of midrashic tradition.[28] Based upon the traces of post biblical Jewish legends in the film *Noah*, Aronofsky seems rather well versed in the Jewish cultural tradition that he claims.

Over the course of his interview with Peter Chattaway, Aronofsky exhibits a sophisticated relationship with the biblical text. On the midrashic tradition, Aronofsky states, "The text is what the text is. The text exists and is truth and the word and the final authority. But how you decide to interpret it, you can open up your imagination to be inspired by it."[29] While clearly giving a great deal of authority to the text as a source for truth, Aronofsky intentionally allows for the play of interpretation and imagination. It is something he embraces. On the other hand, at the Creation Museum and the Ark Encounter, imagination and interpretation are on display despite the fact that AiG writers deny employing these tactics in reaching their understanding of the text. For readers like Ken Ham, and others who share his horizon, the type of imaginative interpretation advocated by Aronofsky is an improper method of reading the text. Ham views the difference between exegesis and eisegesis as critical for adopting a proper hermeneutical approach. Ham advocates for exegesis, which he describes as an attempt "to flesh out meaning based on the plain words, the genre, the context, and other scriptural references."[30] This stands in contrast to eisegesis, which Ham describes as a reading that taps into preconceived ideas and ideas outside of scripture.[31] As it relates to Aronofsky's approach, Ham would accuse him of an eisegetical hermeneutic by forcing his own views onto the text.

Still, the role of interpretation in the Creation Museum's presentation of Methuselah is clear. There is little scriptural context into which one may place the display. In Gen 5 he is a link in a genealogical chain stretching from Adam to Noah. 1 Chronicles 1:1 and Luke 3:23 place Methuselah in the lineage of Abraham and Jesus, respectively, but otherwise provide even less detail than Gen 5. Thus, Methuselah's function at the Creation Museum as a harbinger of apocalypse is the result of an interpretative reading of the Bible. In addition, Methuselah's script also contains elements that purportedly relate to Noah that are not biblical. Methuselah's statement that nobody believes Noah draws upon the long-held tradition that Noah's neighbor's mocked him for his efforts. Utilizing this trope in the Methuselah exhibit says as much about Ken Ham and AiG as it does about Noah's neighbors. Mocked and derided himself, Ken Ham is able to use Methuselah's words as a source of comfort, and vindication, in the face of a skeptical public.

Much of what Gadamer and Jauss write on horizons of expectations is an effort to explain why classic literary works have artistic value. Both Gadamer and Jauss explain this by pointing to defamiliarization and disruption that changes or

---

28. Chattaway, "Darren Aronofsky Talks to CT about 'Noah.'"
29. Chattaway, "Darren Aronofsky Talks to CT about 'Noah.'"
30. Ham, *Six Days*, 187.
31. Ham, 187.

expands the reader's horizon. Gadamer describes this as part of the hermeneutic circle with outward and returning movements. In the outward movement, the reader, encountering the alien in a text, comes to recognize him or herself and finds the familiar in the work. The returning movement represents the reflexive phase wherein the reader recognizes change in him or herself. This change then shifts the reader's horizon.[32] Jauss wrote in a similar manner, but rather than the stronger language of disruption, he wrote about the mediation of the reader's horizon and that of the text. According to Jauss, the more distance that exists between a text's horizon and the reader's horizon, the greater the change in the reader's horizon and the greater the likelihood of a text being seen as having artistic merit. Parris further expands on this: "The tension between the two horizons not only allows us to recognize what is foreign in the text, it also challenges or questions our own prejudices."[33] The reader's expectations are disrupted through a process of defamiliarization creating the potential for the text to push a reader toward new perspectives. Such texts are considered innovative and will become part of the "literary competence of successive generations of readers."[34] In other words, these texts are incorporated into successive horizons of expectations. Not all texts are disruptive in this manner. Thus, if a given text closely reflects the reader's horizon of expectations then there is little to no change in that horizon. Parris maintains that without this provocation there can be no experience. Over time, even the classic works lose this provocation leading to new efforts to "read against the grain" in order to help a work maintain its classic or artistic merit.[35]

Given the argument outlined above, it then seems possible to examine which of the two Methuselahs have the greatest potential to unsettle the reader's horizon of expectations. In this regard, it is useful to recall Ken Ham's strong reaction to Aronofsky's presentation of the Noah narrative and to Methuselah in particular. It is no exaggeration to say that Ken Ham despised this movie, describing it as perhaps "the worst film I've ever seen."[36] Ham states that the film was disgusting, pagan, and evil. So disgusting, in fact, that Ham felt he needed a shower afterward.[37] He levels some of his most biting criticisms toward Aronofsky's depiction of Methuselah as a witch doctor and magician.[38] It is unlikely, however, that Aronofsky's film

32. Parris, *Reception Theory and Biblical Hermeneutics*, 16.
33. Parris, 152.
34. Parris, 133.
35. Parris, 133–35.
36. Ken Ham, "Ken Ham: The Unbiblical Noah Is a Fable of a Film," *Time*, accessed March 28, 2014, http://time.com/42274/ken-ham-the-unbiblical-noah-is-a-fable-of-a-film/.
37. Bielo, *Ark Encounter*, 95. "The Noah Movie Is Disgusting and Evil—Paganism!" Answers in Genesis, accessed January 19, 2017, https://answersingenesis.org/blogs/ken-ham/2014/03/28/the-noah-movie-is-disgusting-and-evil-paganism/. According to Bielo, Ark Encounter designers kept close track of the production of *Noah*.
38. "The Noah Movie Is Disgusting."

will move Ham's horizon on the Noah story because the sympathetic reading required by Gadamer's hermeneutic circle is not complete in Ham. The reader, on the outward movement, finds the homely in a seemingly strange text, seeing oneself in it, and returns having one's horizon of expectation expanded. There is little evidence, based on Ham's public statements about the film, that a fusion of horizons occurred.

Why Methuselah and Why Now?

In their introduction to *Material Varieties of Religious Expression*, Keenan and Arweck define a six-point habitus of religious material expressions that provides a useful framework for analyzing the Creation Museum's animatronic Methuselah. First, the habitus of religious material expressions emphasizes spectacle, representation, performativity, and display.[39] Without doubt AiG takes very seriously the theological content of the Methuselah display; his narrative and his appearance are all meant to lend authority to the AiG hermeneutic. Just as important, however, is the performative aspect of the display. On one hand, material objects reveal what religious ideas "look like."[40] Shared images create a sense of community and can be the starting point from which communal communication is built. However, while material expressions of religion can show us what religious ideas look like, the same material expressions can limit identity and create boundaries and margins.[41] Faced with an animatronic Methuselah, the viewer is not as free to imagine any Methuselah he or she wishes (and there are other types of Methuselah's in popular culture) but is encouraged to see the Methuselah that AiG wishes to present. Borrowing from Stuart Hall, the viewer is likely to adopt a stance of acceptance, accommodation, or resistance to the presented image. The visitor who comes away from the animatronic Methuselah resisting the AiG presentation, "that's not what Methuselah is like," represents the place where differing horizons of expectations are in friction.

Many of the richest receptions of biblical narratives exploit inherent ambiguities in the text, and the short Methuselah narrative is no exception. The paucity of details about Methuselah and his life allows him to become a Rorschach for Bible interpreters. If people know anything about Methuselah (surprisingly, many of my interview subjects knew nothing of him), it is his being the oldest person recorded in the Bible. His age then becomes the launching point into other potentially related discourses—like health and vitality—which play a central role in *Noah*. In *Noah* the land is not rotting so much as it is drying up, like the wrinkled, dry, old skin of a 969-year-old man. It is, moreover, a premature aging and can be reversed with the application of a little bit of moisture—but on a global scale. A

---

39. Keenan and Arweck, "Introduction: Material Varieties of Religious Expression," 14.
40. Keenan and Arweck, 2.
41. Keenan and Arweck, 14.

general sense of unwellness is conveyed not just in the arid landscape but also in the opening scenes when the greens of the serpent and the reds of the fruit are followed by a black shadow that creeps over the earth as the descendants of Cain spread across the land, like a parasite consuming its host. The film's muted color palette, largely of grays and browns, further contributes to this impression. As we know, Aronofsky works with environmental themes and the arid landscapes of *Noah* suggests a world of global warming caused by exploitation. So, in addition to being prematurely old, and frail, the world has developed a fever.

Turning to Methuselah himself, though he appears very aged in *Noah* he nonetheless conveys a general sense of health. He lives on a very lush, green, mountain and, in pointed contrast the industrialized lifestyles of Tubal-Cain and his followers, lives a lifestyle more in tune with the earth. He guards the last seed of Eden, the fecundity of which saves humankind.

The Creation Museum's Methuselah portrays a greater sense of frailty. Though perhaps limited by the technology, here Methuselah remains seated, propped up by his staff and rather bony arms while a thin face gazes at the viewer from beneath the fold of his keffiyeh. This Methuselah exudes a sense of things passing away. The first age of humankind is passing and the last human alive who knew the first human is introducing the transition to a new age.

The third characteristic of Keenan and Arweck's habitus of religious material expressions is a post-secular interest in religious renewal and a "return to the sacred."[42] Here I would again introduce the concept of *biblical hiraeth*. Both Methuselahs manifest in visual form a longing for things that have passed away. The Creation Museum's Methuselah suggests a time when God could be counted upon to punish the ungodly, when His activity is clearly and unambiguously present in the world. In *Noah* Tubal-Cain complains that God no longer talks to humans, thus, Methuselah comes to represent a *hiraeth* for a time when humans were not forgotten. In each instance this is a *hiraeth* for a re-enchantment of the world, a call for God to once again pour out his will upon the earth.[43]

Perhaps, therein, lies the appeal of Methuselah for audiences today. Regardless of which end of the social and political debate spectrum one occupies, there is palpable sense of impending doom pervading American culture. Many see an apocalypse coming in the form of global warming and environmental degradation. Others see a continuous cycle of cultural decay linked to an abandonment of God's Word. In both cases, Methuselah has become a prophet of the apocalypse, a romanticization of the past, and a beacon of hope for the future. *Noah*'s Methuselah preserves the memory of a better day when the earth was a garden and also provides the means of saving the human race. Aronofsky makes no secret of his interest in apocalyptic themes, so it is no surprise that the Noah story, which he

---

42. Keenan and Arweck, 14.

43. Bielo, *Ark Encounter*, 79. Bielo found that re-enchantment is a goal of creation science generally. "Creationists infuse modern science with religious meaning, reshaping science to fit their religious worldview."

describes as the "first apocalypse story," would attract his attention.[44] The Creation Museum's Methuselah is also linked, through Adam, to a golden age of innocence and gardens and offers salvific knowledge to the museum visitor.

The Creation Museum's Methuselah serves as an introduction to Noah, so it seems natural that this should be where we next turn our attention. Though AiG professes to present the Bible without interpretation, there is a fascinating film screened at the Ark Encounter that serves as an excellent example of how AiG uses biblical narratives as social and political commentary.

44. Chattaway, "Darren Aronofsky Talks."

Chapter 7

NOAH STOPS A KNIFE FIGHT

The Creation Museum's Methuselah introduces the visitor to Noah who awaits the visitor in an impressive, to scale, partial recreation of Noah's Ark. However, to get the most of one's Noah fix, a trip to the Ark Encounter is necessary. Had designers strictly adhered to the Bible in their design of the Ark Encounter, the attraction, like the biblical flood narrative, would have lacked in detail. The decision to use artistic license not only makes for a richer attraction but also makes the Ark Encounter an excellent material representation of how AiG imagines the flood narrative of Gen 6–9. Within the walls of this ark the visitor can witness Noah stopping a knife attack, can read about the dangers of story book illustrations of the ark, and can learn how animals walking on treadmills could have helped dispose of waste.

Variously termed by AiG as creative license, educated guesses, or artistic license, the manner in which AiG fills the biblical gaps represents a considerable amount of hermeneutic play. As Hans-Georg Gadamer pointed out, play is an important aspect of the hermeneutical process and represents that middle ground between the text and the interpreter where hermeneutics occur.[1] By employing a system of educated guesses, AiG engages in a process of self-presentation, a central concept in Gadamer's formulation of play. Using a game analogy, he writes: "The self-representation of the game involves the player's achieving, as it were, his own self-representation by playing, ie, representing, something."[2] To relate this to Ken Ham, AiG, and the Ark Encounter, to view Bible interpretation as play at the Ark Encounter is as much about the presentation of AiG as it is about the ark replica as a product.

Hermeneutical play should not be understood as trivial or frivolous—though a comparison to a game is not inappropriate.[3] Considering games and how they are played, individual players are not self-contained and participate in a system

---

1. Parris, *Reception Theory*, 66.
2. Gadamer, *Truth and Method*, 97; Lauren Swayne Barthold, "Gadamer, Hans-Georg," in the *Internet Encyclopedia of Philosophy*, accessed June 12, 2017, http://www.iep.utm.edu/gadamer/.
3. Gadamer, *Truth and Method*, 96; Nicholas Davey, "Gadamer's Aesthetics," in *The Stanford Encyclopedia of Philosophy* (Fall 2018 Edition), ed. Edward N. Zalta, https://plato.stanford.edu/archives/win2016/entries/gadamer-aesthetics/.

larger than themselves. Likewise, spectators must also allow themselves to be drawn into the game. For the game to be comprehensible to both player and spectator a willing immersion must occur, requiring that the "spectator play along with what they bring into being."[4] Because the game draws together both player and spectator, within the bounds set by the game's equipment, conventions, and rules, the communicative nature of the event cannot be measured in the mind of the player alone. Thus, the plays made by AiG at the Ark Encounter must be understood in light of the game and its rules counterbalanced by the spectator's understanding of the event. This chapter takes us further into the mind of the player. The spectator will be the subject of coming chapters.

Naturally, Ark Encounter designers would not view their efforts as being the result of play; rather, AiG views itself as engaged in a process that is designed to prevent misinterpretation. The manner in which AiG plays with the Genesis flood narrative is likely a consequence, as Heidegger pointed out, of the human desire to find reasons for everything, which is an outgrowth of our desire to control things.[5] As any reader of Gen 6–9 can attest, there are peculiarities—gaps and oddities—in the narrative that entreat interpretation. There is a natural impulse to bridge those gaps in order to make sense of the narrative.

Gadamer would argue, however, that play is not without its rules. Tradition is the playing field and "a playful event of understanding is possible only because of what is handed down to us in our tradition and how what is handed down addresses and strikes us."[6] The playing field for AiG is the collection of traditions that inform their understanding of the Bible. Within the bounds of these traditions many different plays are possible, but the boundaries of tradition prevent AiG from completely subjective interpretations. To use a term popularized by Nietzsche, but here best understood as employed by the anthropologist Marshall Sahlins, there are no immaculate perceptions, "the seeing eye is the organ of tradition."[7]

While play is evident at the Ark Encounter, the ideas presented there are decipherable because they emerge on a field of play bounded by a particular hermeneutic maintained by interpretative communities. This includes, as examined above, young-earth creationism and its drive for scientific credibility and the rules and styles of literalist Bible interpretation. While there are many examples at the Ark Encounter to focus on, for this extended analysis of hermeneutical play, I have chosen a short, but remarkable, film shown at the Ark Encounter. *The Noah Interview* represents one of the most playful interpretations of the Bible at the Ark Encounter.

The Ark Encounter has two theaters, one on deck two and another directly above on deck three. During my visit to the Ark Encounter (March 22, 2017) the

---

4. Davey, "Gadamer's Aesthetics."
5. Parris, *Reception Theory*, 76.
6. Parris, 82. Gadamer, *Truth and Method*, 98, where he discusses the players' roles.
7. Marshall David Sahlins, *Islands of History* (Chicago, IL: University of Chicago Press, 2004), 145.

theaters were playing two different films related by virtue of being variations of a journalist who encounters the ark. The 22-minute film playing on deck two, titled *The Noah Interview* is set in Noah's lifetime close to the completion of the ark. In this film, Noah agrees to speak to a reporter from a local tabloid, the "Pangea Independent Tabloid," otherwise known as the "PIT." Pangaea is a nod to the supercontinent that the Ark Encounter proposes must have existed prior to the flood. As described above, the global flood was responsible for breaking this supercontinent apart.

The film opens with Noah hard at work supervising ark construction. Opening scenes show Noah pouring over ark blueprints, with sketches of various cranes sitting on a trackway reminiscent of railroad tracks. While ancient trackways existed, these images introduce the Ark Encounter's argument that Noah had access to more and better technology than secular academic archeology or history supports. If the Ark Encounter visitor follows a clockwise path upon entering the second deck, the deck two theater and its showing of *The Noah Interview* serves as an introduction to following exhibits that make explicit proposals about the construction and maintenance of the ark.

Noah's interview occurs on a very gloomy day. In fact, the unnatural green tint in the stormy sky accentuates a sense of doom. As a harbinger of violent weather, this eerie green-tinted sky will seem familiar to anybody who has lived in tornado alley. The only place where the sun breaks through the roiling clouds is directly above the ark, which rests upon a hill behind Noah. Noah clearly would have forgotten about the interview were it not for his wife's (Emzara) reminder just prior to the arrival of the interview team.

The PIT interview team travels from a local city, thus setting up a city/rural contrast that is evident in the remainder of the film. This dichotomy is evident in the Hebrew Bible in the romanticization of Israel's pastoral past contrasted with cities as dens of wickedness (as, for instance, the city of Sodom). This idealized vision of the rural versus the degradation and wickedness of the city is still evident in Christianity (note the rural locations of both the Creation Museum and the Ark Encounter discussed in Chapter 1). The PIT interview team consists of three individuals. Adah (Heb. "to adorn") is the journalist interviewing Noah and her appearance in this film is quite startling. While Noah and Emzara are wearing AiG's interpretation of period clothing, robes perhaps modeled on the *simlah* (resembling the *himation* of the ancient Greeks), Ark Encounter designers made no effort to cloth Adah in authentic period garb. In fact, Adah looks like she just stepped from a Goth metal music video. Adorned from head to foot in black leather, from her waist hangs dozens of long gray and black tatters, and black leather vambraces wrap her forearms. Partially braided on one side, various feathers decorate her long black hair. Her eyes are heavily shadowed and upon her face is a stylized red W, the arms of which start on her forehead and the middle of which arcs across her nose. Various other red stripes mark her face. A very large, muscular transcriptionist named Kenan accompanies Adah. He is shirtless and heavily tattooed and his disposition is surly and gruff. He also has feathers woven into a small braid that hangs from the left side of his head. Finally, the sketch artist for the PIT is Jared. Jared is slightly more clothed than Kenan and wears a short cape from which hang feathers and a few furs. His personality reflects the stereotypical temperamental artist and is likely meant to be perceived as gay.

Adah is many things that Emzara is not. Seemingly tempered by age and righteous living, Emzara is salt of the earth, possessing a plainer, more imperious, beauty than Adah. Like Noah, Emzara wears plain robes, minimal jewelry, and works with her hands tending to the garden. True to her name, Adah fosters a more cultivated beauty, relying on heavy makeup and more jewelry. The basic honesty of land cultivation seems contrasted to Adah's profession as a journalist, further recalling the dichotomy between city and rural life that pervades much of the Hebrew Bible. Even Adah's coworkers give little credence to her profession. When Adah refuses to help Jared carry his sketching materials, Kenan states that she "doesn't even do anything except sit there and gab."

If there is something more trustworthy about Noah and Emzara's work, it is contrasted with the distrust each express about Adah. As Adah's team approaches Noah's work site, Noah expresses concern that he and his work will be the object of the PIT's scorn. Emzara halfheartedly suggests that Adah might be fair, an assertion that is met with a scoff from Noah. Noah's incredulity foreshadows the skepticism that abounds in the internal structure of this story, which reflects the real-life pressures faced by the Ark Encounter as they worked to construct the ark replica. Noah's skepticism toward the local press (the PIT) is a direct reflection and commentary on real-life press coverage, much of it skeptical, heaped upon the Ark Encounter. Indeed, when construction of the Ark Encounter had sufficiently progressed, Ken Ham published an article on the AiG website titled "Answering Claims about the Ark Project" wherein he addressed many of the popular misperceptions about the Ark Encounter. Therefore, *The Noah Interview* is a creative reimagining of what Noah might have faced as well as being a commentary on the relationship between the Ark Encounter and various hostile media outlets. Throughout Adah's interview with Noah, she seems variously bored, sarcastic, impatient, and rude—cartoonishly so. In the film, and in real life, the media is not only misguided but also corrupted by the influence of Satan, as the acronym "PIT" (Pangea Independent Tabloid) suggests without any subtlety.

The Ark Encounter's presentation of the press in this film echoes claims made about the media from some in the evangelical right. Though Noah exhibits a little more patience, one can see echoes of President Trump's perspective on the mainstream media as the "enemy of the people" in this film's discourse. The notion that the press has a barely disguised agenda, so prevalent in today's social and political discourse, is woven in the presentation of Adah and her team. Furthermore, this discourse is parallel to, and supports, the young-earth creationist disdain for other mainstream figures of authority, like secular scientists, who are also thought to be harboring an agenda. Thus, this discourse that purports to be about a biblical figure in the distant past actually becomes a commentary on society today.

Examining the various Adahs that appear in the Hebrew Bible and their roles in later Jewish religious thought provides a richer understanding of Adah's role in this film. Adah appears in Gen 4:19 as one of two wives (the other being Zillah) of Lamech, son of Methushael of the Cainite lineage. Adah gave birth to two sons. Jabal would be the progenitor of those who live the nomadic lifestyle of animal herding and tents while Jubal would be the father of those who play stringed instruments and pipes (Gen 4: 20–21). As Carol Meyers points out, Adah's songs, coupled with Tubal-Cain's (the son of Lamech's second wife, Zillah) metalsmithing, represent the founding of the civilized arts "which are thus presented as a fully human product and not as a gift of the Gods."[8] In *The Noah Interview* Adah is more clearly associated with the cultural heritage of her son Jubal and her nephew Tubal-Cain than she is the legacy of her son Jabal, who represents the romantic pastoral phase of ancient Israel.

In non-biblical Jewish tradition, events surrounding Adah are symptomatic of the degradation of society prior to the flood. For Jewish exegetes the name "Adah," suggesting beauty, was also linked to sex. According to these traditions, Lamech took two wives, one for child rearing and the other for sexual pleasure. The Jerusalem Talmud suggests that Adah was the wife used for Lamech's sexual desires.[9] On the other hand, the Genesis Rabbah (an early Jewish interpretation of Genesis) maintains that Adah was the wife reserved for childbearing. Of the two traditions, that of the Genesis Rabbah more closely adheres to biblical tradition. However, the depiction of Adah in the Jerusalem Talmud seems closer to that presented in *The Noah Interview*. In this film Adah is the corrupt beauty closely associated with the city and the deviant civilization surrounding Noah.

Adah's appearance, clad in black leather, adorned with bird feathers, and face painted with designs that look like a Hollywood depiction of Native American war paint, evokes a culture that has abandoned God and given itself over to paganism. Adah's affected British accent, a common conceit used in film villainy, further reinforces her role as the villain. It is true that people with posh British accents present as upper class, sophisticated, and elegant; however, it is equally the case that such accents are perceived as nefarious. As linguist Chi Luu writes, "At the same time, in terms of social attractiveness, those same posh RP [received pronunciation] speakers are consistently rated less trustworthy, kind, sincere, and friendly than speakers of non-RP accents."[10] Kenan, the tattooed transcriptionist, who also speaks in an accented, gruff voice, further reinforces the association between accents, villainy, and the alien other.

---

8. "Adah 1: Bible," Jewish Women's Archive, accessed March 23, 2017, https://jwa.org/encyclopedia/article/adah-1-bible.

9. "Adah 1: Midrash and Aggadah," Jewish Women's Archive, accessed March 23, 2017, https://jwa.org/encyclopedia/article/adah-1-midrash-and-aggadah. *The Jerusalem Talmud*, comprised between 400 and 500 CE, contains much of the same material as *The Babylonian Talmud* (ca. 600 CE) though differences in the Gemara are evident.

10. Chi Luu, "Very British Villains (and Other Anglo-Saxon Attitudes to Accents)," *JSTOR Daily*, accessed January 18, 2017, https://daily.jstor.org/very-british-villains-and-other-anglo-saxon-attitudes-to-accents/.

Kenan is a very large, muscular, bare-chested man sporting many Polynesian-inspired tribal tattoos. He sounds like his throat is filled with gravel and he challenges Adah's authority. Unlike Adah, who indicates her disapproval with bored sighs and sarcasm, Kenan directly confronts Noah. As Noah explains the reasons for the coming flood, emphasizing the sinfulness of humans, Kenan stands and passionately asserts, "You know what you call sin, I call freedom, you bigot." Exchanges like this are not biblical, despite the fact that many people, and the Ark Encounter, imagine the masses ridiculing Noah. This is another example of how a little creative license, meant to depict Noah's negative relationship with his neighbors, also functions as a commentary on AiG's understanding of modern social degradation. This link between the modern and the ancient is often justified biblically by Matt 24:37, which reads, "For as the days of Noah were, so will be the coming of the Son of Man." For many, this passage suggests that one sign of the eschatological return of Jesus is a human descent into wickedness that mirrors the state of society in Noah's own lifetime. The specific details of this wickedness, however, are found nowhere in the Bible. At most the reader finds the Gen 6:5 statement that humans were wicked and inclined toward evil and the Gen 6:13 contention that violence filled the earth. Kenan's outburst against Noah is a commentary against a modern, liberal, society that views things like same-sex marriage and transgender acceptance as matters of human rights (freedom in Kenan's words). From the perspective of this liberal and progressive segment of society, anybody who stands against these values is, in Kenan's terms, a bigot. Kenan's outburst is also a narrative of reverse victimization from a Christian audience reacting against what are perceived as false accusations of bigotry and discrimination. AiG wants the audience to understand that the last laugh is Noah's because Kenan, and all he represents, is about to be judged.

The bickering between Adah and her staff emphasizes discord in the broader culture. The interactions of others in the film, who are not of Noah's family, also illustrate this. For instance, the film features a short, and rather peculiar, exchange between two characters listed in the credits as "Bronze Breath" and "Iron Brains." Bronze Breath and Iron Brains interrupt Noah's interview with a dispute about the proper metal to use when building hinges. Like Adah and her staff, Bronze Breath and Iron Brains speak in voices that come across as unnaturally gruff or foreign. Their voices stand in contrast to the dulcet tones of Noah and his wife (who sound very American), further enhancing the difference between the civilized/uncivilized and rational/irrational. Iron Brains passionately maintains that iron is the best material for hinges because of its strength. Bronze Breath holds that bronze is the better material because it resists corrosion. The argument degenerates until Bronze Breath and Iron Brains find themselves in a shoving match and Bronze Breath pulls a knife. At this point Noah steps in, puts a slightly jiu-jitsu move on Bronze Breath, forcing him to drop the knife, and works out an equitable solution between the two men.

Though amusing, I believe the figures of Bronze Breath and Iron Brains also represent a short Ark Encounter discourse on history. It is well established, in both ancient historical and mythological narratives and in modern archaeological dating conventions, that the march of civilizations can be identified in ages associated with various metals. For instance, in *Works and Days* the Greek poet Hesiod identified the earliest ages of history as the Golden, Silver, Bronze, Heroic, and Iron Ages. Note that each subsequent age represents a degeneration from the Golden Age with the Iron Age being an age of labor, trouble, and sorrow. Similar schema are evident in the Hebrew Bible. Perhaps best known is the Dan 2 progression of ages as represented in Nebuchadnezzar's dream vision of an anthropomorphic statue. The head of the statue is gold, chest and arms are silver, belly and thighs are bronze, legs of iron, and the feet are a mixture of iron and clay. There have been many proposals about what historical periods and cultures are represented in this image, but that need not detain us here. One recognizes that, like the Hesiod progression, the Dan 2 statue also represents a degeneration from a golden age. However, in Daniel the progression of ages is also used in an apocalyptic context because, according to Daniel's interpretation of the dream, the statue falls when the feet of iron and clay crumble and the eternal kingdom of God arises in its place. This apocalyptic progression of ages is evident in *The Noah Interview* as the cultures represented by Bronze Brains and Iron Breath will shortly pass away in God's flood judgment. Of course, the Bible itself demonstrates that the age following the flood was not the kingdom of God. Nonetheless, for many Christians the biblical flood is a type for the coming final judgment. Today, non-Christian cultures are Bronze Breath and Iron Brains and AiG looks forward to a coming vindication and establishment of the final kingdom.

The Noah Interview addresses concerns about the perceived selfishness of Noah's actions. In fact, Adah bluntly suggests that Noah building an ark for his family alone is selfish. She states, "It just seems a big life boat for you and your family alone is a little selfish, don't you think?" Noah insists, however, that he is not in control of who or what goes on the ark and that he will accommodate anybody that God chooses to bring. Speculation on Noah's selfishness has a long history in exegetical work derived from Gen 6–9. Some have speculated that Noah should have done more to spare lives, perhaps acting in a manner reminiscent of Abraham's argument on behalf of Sodom and Gomorrah. Like many other traditions derived from this narrative, Genesis is actually silent on Noah's objections or concerns, if he had any, they remained unexplored. The Ark Encounter addresses the issue of Noah's selfishness by taking the issue out of Noah's hands and placing it in God's. This is important enough that it gets addressed a second time toward the end of the film when Noah asserts, again, that he has no control over who God brings to his ark, but he will welcome all God sends.

When the disastrous interview finally ends, Emzara, who had returned to her gardening, approaches Noah and asks how the interview went. "About as bad as I thought it would," Noah replies. Emzara states, "Well, scoffers gonna scoff." The idea that ridiculing and scoffing masses surrounded Noah is firmly entrenched in the popular imagination. Even at the Creation Museum an animatronic character mixing pitch scoffs at Noah's efforts (though admittedly in a more gentle manner than Adah and her crew). Sermons, works of art, and Sunday school lessons continue to perpetuate this tradition. Oddly enough, AiG recognizes the problematic nature of this imagined aspect of the Noah narrative. In an article titled "We Just Don't Noah," published on the AiG website on September 23, 2013, Tim Chaffey writes that there is nothing biblical about scoffers living near Noah. He further states that while one can make reasoned deductions, the reader must be careful not to introduce anachronism or their own thoughts into the text.[11]

While maintaining the distinction between Bible narrative and educated guesses may be easy for the biblically literate staff of AiG, the Bible literacy of Creation Museum and Ark Encounter visitors, even among those who are ardent believers in the AiG message, is a matter of concern. My interview subjects could rarely cite chapter and verse about these well-known narratives and many could not correctly identify the book in which these narratives appear. Because of this, AiG runs the risk of doing what Chaffey claims AiG must avoid: creating in the visitor's mind a blending, or confusion, of Ark Encounter educated guesses and information that actually appears in the Bible. Furthermore, if the confusion between the Bible and the educated guesses runs too deep, then the narrative presented by AiG at the Creation Museum and the Ark Encounter, and the educated guesses contained therein, takes on the authority of the Bible among visitors who fail to distinguish the guesses from the Bible. This fusion of biblical authority with the Creation Museum and the Ark Encounter, because the contents contained therein are considered biblical (even though AiG admits to engaging in guesswork), is evident among some of the subjects interviewed for this study.

It is true that artistic license is a feature of many pop-culture representations of classic texts. For instance, Homer's *Odyssey* is retold in the Jim Crow era South in the film *O Brother, Where Art Thou?* Some people quip that the worst person to see a movie with is the one who "has read the book." Perhaps we all know somebody who left one of the Lord of the Rings films complaining about the artistic license taken by Peter Jackson in his adaptation of the Tolkien trilogy or how the Harry Potter films may have deviated from the canon. Among my interview subjects, and in TripAdvisor and Facebook reviews, complaints about these attractions drifting from the Bible are rare.

The general lack of concern about the educated guesses made at the Creation Museum and the Ark Encounter likely results from the trust that patrons have already placed in Ken Ham and AiG. After all, Ken Ham and AiG engaged in an extensive ministry before either of the flagship attractions was built and the success of this ministry is one of the factors that made building the Creation Museum and the Ark Encounter possible. Having established his trustworthiness as a Bible exegete, Ham can speak about issues related to the Bible with a great deal of authority without arousing the suspicions of his audience. Peter Jackson, in the early days of the Lord of the Rings films, or Chis Columbus, when he directed *Harry Potter and the Sorcerer's Stone*, lacked that kind of authority. In the early days of those franchises, neither had widely established their credibility as interpreters of the works of Tolkien and Rowling.

---

11. "We Just Don't Noah," Answers in Genesis, accessed April 18, 2017, https://answersingenesis.org/noahs-ark/we-just-dont-noah/.

The willingness of many Creation Museum and Ark Encounter visitors to trust the materials presented therein as biblical has consequences regarding biblical authority and the way in which AiG interpretation blurs with actual Bible content. This transfer of biblical authority to non-biblical presentations of the Bible at the Ark Encounter occurs despite the fact that ark designers included some disclaimers about educated guesses and artistic license. One sign introducing a display called "Workable Models" reads: "Have you ever wondered how Noah's family fed all the animals and removed their waste? How did they provide fresh air and water? And how did they light the ark? The concepts displayed in this exhibit are models showing plausible solutions to these challenges. While we may not know all of the details, we know they successfully accomplished their tasks since all eight people and the animals God sent to them survived the Flood." Another display, with a header that reads "Artistic License," reads: "This exhibit provides a plausible backstory based on clues from Scripture to explain how the Lord may have prepared His faithful servant to fulfill such an important mission." Artistic license is invoked again in the ark's living quarters display where ark designers were more explicit. "Since we don't have a time machine, we can only make educated guesses about the looks, skills, and personality of each individual. Any attempt to represent historical events necessarily involves using artistic license, and we took great care not to contradict biblical details." One should note, however, that *The Noah Interview* contains no such disclaimer. The Ark Encounter does avoid contradicting the biblical text (at least as AiG understands it); however, contradiction is not the primary concern.

Take, for instance, several details from *The Noah Interview*. This short film, along with other displays at the Ark Encounter, works very hard to certify Noah as a ship builder. At one point, Noah launches into the particulars of using pitch. In another instance, Noah begins a technical explanation of his tri-keel ark design and scarf joints. This establishes Noah's engineering credibility despite the fact that the biblical narrative says nothing about Noah's expertise in this area. In the mind of the hurried, uninformed, visitor, the distinction between "Noah may have had shipbuilding expertise" and "Noah had ship building expertise" is easily lost.

Though the artistic license and educated guesses disclaimers are absent from *The Noah Interview*, the film is, nonetheless, an extended exercise in speculation. It is just one small example—among many—of speculative displays found in the Ark Encounter. In these displays AiG is encoding a particular message about biblical narratives that they want the visitor to accept as authoritative, disclaimers notwithstanding. I have found in interviews and the online reviews that, despite the disclaimers offered that the Ark Encounter, educated guesses are becoming part of the Bible literacy of museum visitors, taking on the authority of biblical narrative, and becoming part of a new horizon of expectations for visitors. Before we get to that material, however, I have one more deep dive into an Ark Encounter display. The Ark Encounter's *Fairy Tale Ark* exhibit, which is quite critical of many images of the ark for children, provides an opportunity to examine how material objects, like bath tub arks, can be employed as "bad objects" in support of AiG's interpretation of Genesis narratives.

Chapter 8

THE FAKE ARK DELUGION

Ask any American what images come to mind when they think of quality handmade objects made in America and chances are that they will think of Amish craftsmen. There can be no doubt that the Amish are romanticized in American culture. From quaint farms and horse-drawn plows to quality handmade items, Amish goods, made using techniques from a bygone era, suggest quality and durability, and are superior to modern machine-made goods. For Americans, the Amish are what Dachang Cong calls "fashionably old fashioned," embodying the cultural cache of the "values and strength of rural America."[1] As such, the Amish are a powerful symbol for tradition, simpler times, and a community governed by biblical values.[2] In a word, there is something more authentic about the Amish. Orie and Ernest Lehman, Amish contractors from Indiana, oversaw the construction of Ark Encounter's timber frame.[3] Though they, and many other Amish, use power tools and other modern building techniques, the Ark Encounter, nonetheless, benefits from this Amish cultural mythology.

Realism and authenticity are paramount concerns for AiG in its Creation Museum and Ark Encounter attractions. From employing Amish craftsmen to creating realistic zoological specimens, one goal is to rationalize the fairy-tale and mythological elements of biblical narratives in an effort to repudiate the scoffers. After all, employing the Amish in the ark's construction recalls large things (like barns) quality built by hand, thus reinforcing the plausibility of Noah hand-building an ark. The existence of the Creation Museum and the Ark Encounter suggests that visitors need the tangible and the material to enhance the credibility of biblical narratives.

Representing a type of heritage tourism, focused on the "re-creation of ethnic or cultural traditions," a perceived authenticity is critical to the success of a venue like the Ark Encounter.[4] As Chhabra et al. write, heritage tourism is

---

1. Dachang Cong, "The Roots of Amish Popularity in Contemporary U.S.A.," in *Journal of American Culture* 17, no. 1 (Spring 1994): 59.

2. Cong, 61.

3. "Lehman Brothers Visit the Ark Site," Ark Encounter, accessed May 19, 2019, https://arkencounter.com/blog/2014/06/11/lehman-brothers-visit-the-ark-site/.

4. Deepak Chhabra, Robert Healy, and Erin Sills, "Staged Authenticity and Heritage Tourism," *Annals of Tourism Research* 30, no. 3 (July 2003): 702, https://doi.org/10.1016/S 0160-7383(03)00044-6.

"representative of many contemporary visitor's desire . . . to directly experience and consume diverse past and present cultural landscapes, performances, foods, handicrafts, and participatory activities."[5] The Ark Encounter theme park, with its authentic ark replica and ancient Middle Eastern village, dovetails nicely with the expectations of heritage tourism. The draw of heritage tourism is powerful enough that even museums like the MotB attempt to incorporate heritage elements. This is particularly evident in the MotB's *World of Jesus of Nazareth* display that features a replica of first-century Nazareth complete with costumed historical interpreters.

Studies have shown that actual authenticity is less important than perceived authenticity.[6] For organizations like AiG, this perceived authenticity is critical because, in American culture, authenticity is nearly synonymous with objectivity.[7] This was evident in James Bielo's observations of an Ark Encounter design team who worried that "small artistic details could make or break the immersive effect and the demonstration of scripture's historicity."[8] This means that, while material representations of Genesis narratives are clearly important to AiG, one notes that the correct kind of material object is also necessary—not just any representation of the ark will do. At the Ark Encounter AiG makes an extended argument for the theological necessity of representing Noah's Ark in realistic (authentic) proportions and in properly reflecting the flood's tragedy. The *Fairy Tale Ark* display makes this argument in a no-holds-barred attack on children's Bible literature.

Located on the Ark Encounter's second floor, the *Fairy Tale Ark* display has the most elaborate façade of the Ark Encounter exhibits. The display's faux wood entrance is topped by a lintel upon which crouch cartoon versions of animals, including a cow, elephant, and monkey, arrayed against a rainbow backdrop. Stepping into the display one faces a wall of children's books that feature Noah and the ark. These books feature images of brightly colored arks, smaller than biblical specifications, loaded with smiling, happy animals that flank a beaming Noah. Dubbed "fairy tale arks," Ark Encounter designers see a real danger in these seemingly innocuous images.

The *Fairy Tale Ark* display warns visitors about the dangers of fairy-tale arks found in depictions of Noah's flood marketed to children. A large plaque, hanging on the left wall, over which a large serpent drapes, summarizes this issue. The caption reads, "If I can convince you that the flood was not real, then I can convince you that heaven and hell are not real."[9] According to the Ark Encounter, fairy-tale arks are misleading because they downplay the reality of the flood and place the ark on the same footing as other myths and legends. To explain what is at stake,

---

5. Chhabra, Healy, and Sills, 703.

6. Chhabra, Healy, and Sills, 703.

7. John P. Taylor, "Authenticity and Sincerity in Tourism," *Annals of Tourism Research* 28, no. 1 (January 2001): 7, https://doi.org/10.1016/S0160-7383(00)00004-9.

8. Bielo, *Ark Encounter*, 18.

9. Wall text, untitled.

the Ark Encounter uses a device it calls the "7 Ds of Deception" (a companion to the 7 Cs of Creation found at the Creation Museum). The 7 Ds of Deception are described in a series of large, faux books that sit in a horizontal line about halfway up the wall of children's books. Fairy-tale arks *disregard* God's Word by misrepresenting the size of the ark and are *deceptively* cute. Fairy-tale arks *distort* the message by focusing on "cute animals on a fun boat ride" and *discredit* the truth because atheists and skeptics use these images to "mock the Bible." These images are *destructive* for people of all ages and *disorient* the reader by sending mixed messages. Finally, these whimsical images *defame* God's character by treating what is sober and serious as lighthearted and fun.[10]

AiG writers were addressing this issue prior to the building of the ark replica. Bodie Hodge, speaker and researcher for AiG, once wrote that the purpose of children's Bible illustrations and stories is to properly educate the next generation.[11] Illustration errors impede this goal and ultimately undermine the Bible. Hodge offers several comments on what he perceives as common errors in children's ark illustrations. First, he notes that the flood event was not a happy event; therefore, images of happy animals and a grinning Noah undermine the seriousness of the flood. Second, children's illustrations err in placing modern animals on the ark. According to AiG, evolution has only occurred since the flood and only happens within species. As Noah was instructed to bring two of each animal "kind" onto the ark, this argument allows AiG to propose a more manageable number of animals. AiG maintains that modern species resulted from intraspecies evolution descending from the original kinds placed on the ark. Thus, modern animals would not look like their ark-dwelling ancestors. For example, whatever the dog *baramin* looked like in Noah's time, it certainly would not have resembled the dogs we know today. Thus, Hodge would argue, depicting modern animals in children's bibles does not accurately represent animals that were actually brought onto the vessel.

Finally, Hodge claims that honest and accurate depictions of Noah's Ark for children should include dinosaurs.[12] Young-earth creationists argue that dinosaurs would have been created on day six with the other land creatures. Furthermore, there is no reason to assume that the dinosaurs were gone by the time of the flood. (In fact, in the Creation Museum's *Dragon Legends* display, AiG teases the possibility that dinosaurs were seen on earth as recently as the late eighteenth century.)

These cartoonish images are problematic for Ark Encounter designers because they undermine the Bible's historical veracity. The display maintains that the

---

10. This summary of the *Fairy Tale Ark* display is based upon my own observations during a March 2017 visit to the Ark Encounter.
11. "Top 15 Illustration Problems in Genesis 1–11," Answers in Genesis, accessed November 10, 2017, https://answersingenesis.org/bible-history/15-illustration-problems-genesis/.
12. "Top 15 Illustration Problems in Genesis 1–11," 15.

viewer is more likely to understand the ark narrative as plausible if "realistic" proportions are presented. Cartoon arks are just too difficult to take seriously. The Ark Encounter has expressed concern that children viewing these images see them as toys. Furthermore, the lack of seriousness in the imagery increases the likelihood that the flood narrative will be seen as something fantastic. Too much grinning, on the part of both Noah and the animals, undermines the gravity of God's judgment. Noah's smile can never belie the deadly nature of God's judgment, why it was horrible, and why it was necessary. Connecting the past to the future, AiG writers maintain that the flood event, and world conditions leading up to the flood, reflect conditions that will exist prior to God's future judgment (Matt 24:37–39). Thus, a proper understanding of the events of Noah's time will only enhance the observer's ability to recognize when conditions are right for the next judgment.

On this issue AiG is out of step with a lot of modern trends in relating violent stories to children. AiG materials suggest that children should not be sheltered from the violence of the flood narrative. In this respect AiG reflects an earlier period in American history less concerned with nurturing childhood innocence. Even so, as Bielo illustrated, Ark Encounter design teams struggled with the "themes of judgement-worthy sin" while trying to keep the attraction family friendly.[13] Some patron comments illustrate that AiG was only partially successful in this endeavor.

The Filthy and the Odious

The recent flood of sanitized images and stories about Noah's Ark, and AiG's reaction to these images, can be contextualized within a longer history of ark images designed for children. Softening the rough edges of the flood narrative for children follows changing perspectives on childhood exposure to violent imagery. As communicated in the *Fairy Tale Ark* display, AiG objects to sugar coating the nature of God, His wrathfulness, the terror of His judgment, and His just punishment for disobedient people. In arguing that children should be exposed to these aspects of God's nature and His judgment, AiG hearkens back to a standard that seems more Puritan than those modern approaches that shelter children from these uncomfortable images.

Generally speaking, the Puritans viewed parents as responsible for a child's spiritual upbringing.[14] In many ways, this meant exposing children to the harsh realities and consequences of original sin. Sentimentalizing childhood was avoided, and children were not sheltered and protected from the consequences of God's wrath. As Steven Mintz argues in his study of childhood in America, for the Puritan, "children were adults in training who needed to be prepared for

---

13. Bielo, *Ark Encounter*, 101.
14. Steven Mintz, *Huck's Raft: A History of American Childhood* (Cambridge, MA: Belknap Press of Harvard University Press, 2004), ix.

salvation" and a proper education served as the primary mechanism for creating a Godly society.[15] Even babies and toddlers were viewed as fallen creatures, embodying "aggressive and willful impulses that needed to be suppressed."[16] Mintz cites the words of Reverend Benjamin Wadsworth who claimed that babies were "filthy, guilty, odious, abominable . . . both by nature and practice."[17] Reverend Wadsworth's words recall the Protestant preachers cited by Peter Stearns in his study of childhood in world history, many of whom railed on the topic of original sin in children and used the concept of death, as a consequence of original sin, to mold behavior.[18]

Not only did these perspectives emerge from the pulpit but they were also found in children's bibles and Bible story collections. Puritan parents were clearly concerned with obedience and the flood narrative provided a convenient record of the consequences of disobedience. Thus, in early children's bibles, there is no attempt to "sanitize or minimize the judgment and death upon those who are disobedient."[19] Indeed, much like the Ark Encounter, early children's bibles and storybook publishers were interested in expanding on these themes.[20] One notable example is Nathaniel Crouch's *Youth's Divine Pastime* (1691) which focused on the darker Bible stories and did not avoid nudity and violence. Thus, Crouch's retelling of the flood ends with this dark verse:

Then some unto the Mountains flee,
And others climb the Trees,
Here one cries out "Ah! Woe is me,
He Death and Judgment sees."[21]

A dark message indeed, but perhaps not even as direct and unfiltered as the message delivered in Jonathan Edward's famous 1741 sermon "Sinners in the Hands of an Angry God" which concluded with a message to unconverted children about God's growing wrath and their risk of going to hell.[22]

In the *Fairy Tale Ark* display, Ark Encounter designers lament the softening of the death, destruction, sin, and judgment themes in many modern depictions of the flood narrative for children. The Ark Encounter rightly points out that this

---

15. Mintz, 10.
16. Mintz, 10.
17. Mintz, 11.
18. Peter N. Stearns, *Childhood in World History*, 3rd ed. (New York: Routledge, Taylor & Francis Group, 2017), 48.
19. Russell W. Dalton, *Children's Bibles in America: A Reception History of the Story of Noah's Ark in US Children's Bibles*, Scriptural Traces : Critical Perspectives on the Reception and Influence of the Bible 5 (London: Bloomsbury T&T Clark, 2016), 46.
20. Dalton, 46.
21. Dalton, 48.
22. Dalton, 49.

soft approach to the flood narrative is currently very common. Clearly the tide has shifted since Puritan days.

Reflecting changing conceptions of childhood and what is appropriate for childhood consumption, more recent children's bibles and Bible story collections downplay the violent aspects of many biblical stories. The Puritan approach to childhood began to recede in the mid- to late eighteenth century. Inspired by John Locke and his concept of the *tabula rasa* mind, children came to be seen as blank slates instead of innately depraved and sinful. As blank slates children could be viewed as morally innocent and all the features we associate with protecting childhood innocence began to emerge.[23] In contrast to Reverend Wadsworth's images of sin-corrupted, odious, and filthy creatures, parents in the mid-1700s began to see children as "innocent, malleable, and fragile creatures who needed to be sheltered from contamination."[24] Thus, the mid-eighteenth through the late nineteenth centuries represent something of a transition period in how violent biblical stories are presented to children.

During this transition some horrible flood depictions for children remained relatively common. In Lucy Barton's *Bible Letters for Children* (1831) children learned "how dreadful it is to disobey such a powerful God, who can destroy us in a moment, if he please!" This God is the "same Being who commanded the waters to destroy the earth [but] condescends to love little children, if they do but wish to try to please *Him*."[25] Even though the Bible is relatively silent on what happens outside the ark, some children's bibles speculate about the fate of people facing the flood. In many publications where illustration space was lacking it is telling that of all the possible images to accompany the Noah's Ark story, images of drowning people were not uncommon. Dalton speculates that "drowning animals may have been especially poignant to the children, who may have identified with the sorrowful, innocent faces."[26]

As new theories about education and mental and emotional development took root these images became less common. More people began to dispute the idea that people were corrupt from birth, as original sin seemed to dictate.[27] If there is no original sin, there is less emphasis on punishment, and biblical narratives that featured these punishments became less urgent. Additionally, the advent of the Industrial Revolution and the transition away from an agricultural economy meant smaller households and a decrease in infant mortality. These social and economic changes heralded shifting emotional attachments to children and a move away from "using anger and fear to discipline children."[28] Stearns

---

23. Gregory S. Jackson, *The Word and Its Witness: The Spiritualization of American Realism* (Chicago, IL: University of Chicago Press, 2009), 62.
24. Mintz, *Huck's Raft*, 3.
25. Dalton, *Children's Bibles in America*, 59.
26. Dalton, 61.
27. Stearns, *Childhood in World History*, 57.
28. Stearns, 61.

maintains that this period brought with it an image of children as "wondrous innocents" and with this "loving innocence" came a desire to protect children from corruption.[29] This was supported by the young discipline of psychology and new perspectives on childhood mental development. There emerged a view of children as "psychologically vulnerable" needing careful treatment. "Not only should they not be frightened as part of discipline, they should not even be made to feel guilty, because this would damage their self-esteem and lead to later problems."[30]

By the end of the nineteenth and into the twentieth centuries, the seemingly harsh features of the biblical flood story were being softened. Some narratives focused on Noah warning his recalcitrant neighbors about the impending flood (even though this event is absent from the biblical narrative) thus shifting responsibility from Noah and God to the people and further justifying their deaths. In other cases, a narrator is placed in the story to serve as a buffer between the horrible events of the biblical narrative and the child. Such is the case in Mary Sherwood's *Scripture Prints: With Explanations in the Form of Familiar Dialogues* (1832). In this retelling a grandmother narrates the events and explains the reasons the flood had to occur.[31]

In addition to changing conceptions about childhood exposure to violence, in the early twentieth century children's bibles began to compete with animated films and eventually television shows. As Dalton argues, comic books and Walt Disney pushed children's bibles and storybooks in a more entertaining direction.[32] By the early 1990s there was a noticeable shift away from "realism" in depictions of the flood narrative for children toward a more animated and cheerful story featuring a boat ride. Images of death and destruction became far less common. Many of these texts featured anthropomorphic animals which pushed the narrative even closer to the format of a fable. The age of the fairy-tale ark had begun. Today, even the theologically conservative presses—Zondervan, Cook Communications, and Thomas Nelson—have been engaged in publishing what Ham calls "fairy tale" versions of the flood. While these presses may be, as Dalton suggests, trying to make Christianity more fun and approachable, they do so, according to Ken Ham, at the cost of biblical accuracy.[33]

In his call for greater accuracy in storybook depictions of the flood, Ham also argues for the necessity of exposing children to the horrible nature of the event. As the preceding short history of the flood narrative in children's literature demonstrates, in this respect Ken Ham has much more in common with seventeenth- and eighteenth-century approaches to children's Bible literature than he does with modern publishers. In both the Creation Museum and the

---

29. Stearns, 61.
30. Stearns, 104.
31. Dalton, *Children's Bibles in America*, 89.
32. Dalton, 245.
33. Dalton, 250–53.

Ark Encounter, Ham includes displays that illustrate the more disconcerting elements of the flood story. This includes a remarkable miniature flood diorama at the Creation Museum. This diorama features the ark, floating on an angry gray ocean some distance behind a rocky peak jutting from the water. People trample other people ascending the mountain in panic, others cling to it in desperation, and others are engaged in fistfights as the flood waters continue to rise. Across the room a short video dramatization features two children playing a game while seemingly alone in their home. The viewer's attention is drawn to the window behind the children that frames a flood tidal wave approaching the house. There is no question that the children are doomed.

The similarities between the Puritan and Ham's approach to exposing children to these biblical topics does not seem accidental. In delving into Ham's literature, one notices an admiration for Puritan Christianity and the English reformers. Note, for example, that Ham is a big fan of John Bunyan's (1628–1688) *Pilgrim's Progress* (1678). Ham admires Bunyan for being a non-compromiser and a hero who stood firm in his convictions.[34] Steven Fazekas writes, in an AiG articled titled "To Be a Pilgrim," that there is no better book to have occupying the space next to the Bible.[35] The fact that Bunyan, as claimed by Ken Ham, believed in the literal six-day creation of Gen 1 further bolsters his reputation. AiG has worked with Master Books on a special reprint of Bunyan's books and has even created a *Pilgrim's Progress* study curriculum. Though he is a late arrival on the Puritan scene, and Puritanism had changed since the days of Increase and Cotton Mather, Jonathan Edwards (1703–58) is also greatly admired by AiG. In a 2007 AiG article, Becky Stelzer exhorts Christians to follow the example of Edwards.[36] In a 2008 AiG article titled "How Young Is Too Young," the author recommends educating children with *The New England Primer*, a text used by Puritans to educate children about serious biblical issues.[37] Many Creation Museum and Ark Encounter visitors, however, find this approach to children a bit off-putting and they maintain that some of the information on display is not suitable for kids.

---

34. "The 'Pilgrim' Who 'Preaches' from a Grave," Answers in Genesis, accessed December 1, 2017, https://answersingenesis.org/ministry-news/ministry/the-pilgrim-who-preaches-from-a-grave/.

35. "To Be a Pilgrim," Answers in Genesis, accessed February 15, 2018, https://answersingenesis.org/christianity/to-be-a-pilgrim/.

36. "Taking a Look at Jonathan Edwards," Answers in Genesis, accessed December 8, 2017, https://answersingenesis.org/ministry-news/ministry/taking-a-look-at-jonathan-edwards/.

37. "How Young Is Too Young?" Answers in Genesis, accessed February 15, 2018, https://answersingenesis.org/train-up-a-child/raising-godly-children/how-young-is-too-young/.

Scaring the Kids

The notion that Ken Ham and AiG overexpose children to violence, and other topics some deem inappropriate, is evident in some patron responses to Creation Museum exhibits. There are three displays in the Creation Museum that elicit criticism for their potential negative effect on children. The Creation Museum's *Graffiti Alley* is a scary place and the display's interior is clearly designed to create discomfort. The *Culture in Crisis* display elicits criticism from patrons who feel the content (pornography and abortion) are not appropriate for children. For instance, in one online review a patron complained that the displays about drugs and pregnancy were not child friendly.[38]

Museum patrons, otherwise sympathetic to the message of the Creation Museum, have remarked on the inappropriate nature of these displays for children. Some parents coped with the situation by covering their children's eyes and rushing them through the space. Regarding *Graffiti Alley*, a September 23, 2013, TripAdvisor review by nofitpitchinkids stated that the alley of sin (she likely means Graffiti Alley) confused her kids.[39] In a reference to the *Culture in Crisis* display, a TripAdvisor reviewer called T S complained that many areas might have been appropriate for tweens and teenagers but were otherwise inappropriate for the younger children. T S shielded the eyes of his young grandchildren through the displays dealing with pornography and teen pregnancy.[40]

Perhaps the most potentially disturbing display at the Creation Museum is the so-called *Cave of Sorrows*, the portion of the Creation Museum described above as adorned with images of skulls, childbirth, tornados, drug addiction, starvation, mushroom clouds, and Nazis on the walls.[41] Some museum visitors make explicit reference to this room. For instance, KentuckyTravelBug80 notes that some displays, especially those of drug use and animal sacrifice, were too graphic and violent for children.[42] Missy J writes that not only was she uncomfortable with the

---

38. Larry G., "Not for Children," TripAdvisor, October 17, 2016, https://www.tripadvisor.com/ShowUserReviews-g39743-d619562-r428850439-Creation_Museum-Petersburg_KentucKY.html.

39. nofitpitchinkids, "Liked It a Lot . . . But," TripAdvisor, September 23, 2013, https://www.tripadvisor.com/ShowUserReviews-g39743-d619562-r178325657-Creation_Museum-Petersburg_KentucKY.html.

40. T S, "Great for Older Kids," TripAdvisor, July 10, 2016, https://www.tripadvisor.com/ShowUserReviews-g39743-d619562-r390957595-Creation_Museum-Petersburg_KentucKY.html.

41. T S, "Great for Older Kids," pp. 40–50.

42. KentuckyTravelBug80, "Really Disappointed," TripAdvisor, June 27, 2010, https://www.tripadvisor.com/ShowUserReviews-g39743-d619562-r68813949-Creation_Museum-Petersburg_KentucKY.html.

displays but her children also expressed discomfort as well.[43] Parent reactions to these displays demonstrate the power of images to mold opinion. For AiG, these images are part of the rhetoric defining good and bad theology.

Fairy-Tale Arks as Bad Objects

Among other things the *Fairy Tale Ark* display is a battle about pictures and images. In his 2004 monograph titled *What Do Pictures Want? The Lives and Loves of Images*, W. J. T. Mitchell notes that pictures engage in world making.[44] Understood in light of the "pictorial turn" where images have replaced words "as the dominant mode of expression in our time"[45] it becomes evident why the Ark Encounter places much emphasis on images and pictures of the ark.

Though related, images and pictures are not synonymous. Mitchell describes images as "a family of immaterial symbolic forms" and pictures as the "material medium" that may reflect the image.[46] Mitchell continues by asserting that images are often viewed as "destructive forces that lead us astray"[47] and that pictures are often approached as living things with "agency, motivation, autonomy, aura, fecundity."[48] As such, there is something about the picture, when viewed in this manner, that recalls discourse on idols and suggests that the *Fairy Tale Ark* display is, in part, a discourse on idolatry.

Idol worship, one of the great bugbears of the Hebrew Bible, is steeped in the language of agency and deception. Thus, Jer 10:14 states that idols are false images. For the prophet, the idea of the idol as living, being clothed, fed, and carried into battle, is a misattribution of agency, autonomy, and motivation to a dead object. Approaching dead objects in this manner is deceptive and destructive. As Mitchell points out, this is an example of people who "behave as if pictures were alive, as if works of art [have] minds of their own, as if images [have] the power to influence human beings, demanding things from us, persuading, seducing, and leading us astray."[49] The Ark Encounter assumes that the fairy-tale ark images have the power to distract and deceive. In fact, this is the whole premise of the 7 Ds of Deception. Like a Hebrew Prophet, the Ark Encounter argues that fairy-tale arks are not authentic but are fake and do not represent anything real. Thus, in the words of Jeremiah, "Everyone is stupid and without knowledge; goldsmiths are all put to

---

43. Missy J., "Average," TripAdvisor, January 12, 2012, https://www.tripadvisor.com/ShowUserReviews-g39743-d619562-r122990376-Creation_Museum-Petersburg_KentucKY.html.
44. Mitchell, *What Do Pictures Want?* xv.
45. Mitchell, 5.
46. Mitchell, 85.
47. Mitchell, 19.
48. Mitchell, 6.
49. Mitchell, 7.

shame by their idols; for their images are false, and there is no breath in them" (10:14). Despite the fact that they are fake, they still deceive, and must therefore be destroyed.

The Hebrew Bible teaches that destroying idols is both an object lesson and an act of virtue. Moses acted righteously when he destroyed the golden calf and ordered the Levites to kill the idolaters (Exod 32: 27–28). Mitchell describes such acts of destruction as a very public "holy duty" that functions as an "admonitory exhibition."[50] For AiG, fairy-tale arks are idols, objects mistakenly revered by those who allow these pictures and images to instill a false image of God and the flood narrative. The *Fairy Tale Ark* display is the public admonition of such images and pictures.

Mitchell explains that fetishes, idols, and totems, as encountered and defined by modern Western colonial powers, function as "bad objects." Such objects, Mitchell maintains, were tools of differentiation and became the items through which European colonizing powers defined themselves as superior.[51] The evaluation of such objects as primitive implies an aesthetic judgment that separates the "redeemed from the damned, the purified from the corrupt and degraded object. As an imperial practice, aesthetics enlists all the rhetoric of religion, morality, and progressive modernity to pass judgment on the 'bad object' that inevitably come into view in a colonial encounter."[52] From the perspective of the colonizer, the bad object may be approached with ambivalence or anxiety, may be seen as worthless or disgusting, but remains an object of value in the colonized culture.[53]

To define some things as bad objects and to place them on display are all acts of power. However, one cannot argue that AiG exercises enough cultural hegemony to make its cultural views normative. At this point I found it helpful to turn to Bruce Lincoln's comparative study of myth and classification where he writes about counter hegemonies, counter-hegemonic inversions, and counter-taxonomic discourses. About counter taxonomic discourses, Lincoln writes that they are "alternate models whereby members of subordinate strata and others marginalized under the existing social order are able to agitate for the deconstruction of that order and the reconstruction of society in a novel pattern."[54] If we therefore view AiG as attempting a counter-hegemonic discourse, then the ideological content of the *Fairy Tale Ark* exhibit can be seen as having some similarities to Mitchell's concept of the bad object, even though AiG is not a hegemonic power.

Even the act of display draws upon this discourse. The modern museum has its roots in early modern cabinets of curiosities, many of which featured New World objects brought back to Europe by colonial explorers. The act of display and categorization is a statement of power and dominance. Consider then that the

50. Mitchell, 18.
51. Mitchell, 165.
52. Mitchell, 147.
53. Mitchell, 158.
54. Lincoln, *Discourse and the Construction of Society*, 8.

children's books in the *Fairy Tale Ark* display sit on shelves like an old-fashioned display of fetishes and totems. The very act of displaying these children's bibles and storybooks is an exercise that recalls the ideological function of the museum as a place supporting a specific (colonial) ideology. By putting these objects on display AiG is setting them apart as exotic and as nonnormative.

In categorically rejecting popular images produced for children's bibles and storybooks, AiG furthers the distinction between us and them and sets up what Birgit Meyer terms a contest over the categories of good and bad, each of which are inherent in the concept of the bad object.[55] Like Mitchell, Meyer further maintains that the bad object functioned as a marker of distinction that demonstrated the superiority of Christianity over other religious systems.[56] Fairy-tale arks allow AiG to do this within the unique context of both an intra-Christian debate and AiG's dismissal of secular culture. As part of AiG's intra-Christian debate the bad object is a representation of a bad theology based upon an incorrect reading of scripture. As serious as this sounds, AiG claims that this bad theology is ultimately not a matter of salvation. In other words, viewing, or even producing, fairy-tale images of the ark is not the basis upon which individual salvation hangs. Instead, for AiG the risks embodied in these bad objects is found in both the shortcomings of the culture that produces them and in their continued cultural impact. AiG places fairy-tale arks within the context of the culture wars and the diminished role of biblical authority of America. As bad objects, these images lead us further away from biblical authority, further away from God, and contribute to cultural decay.

As the bad object results from distinguishing the legitimate and the illegitimate, the superior and the inferior, the concept raises questions about authenticity. As AiG works to delineate between the real and the fake, authenticity remains central to AiG's criticisms of fairy-tale arks. AiG asserts that the problem with many modern children's ark illustrations is a failure to authentically represent the ark as described in the Bible. AiG uses the language of counterfeit and Ham argues that bathtub arks attempt to pass themselves off as (bad) representations of the real thing. Considering AiG's use of the language of counterfeit in its presentation of ark images helps us understand part of the moral framework from which AiG evaluates fairy-tale arks. In her analysis of counterfeiting and authenticity, Magdalena Crăciun writes about authentic and inauthentic objects and the manner in which they are produced and how consumers engage with them. In her analysis, Crăciun argues that fake or inauthentic objects can pose moral dilemmas and that these objects embody moral values.[57] "All types of inauthentic objects," she writes, "represent transgressions against identity, property, morality, and the

---

55. Birgit Meyer, "How Pictures Matter: Religious Objects and the Imagination in Ghana," in *Objects and Imagination: Perspectives on Materialization and Meaning*, ed. Øivind Fuglerud and Leon Wainwright (New York: Berghahn Books, 2015), 166.

56. Meyer, 166.

57. Magdalena Crăciun, *Material Culture and Authenticity: Fake Branded Fashion in Europe* (London: Bloomsbury, 2014), 25.

authority of law."[58] Central among these moral issues is deception. Not only do inauthentic objects deceive others, they also deceive the producer. In fact, "people who engage with these objects are portrayed not only as deceivers, but also self-deceivers who hide from themselves and others who they truly are."[59] Counter to this is the notion that engagement with authentic objects is coded as morally positive and is a vehicle for producing a more authentic self.[60]

Dan Leitha's AiG website article titled "Mything the Boat: How the World Sees Noah's Ark" reflects these ideas. Leitha accuses illustrators of ignoring information in scripture. Furthermore, he claims that some artists simply do not believe the story, giving them the freedom to treat the narrative in any manner they see fit.[61] This thinly veiled accusation of deception echoes the central moral claims against counterfeiters. Leitha's argument suggests a concern with authenticity and how authenticity can be undermined by trickery. Atheists like fairy-tale arks because it allows them to undermine biblical narratives.[62] Since seeing is believing, viewing an inauthentic image paves the way to wrong belief. Leitha's scorn is reserved not just for illustrators of Noah's Ark but for all who engage in these inauthentic illustrations. He draws upon 2 Pet 3, condemning scoffers and skeptics of the last days, and claiming that the world desires ignorance rather than facing final judgment.[63]

AiG clearly objects to Bible illustrations that are too cartoonist and that fail to capture a certain amount of realism. However, it would appear that this insistence on realism does not extend to items sold online. In prior chapters we encountered the concept of the *baramin* and the notion that the animal kinds Noah brought onto the ark would not have looked like their modern descendants. Nonetheless, the AiG website sells several Noah's flood books for children that feature modern elephants, sheep, giraffes, and gazelles, just to name a few. In fact, the children's book titled *Remarkable Rescue: Saved on Noah's Ark* (for sale on the AiG website) violates many principles set forth in the *Fairy Tale Ark* display. The book's cover features smiling giraffes, elephants, and bears together with a beaming Noah. All are seemingly ready for their boat ride. Likewise, the Ark Encounter gift shop is filled with stuffed elephants, lions, zebras, and rabbits, all represented in their current forms. The Ark Encounter lunch box features all these and adds panda bears, kangaroos, and buffalo.[64]

---

58. Crăciun, 25.
59. Crăciun, 103.
60. Crăciun, 103.
61. "Mything the Boat."
62. Doulos Iesou Christou, *Stop Mything Noah's Ark*, https://www.youtube.com/watch?v=NQDgnFgx2Js.
63. "Mything the Boat."
64. "Store Home," Answers in Genesis, accessed June 18, 2018, https://answersingenesis.org/store/?sitehist=1529337769738.

From Fisher-Price to Williamstown

The biblical description of the ark is such that both the "realistic" reconstruction of AiG and fairy-tale arks can emerge from the same narrative space. The eddies and undercurrents that result from a narrative that just does not have enough information have produced everything from the behemoth that sits in the Kentucky countryside to Fisher-Price Little People's Noah's Ark. They do not, however, occupy the same ideological space and the *Fairy Tale Ark* display illustrates that this struggle over imagery, and relegating some images to the status of bad objects, is a reflection of a larger cultural struggle about the Bible, how to read it, and which reading ought to have cultural dominance. For AiG, taking the text as literally as possible enhances their argument that this is a historical document. For others, the historicity matters less than the metaphors and the lessons that can be drawn from the story. When the ark is depicted as a toy overloaded with animals, the concept of the Bible as story is being emphasized. As Americans understand story, there is room in story for imaginary people, places, and events.[65] This is why AiG insists that the Bible is not *just* a story but history. Bodie Hodge, in response to a letter written to AiG, complains that the author, in calling the Bible a story, discounts it as history.[66] For AiG, recent trends on attitudes toward the Bible are cause for concern. According to the most recent American Bible Society State of the Bible Survey, 25 percent of adults now believe the Bible has too much influence in society (up from 13 percent in 2011).[67] The same survey found that "more adults believe the Bible is *inspired* (with some symbolism) than *literal*."[68] Only 22 percent believe the Bible is the "*actual* word of God and should be taken literally, word for word," a number that has stayed fairly consistent in recent years.[69] It seems clear that, for AiG, if these trends are going to be reversed, then the truth (as they see it) needs to be presented to the children. If they are taught that God is serious, the things done by God are serious, and that the Bible is serious, then perhaps the road to viewing the Bible as a collection of fairy tales will be curtailed.

For some, the flood narrative, the Culture in Crisis, and the Cave of Sorrows are potentially disturbing. For others, it is not the doom, destruction, and decay that are the problems. Rather, the problem is the potential of Adam's bare chest setting hearts aflutter. In the next chapter we will delve much deeper into patrons' perspectives on AiG attractions and will encounter thoughts about Adam's sexy body.

---

65. The difference between history and story is not evident in many foreign languages. Thus, the difference between history and story in American English will often confuse those learning English.

66. "The Message, Not the Literal Meaning, Is What Matters," Answers in Genesis, accessed March 29, 2019, https://answersingenesis.org/theistic-evolution/god-and-evolution/the-message-not-the-literal-meaning-is-what-matters/.

67. Barna Group, *State of the Bible, 2018* (Ventura, CA: Barna Group, 2018), 19.

68. Barna Group, 22.

69. Barna Group, 22.

Chapter 9

ADAM IS TOO SEXY!

It is now time to turn our attention to how visitors of the Creation Museum and the Ark Encounter receive the messages embodied in each. In earlier chapters I described the multilayered nature of this reception study and examined specific examples of how AiG represents the Bible in the material objects at the Creation Museum and the Ark Encounter. The next two chapters will focus on patron responses to each with specific attention given to how patrons view the Creation Museum and the Ark Encounter as representations of the Bible. Many corollary questions arise from this topic, including, do the Creation Museum, and the Ark Encounter, as representations of the Bible, perform the authoritative work of the Bible? Also, do museum patrons view the Creation Museum and the Ark Encounter as faithful representations of the Bible? To what degree do these attractions challenge or confirm what patrons know about the Bible? Following Jauss, we will reconsider the idea that works that push the reader's expectations have greater potential to expand the reader's horizon of expectations. Some readers do not desire this expansion and thus seek, in the Creation Museum and the Ark Encounter, something that closely conforms to their horizon of expectations. Even among this audience there are signs of resistance that demonstrate that patrons are not all hegemonic readers. Others, some counting themselves as Christians, are profoundly challenged by the displays and offer signs of resistance to AiG's interpretation of the Bible.

I used two sources of data for the analysis I lay out in these next two chapters. First, I have analyzed visitor reviews of the Creation Museum and the Ark Encounter from TripAdvisor and Facebook. TripAdvisor is a website that collects user reviews of hotels and attractions. In total I have gathered and coded nearly two thousand user comments/reviews on these attractions. This data is useful in that it represents a somewhat spontaneous and unprompted reaction to the Creation Museum and the Ark Encounter. The sheer volume of reviews also allowed for a broad overview that could not be accomplished with a more limited set of face-to-face or phone interviews. As such, this data set provided hints about what was catching the visitor's attention, which then suggested topics that might benefit from my attention. While it is a rich source of data, there are, nevertheless, qualifiers on its use. First, the sample is self-selected and is comprised of people with the technological resources, savvy, and proclivities to leave reviews on travel websites.

Additionally, unlike interviews, there is no opportunity to ask questions and probe subjects for further detail.

My second source of information about visitor perceptions of the Creation Museum and the Ark Encounter comes from a series of in-depth interviews conducted during the spring months of 2017. I contacted some Facebook and TripAdvisor reviewers through the respective apps, requesting phone interviews about their visits to these AiG attractions. Requests for on-site interviews were denied by the Creation Museum owing to the organization's policy of no guest solicitation. These interviews provided an excellent opportunity to probe some of the themes that were emerging in the coding of online written reviews. From these interviews I learned that patrons do not know as much about the Bible as I imagined. This realization inspired me to think about visitor engagement with the Creation Museum and the Ark Encounter in different ways. As the Creation Museum and the Ark Encounter largely focus on Genesis, I limited my questions to that portion of the Bible. During the interviews I asked participants to reflect upon their state of knowledge about select Bible passages before their visit and then to reflect on how their understanding of those passages may have changed because of the visit. Most interviews lasted at least thirty minutes though a few lasted as long as one hour.

Sexy Adam

That authorial intent is not always realized in audience reception is canon in reception studies. A long-term study of the Kentucky Creation Museum and the Ark Encounter was bound to turn up some interesting ideas; however, finding that Noah may have employed a Flintstones-inspired method for animal waste disposal, or that Adam may have been too sexy, reveals the creativity of both Creation Museum and Ark Encounter designers and the audiences visiting these attractions. Though there is no evidence indicating otherwise, it is doubtful that Ken Ham intended for the mannequins of biblical figures on display at the Creation Museum to become sex objects. It turns out, however, that some visitors find the mannequins rather sexy. From my perspective as a reception scholar, the responses I received in interviews and the various online comments revealed the creativity, agency, and sometimes conflicted nature of the way visitors interacted with these attractions.

Pop-culture presentations of the Bible are inherently interesting because they reveal what people do with biblical narratives outside more formal channels of interpretation, like church councils, published commentaries, or seminary classes. Presentations like those found at the Creation Museum and the Ark Encounter are doubly interesting because of the edutainment context and the high production values (which has not been the norm for attractions like this). As edutainment these attractions set themselves apart from other popular culture presentations of the Bible, like Darren Aronofsky's 2014 film *Noah*, discussed in a prior chapter.

While a film like *Noah* may play with biblical narrative and exhibit midrashic qualities, the Creation Museum and the Ark Encounter are different because they are presented simultaneously as entertainment and as biblically authoritative and educational.

Despite AiG's declaration of biblical authority, much of what the visitor finds at the Creation Museum and the Ark Encounter is not biblical. At these attractions, as AiG admits, educated guesses, plausible reconstructions, and artistic license are employed. In the interest of disclosure, this research makes no claims that applying artistic license or educated guesses to biblical narratives is right or wrong. Instead, my interest lies solely in what Yvonne Sherwood called the "afterlives" of the Bible, the various ways the Bible is employed and what influences people to read the Bible in a particular manner.[1] Bielo views artistic license at the Ark Encounter as an invitation to the visitor to "close the intertextual gap between the literalist ideology of scripture and the creative team's artistic labor."[2] I was curious, however, about how this invitation plays out in visitor responses to the Ark Encounter. I would suggest that some patron responses reveal that the boundary between the text and artistic license is fuzzy and that the educated guesses of AiG are becoming part of the biblical literacy for Ark Encounter visitors. For some visitors the embedding of educated guesses in a biblical framework, aided by the authority of AiG and Ken Ham as interpreters of the Bible, confers upon these guesses an aura of biblical authority.

Methus-a-who?

Examining how patrons respond to claims made at the Ark Encounter and the Creation Museum required gauging how much visitors seemed to know about the Bible. On the topic of Bible knowledge, interview subjects consistently rated their knowledge of the Bible higher than their specific responses to questions about the Bible seemed to warrant. Each subject was asked to rate their general knowledge of the Bible on a scale from one to ten, with one being least familiar to ten being most familiar. A response of five was determined to indicate average familiarity, a response of six or seven to be above average familiarity, and a response of eight or higher to be well above average. As the Creation Museum and the Ark Encounter maintain a tight focus on Genesis narratives, interview subjects were also asked to rate their familiarity with Genesis. The same scale was maintained for the Genesis rating.

Many patrons who rated themselves at six or higher failed to identify information about well-known biblical narratives. Take, for example, Methuselah, famous for being Noah's grandfather and, at 969 years, the oldest person recorded in the Bible (Gen 5:21–27). This is such an outstanding and concise statement that it often

---

1. Sherwood, *A Biblical Text and Its Afterlives*, 3.
2. Bielo, *Ark Encounter*, 145.

appears in various forms of Bible trivia.[3] Despite the Old Testament recording no other information about Methuselah, the Creation Museum devotes an entire display to this enigmatic character, as I previously detailed. To determine how patrons received the Methuselah display, interview subjects were asked to describe what they know about Methuselah from the Bible. One subject, who indicated a high level of knowledge about the Bible and the book of Genesis, was unable to recall anything about Methuselah. Another subject, who indicated a high level of Bible literacy prior to visiting the Creation Museum, learned about Methuselah as a result of the trip, stating, "I wasn't really aware who he was [or that he was] the oldest person in the Bible . . . until we went there and [saw] that display."[4] Another person stated: "When I was at the Creation Museum and we stopped at that display, I was like, 'Oh, that's why people say it's older than Methuselah.' It never even clicked to me."[5] I do not intend to imply that lack of knowledge about Methuselah is the only measuring rod of Bible literacy (though it does continue to surprise me). I had interview subjects unable to recall the story of Cain and Abel (and its place in the text)[6] and many who could not recall basic facts about the flood narrative. If patrons know less about the Bible than they indicate, there are implications for what they may regard as biblically authoritative based on Creation Museum and Ark Encounter displays.

With one exception, all the interviewees were sympathetic to the message of AiG. Likewise, the vast majority of the online reviews were also supportive of the theology on display at the Creation Museum and the Ark Encounter. It is clear, however, that this support does not emerge from detailed knowledge of the Bible passages that AiG's young-earth creationism is based upon. If one assumes that the average Creation Museum and Ark Encounter visitor would be biblically motivated, this might seem surprising. However, that visitors may not know much about the Bible is predicted by recent Bible literacy surveys. For example, a 2014 Barna Group survey on the state of the Bible in America found that 53 percent of Americans read the Bible three or four times per year.[7] According to the same survey, 15 percent of adults read the Bible daily while 13 percent read the Bible several times per week.[8] The average Bible reader will spend about thirty minutes in the text, and, according to Barna, this does not vary according to faith engagement.[9] Additionally, 69 percent of respondents consider themselves to be moderately or somewhat knowledgeable about the Bible while 12 percent claim

---

3. "20 Question Bible Quiz—Bible Trivia—James River Church," JRC, accessed February 2, 2017, https://jamesriver.org/blog/bible-quiz.
4. Kurtis, in discussion with the author, April 2017.
5. Myra, in discussion with the author, May 2017.
6. Isabella, discussion.
7. Barna Group, *The State of the Bible, 2014* (Ventura, CA: Barna Group, 2014), 11.
8. Barna Group.
9. Barna Group, 12.

to be highly knowledgeable (Barna 20).[10] Despite this, only one in four adults can correctly name the first five books of the Bible. However, this number increases to 69 percent for practicing Protestants.[11] These results are generally confirmed in PEW's U.S. Religious Knowledge Survey (2010) which found that Protestant and Catholic Christians score poorly on questions about world religions while performing better on questions about the Bible and Christianity. For example, white evangelicals averaged 4.8 out of 11 questions correct on world religions and 7.3 out of 11 correct on questions about the Bible and Christianity.[12]

Based upon these, and other surveys, some have declared a Bible illiteracy crisis in America. Ed Stetzer, writing in *Christianity Today*, worries that since people do not regularly read their Bible they cannot adequately know the contents of their Bible.[13] Albert Mohler, president of the Southern Baptist Theological Seminary, declared the problem of Bible illiteracy in America to be a scandal.[14] I linger on this issue because there are things that appear in the Creation Museum and the Ark Encounter that are not found in the Bible. If the levels of biblical literacy encountered so far are typical, then a patron's ability to separate the biblical from what Ark Encounter designers call "educated guesses" might be limited. As some of the following patron responses to the Ark Encounter suggest, the "educated guesses" and "artistic license" of the Ark Encounter is becoming part of the patron's Bible knowledge.

Moon Pools for Poop Chutes

There are enough gaps in the biblical description of Noah's Ark and the flood narrative that an attraction based solely on the information provided in the Bible would be pretty boring indeed. Therefore, ark designers decided to make educated guesses and use artistic license to fill the lacunae. Such efforts were deemed necessary because the biblical narrative contains very few details that a reader would want to know about such a vessel and the subsequent flood event. The day-to-day operations on the ark, things like animal feeding, watering, and waste removal, and the living quarters, represent some of the most notable examples of artistic license from ark designers. For example, the Ark Encounter

---

10. Barna Group, 20.
11. Barna Group, 23.
12. "U.S. Religious Knowledge Survey," Pew Research Center, accessed September 28, 2010, https://www.pewforum.org/2010/09/28/u-s-religious-knowledge-survey/.
13. "The Epidemic of Bible Illiteracy in Our Churches," Ed Stetzer, accessed April 19, 2018, https://www.christianitytoday.com/edstetzer/2015/july/epidemic-of-bible-illiteracy-in-our-churches.html.
14. "The Scandal of Biblical Illiteracy: It's Our Problem," Albert Mohler, accessed April 19, 2018, http://albertmohler.com/2016/01/20/the-scandal-of-biblical-illiteracy-its-our-problem-4/.

proposes that a moon pool could have been part of the ark design and would have neutralized the stench created by thousands of animals in a confined space. The up and down motion of the boat and the waves in the moon pool could have forced air to circulate through the ark—functioning much like the pumping of a bellows. Another proposal depicts an animal walking on a treadmill attached to a conveyor belt with a series of scoops that pick up animal waste and deposit it into the moon pool. The moon pool and the animal waste disposal system are not part of the ark design as described in Gen 6.

Ark designers did not hide the fact that they were employing guesswork. One sign introducing a display called *Workable Models* reads:

> Have you ever wondered how Noah's family fed all the animals and removed their waste? How did they provide fresh air and water? And how did they light the ark? The concepts displayed in this exhibit are models showing plausible solutions to these challenges. While we may not know all of the details, we know they successfully accomplished their tasks since all eight people and the animals God sent to them survived the Flood.[15]

Another display, with a header that reads "Artistic License," reads: "This exhibit provides a plausible backstory based on clues from Scripture to explain how the Lord may have prepared His faithful servant to fulfill such an important mission."[16] Artistic license is invoked again in the ark living quarters display where ark designers were more explicit: "Since we don't have a time machine, we can only make educated guesses about the looks, skills, and personality of each individual. Any attempt to represent historical events necessarily involves using artistic license, and we took great care not to contradict biblical details."[17] The Ark Encounter attempts to avoid contradicting the Bible (at least as AiG understands it); however, contradiction is not the primary concern of this research. Rather, I am interested to know if educational guesses become part of the biblical literacy of Creation Museum and Ark Encounter visitors.

Ark designers justify this, in part, with a rather postmodern view of history. First of all, they argue that the Genesis flood narrative qualifies as history and then argue that "any reconstruction of historical events necessarily involves using artistic license."[18] Underlying this is an imperative to prove that biblical narratives are authentic, though why such matters cannot be taken on faith actually comes up in patron responses analyzed below. One might assume that efforts to demonstrate (by filling in lacunae) how the ark and the flood could have happened are done in order to convince Bible skeptics, secularists, and perhaps the occasional atheist. However, Ken Ham has repeatedly stated that Christians, as much as anybody else,

---

15. Wall text, *Workable Models*, Ark Encounter, Williamstown, KY.
16. Wall text, *Using His Gifts*, Ark Encounter, Williamstown, KY.
17. Wall text, *Artistic License*, Ark Encounter, Williamstown, KY.
18. Wall text, *Artistic License*.

are his target audience. Specially, as argued above, he desires to reach Christians who have abandoned the Old Testament as an irrelevant relic superseded by the New.

They Had Me until the Dinosaurs

In my approach to analyzing visitor responses to the Creation Museum and the Ark Encounter, I adapted the audience reception framework outlined by Stuart Hall (1932–2014) in his landmark 1973 article on encoding and decoding. Hall's research focused on the production of television shows, but his argument captures something about the manner in which AiG encoded the Bible in the Creation Museum and Ark Encounter and how patrons receive that message. Hall maintained that mass media products, like television shows, contain messages in the form of sign vehicles. An important concept in semiotics (the study of sign processes and communication), a sign vehicle is a physical manifestation of a sign. A sign, therefore, is a representation of meaning—composed of, for example, words, images, and sounds that allow for the communication of ideas—that points to something other than itself. *Decoding* refers to the meanings that audiences (be they television program viewers, visitors to the Creation Museum, or readers of the Bible) derive from the encoded object. Hall maintains that encoding and decoding both utilize similar processes and that social, political, and economic circumstances inform both production (encoding) and reception (decoding). As it relates to production, Hall asserted that "technical skills, professional ideologies, institutional knowledge, definitions and assumptions" frame the production process.[19]

Though mass communication products might encode certain messages intended for the reader/viewer, there is no assurance that the reader will accept the intended message. Hall proposes that readers will adopt one of three reading positions. The first is the dominant/hegemonic position. From this position, the reader decodes the message in "terms of the reference code in which it has been encoded."[20] A hegemonic reader operates inside the dominant code and accepts the worldview that the text presents. This reading position most fully realizes the author's intent. Hall posits that the second reading position is the negotiated position. The negotiated position is of interest because it potentially produces contradictory readings. Adopting this position, the reader allows for some adaptive and oppositional perspectives that run counter to the position of the encoder. As described by Hall, the negotiated position "acknowledges the legitimacy of the hegemonic definitions to make the grand significations (abstract), while, at a more restricted, situational (situated) level, it makes its own ground rules—it operates

---

19. Hall, "Encoding, Decoding," 509.
20. Hall, 515.

with exceptions to the rules."[21] By making exceptions to the rules at the individual level, the negotiated position often places itself in tension with the dominant-hegemonic position. Finally, the third position is the oppositional. Hall says the least about this position despite its potential for being the most politically charged. Simply stated, the oppositional position decodes in a manner that is contrary to the dominant-hegemonic position.

When analyzing patron interviews and online reviews, special attention was directed at reviews that mention features of the Ark Encounter and the Creation Museum that are based upon educated guesses and artistic license. Following Hall, I divided comments into three different categories. One category represented those who accept the educated guesses, without qualification, as statements of what Noah did or how things functioned. This group represents those who accept the message of AiG without question. A second category accepted the educated guesses as interesting and plausible but still recognized these reconstructions as guesswork. This category represents those who are in negotiation with the presentation of AiG. A third category flatly denied the plausibility of these proposals. This group represents those who are in opposition to AiG's message.

Some of those who accepted the educated guesses of the Ark Encounter as authoritative draw little distinction between Ark Encounter guesses and the Bible. For instance, one reviewer wrote that the Ark Encounter presents what is found in the Bible and that Noah's survival required advanced engineering.[22] For others, there is no equivocation, Ark Encounter educated guesses are not mere proposals but reflect systems designed and used by Noah. After visiting the Ark Encounter another reviewer wrote that Noah would have had a complex engineering solution for animal care on the ark.[23] The Bible says little about animal care on the ark; therefore, one presumes that the writer is referring to the feeding and watering systems presented at the Ark Encounter. That the Bible and the Ark Encounter merge together in these comments illustrates that the Ark Encounter's presentation is becoming part of patrons' horizon of expectations. Indeed, another TripAdvisor reviewer elaborates on the feeding and watering systems at the Ark Encounter while declaring that the Ark Encounter is an exact replica of the biblical ark.[24]

In his 2018 study of the Ark Encounter, James Bielo describes how design teams hope to spark a sense of plausibility in the patron. He describes their goal was

---

21. Hall, 516.

22. Linda S., "Awe Inspiring," TripAdvisor, September 10, 2016, https://www.tripadvisor.com/ShowUserReviews-g39995-d10110346-r416891443-Ark_Encounter-Williamstown_KentucKY.html.

23. Micolski2013, "A Must See on Your Bucket List!" TripAdvisor, September 13, 2016, https://www.tripadvisor.com/ShowUserReviews-g39995-d10110346-r418086402-Ark_Encounter-Williamstown_KentucKY.html.

24. Momcat6, "Impressive!!" TripAdvisor, November 9, 2016, https://www.tripadvisor.com/ShowUserReviews-g39995-d10110346-r435993589-Ark_Encounter-Williamstown_KentucKY.html.

visitors leaving with the impression that "Wow! Maybe that was possible. Maybe that did happen."[25] On that measure the Ark Encounter seems to be succeeding. That the Ark Encounter educated guesses are becoming part of a new biblical horizon for visitors is suggested by many visitor comments. For instance, some indicate that Ark Encounter artistic license changed how they thought about the flood narrative. One reviewer wrote, "The Ark Encounter really gave a feel for what it must have been like for Noah & his family during the flood. It made me think of things I would have never considered before, such as how they dispose[d] of all the animal waste, [and] where and how did they live and eat?" For others, seeing the Ark Encounter made the biblical narrative more concrete. Another reviewer wrote, "I've read the bible story many times and tried to imagine it. I was wrong, it's more, much more."

Others saw AiG educated guesses as plausible and interesting but held the educated guesses apart from the biblical narrative. One reviewer wrote that even though the Bible does not describe the ark's interior and its systems, it was interesting to see how AiG imagined the ark.[26] Others applaud the information contained therein as logical and plausible even if speculative. One interview subject stated they were unable to draw a firm conclusion about the authenticity of the displays, but it nonetheless seemed logical and possible.[27] Another interview subject told me, "Well, I don't know that it changed anything [about my understanding of the flood narrative], but again they made good arguments about how they could have done air flow, how they could have watered the animals and fed them. . . . The most surprising thing to me that I never thought about was that the dinosaurs would have existed during that period."[28] Others saw the educated guesses at the Ark Encounter as grounded in science and used this to bolster the authenticity of the biblical flood narrative. For example, one subject noted, "I think some of their presentations helped show [the] possibility of how it could have happened."[29] For others, showing possible day-to-day functions of the ark shored up the Bible's authority. Katie W wrote on TripAdvisor that while the ark is impressive, being able to go inside and see how it all worked increased the plausibility and historical accuracy of the flood.[30]

Finally, there are those who reject Ark Encounter educated guesses. One of the most controversial aspects of the Ark Encounter is the inclusion of dinosaurs. For

---

25. Bielo, *Ark Encounter*, 26.

26. Sam B., "A Visit to the Ark," TripAdvisor, August 20, 2016, https://www.tripadvisor.com/ShowUserReviews-g39995-d10110346-r407996487-Ark_Encounter-Williamstown_KentucKY.html.

27. Brooke, in discussion with the author, April 2017.

28. Ellen, in discussion with the author, April 2017.

29. Ashton, in discussion with the author, April 2017.

30. Katie W., "Impressive," TripAdvisor, November 1, 2016, https://www.tripadvisor.com/ShowUserReviews-g39995-d10110346-r433622567-Ark_Encounter-Williamstown_KentucKY.html.

many otherwise sympathetic visitors this proves to be a breaking point. Dennis indicated sympathy for the Ark Encounter, however, he said "they lost me when [describing] . . . how they would've done the plumbing situation for all of the sewage. . . . When I saw some animals in the cages being dinosaurs, it just pretty much lost all validity for me."[31] Another reviewer appreciated the biblical aspects of the Ark Encounter but objected to the amount of interpretation ark designers worked into the design. For pamfchang the ark became too rationalized. For her, AiG's interpretative hand was too heavy, Noah's living quarters were too rich, and the ark's engineering systems were overdone. For pamfchang, faith in God's miracles is enough to explain how those aboard the ark survived and rationalized materialistic explanations are not necessary.[32] This review is really the only one in which I saw this tension play out, which suggests that for most, both AiG and visitors, explanations for the flood event grounded in the material explanations are a necessary supplement to faith.

While the above has focused primarily on the Ark Encounter, artistic license is also on display at the Creation Museum. According to AiG theology, the fall of humanity explains many of the things we observe about the world today. The Creation Museum represents the well-known consequences of Adam and Eve's sin. For example, there is a post-Garden of Eden diorama that depicts Adam working the ground with a hoe while a prominently pregnant Eve looks upon the scene. This diorama, of course, depicts Adam as cursed to struggle with the land and hints at Eve's curse to bear children in pain. In addition to these well-known aspects of the story, AiG depicts some lesser-known elements deduced from the narrative. For instance, AiG proposes that prior to the fall, all things existed perfectly in balance and "plants produced exactly the amount of food needed by the animals of the earth."[33] Adam and Eve's sin, however, introduced death into the world and once animals started reproducing at a higher rate to replace the dead, greater demands were placed upon the ecosystem. To accommodate this, God caused plants to overproduce, leading eventually to weeds.

AiG also proposes that all animals (Adam and Eve included) must have been vegetarian prior to the fall and that humans remained vegetarian until God commanded Noah to eat meat. AiG points to Gen 9:3 wherein "every living creature will be food for you." AiG deduces that since there was no death at the time of creation that all animals must have been vegetarian. The argument that there was no death at the creation is derived from God's declaration that everything was good. Thus, a good God would not have introduced design flaws, like death, into His creation. This is further supported by Gen 1:29-30 where God declared

---

31. Dennis, in discussion with the author, May 2017.

32. pamfchang, "Magnificent but Questionable," TripAdvisor, September 4, 2018, https://www.tripadvisor.com/ShowUserReviews-g39995-d10110346-r414753778-Ark_Encounter-Williamstown_KentucKY.html.

33. Display text, *Before Adam's Sin*, Creation Museum, Petersburg, KY.

that plants have been given as food to both humans and animals. AiG continues by claiming that the plants given as food are sufficient for life.[34]

One of the best comments about AiG overreach occurred in response to a model of Adam. As we have seen, some comment about how educated guesses make the ark more rational, plausible, and shore up the Bible's authority. However, apparently too much realism can have some unexpected libidinal consequences. It is true that the Creation Museum's Adam mannequin is conventionally handsome. He has a muscular and tanned body, sports a six-pack, and wears only a large loincloth. One reviewer exclaims that this explains a lot about Eve because Adam is so sexy one might be tempted to sympathize with Eve, something this reviewer views as most unfortunate.[35] That Adam's sexiness might excuse Eve's temptation reflects an understanding of the Genesis narrative that is not supported by the text.

The Genesis narratives offer no description of the appearance of Adam and Eve, so any depiction relies upon interpretation, guesswork, and artistic license. The Creation Museum's Adam looks a bit 1980 James Brolin in *Night of the Juggler* with his messy long hair and his full dark beard. That the Creation Museum's Adam wears very little clothes allows us to see that the museum imagines Adam as having no body hair. This is a peculiar feature considering that Adam has a full black beard and a rich mane of black hair. One might be tempted to write this off as resulting from the difficulty of modeling body hair on a mannequin, but the Creation Museum gives too much attention to detail for this to be plausible. Likewise, there are articles on the Ark Encounter blog that demonstrate how modelers were adding hair to animals, so a process certainly seems to have been in place. This then raises the question as to why the Creation Museum's Adam looks like he uses a bottle of Nair hair remover body cream each week, even though the ideal of a hairless male body is a relatively new standard of physical perfection. I would suggest that the answer lies in the concept of perfection at creation, coupled with socially constructed images of the perfect male body.

The question of Adam's sexiness might partly lie in current conceptions of the sexy male body. While there have been times in American history when body hair was deemed sexy, think 1970s Burt Reynolds or 1980s Tom Selleck, current trends are away from body hair on men. It was, perhaps, the 2005 film *The Forty-Year Old Virgin* that signaled the arrival of the hairless male when Andy's (Steve Carrell) less than helpful friends convince him to undergo a chest waxing because women will not be interested in his "*Teen Wolf* thing." Now, from Daniel Craig to Ronaldo, from Hollywood to soccer, the ripped, bare-chested male is being promoted as the ideal.

---

34. "Creation's Original Diet and the Changes at the Fall," Answers in Genesis, accessed July 2, 2018, https://answersingenesis.org/animal-behavior/what-animals-eat/creations-original-diet-and-the-changes-at-the-fall/.

35. paolobiosas, "Were Dinosaurs Late?" TripAdvisor, June 29, 2016, https://www.tripadvisor.com/ShowUserReviews-g39743-d619562-r387359208-Creation_Museum-Petersburg_KentucKY.html.

While this particular cultural moment in America might support my interpretation, it turns out that artistic depictions of Adam with body hair are relatively infrequent. A tradition of Adam, sans body hair, appears to emerge from Renaissance conventions in depicting the first man. Renaissance art, inspired by Classical depictions of the male body, went to great lengths to explore the ideal male form. This meant depicting exaggerated musculature and proportions. It was thought that depictions of body hair obscured the presentation of this ideal form. Perhaps the most famous of these depictions is Albrect Durer's *Adam and Eve*. In this engraving a "ripped" Adam is shown without body hair. Durer linked this depiction to his study of the male form, stating that "the Creator fashioned men once and for all as they *must* be, and I hold that perfection of form and beauty is contained in the sum of all men."[36] Vaughan Hart further strengthens this connection by explaining that Durer sought to connect the ideal human form and natural order in his depiction of Adam and Eve.[37] Other Renaissance artists followed suit, with some giving Adam a beard but choosing not to depict any other body hair.

AiG's reading of the Genesis creation narrative considers the moment from creation to the fall to be a period of perfection.[38] Therefore, Adam and Eve's bodies, as depicted in the Garden of Eden, needed to reflect something of an ideal body. However, one's view of the ideal body is conditioned by the conceptions of one's culture coupled with, in this case, artistic conventions for depicting the first couple. These combine in the Creation Museum to produce a sexy Adam who meets twenty-first-century American beauty standards while also relying on Renaissance depictions of Adam with the ideal body. Furthermore, one should add that, despite having black hair, the depictions of Adam and Eve in the Creation Museum are nonetheless very Caucasian in their facial features. As the Garden is thought to be a place of perfect beauty, then it is telling that the white ideals for beauty inspired museum designers.

AiG neither adds to nor takes away anything that has not already been part of mainstream depictions of Adam. Because of this, images of Adam and Eve produced in the Creation Museum likely will not exceed or violate visitors' expectations and will do little to move the Jaussian horizon of expectations on this narrative. At best, for the typical evangelical visitor to the Creation Museum, such images more likely affirm rather than edify. As Jauss points out, changes in the horizon of expectations occur when a work challenges expectations. It is in challenging expectations that growth in the horizon is most likely to occur. Affirmation, however, does not imply growth so much as reinforcing a status quo.

Among patron comments analyzed for this study, those who express concern or outrage about the introduction of non-biblical material to the story are a minority.

---

36. Navel Gazing, 6.
37. Navel Gazing.
38. "Story of Adam and Eve," Creation Museum, accessed July 2, 2018, https://creationmuseum.org/eden/adam-eve/.

The general lack of concern about the educated guesses made at the Creation Museum and the Ark Encounter likely results from the trust that patrons have already placed in Ken Ham and AiG. After all, Ken Ham engaged in an extensive ministry before either of the flagship attractions was built. The success of his ministry is one of the factors that made building the Creation Museum and the Ark Encounter possible. Having established his trustworthiness as a Bible exegete, Ham can speak about issues related to the Bible with a great deal of authority without arousing the suspicions of his audience.

"Pushing Our Own Ideas"

AiG seems to be of two minds when it comes to educated guesses and artistic license. In the article titled "We Just Don't Noah," published on the AiG website on September 23, 2013, Tim Chaffey writes about the assumptions often made about the flood narrative and cautions the reader about introducing alien ideas into the text. As noted earlier, logical deductions based solely upon the Bible are okay but introducing our own ideas into God's Word represents faulty reading.[39]

While maintaining the distinction between Bible narrative and educated guesses may be easy for the biblically literate staff of AiG, the Bible literacy of Creation Museum and Ark Encounter visitors, even among those who are ardent believers in the AiG message, was not as high as expected. There was no expectation that visitors would cite chapter and verse; however, many could not even identify the book in which these well-known narratives appear. Because of this, AiG runs the risk of doing what Chaffey claims AiG must avoid, creating in the visitor's mind a blending, or confusion, of Ark Encounter educated guesses and information that actually appears in the Bible. Furthermore, if the confusion between the Bible and educated guesses runs too deep, then the narrative presented by AiG at the Creation Museum and the Ark Encounter has the potential to assume the authority of the Bible among visitors who fail to distinguish the guesses from the Bible. This is evident among some of the subjects interviewed for this study.

The willingness of many Creation Museum and Ark Encounter visitors to trust the materials presented therein as biblical has consequences regarding biblical authority and the way in which AiG interpretation blurs with actual Bible content. This transfer of biblical authority to non-biblical presentations of the Bible at the Ark Encounter occurs despite the fact that ark designers included some disclaimers about educated guesses and artistic license. In the mind of the hurried, sometimes uninformed visitor, however, the distinction between "Noah *may have had* shipbuilding expertise" and "Noah *had* ship building expertise" is easily lost.

---

39. "We Just Don't Noah."

Chapter 10

EXPECTING SOME FLATBREAD SANDWICHES

In my patron interviews and analysis of online reviews of the Creation Museum and the Ark Encounter, I found that patrons generally do not reflect upon specific Bible passages in their interpretation of the Creation Museum and the Ark Encounter. Instead, what seems more important is that these attractions conform to some concept of the biblical. Consequently, that sense of the biblical puts a *biblical hiraeth* on the visitor that finds expression in a feeling of being transported to a biblical time and place. Additionally, there is a chance that others could experience the Bible in this manner if they would only open their minds and give places like the Creation Museum and the Ark Encounter a chance.

As Bielo points out, research has shown that "the Bible" does not refer to just the Book.[1] In my analysis of visitor reviews of the Creation Museum and the Ark Encounter, there were many references to the Bible and much use of the term "biblical." However, there were also references to "God's Word," "the Word of God," "the Gospel," and "scripture." The use of these terms taps into a discourse that includes the Bible but may also extend beyond the Bible. For instance, as Malley points out, "God's Word" is sometimes extended to include sermons, discussions of sermons, and formal church lessons. Furthermore, there are even instances of God's Word used in reference to works in which no Bible verse is cited.[2]

The imprecise nature of this language is illustrated by reviewer comments on the Creation Museum. For instance, a TripAdvisor reviewer wrote that the Creation Museum's scientific data supported a biblical perspective in alignment with scripture.[3] As suggested here, biblical is not necessarily synonymous with Bible. In fact, something can be deemed biblical even if it does not strictly conform to the Bible. This is possible because, as Malley asserts, there is a difference between how evangelicals and their critics understand the concept of interpretation. For the evangelical, something can be deemed biblical if it is derived from the Bible

---

1. Bielo, *Ark Encounter*, 58.
2. Malley, "Understanding the Bible's Influence," 196–97.
3. 639randyr, "A TON of information," TripAdvisor, May 31, 2015, https://www.tripadvisor.com/ShowUserReviews-g39743-d619562-r276300938-Creation_Museum-Petersburg_KentucKY.html.

and is "rooted in the authority of God's word."[4] Malley holds this in contrast to the critic who accuses evangelical interpretation of being "distant, selective, or indirect relation to what the Bible says."[5] It is enough, therefore, to establish a relationship between the Bible and a reader's interpretation of it. Thus, the goal for AiG, to use the terms employed by Malley, is transitive in nature. AiG's Bible interpretation need not be identical to the text so long as "*transitivity* between the text and the reader's understanding is established."[6] This allows, so long as some connection to the Bible is present, for "propositions to be regarded as interpretations of a text even when they are not identical to the text."[7]

The idea that others mocked Noah for his ark-building efforts is often perceived as biblical. When asked to recount what they knew about the biblical flood story prior to their visit to the Creation Museum and the Ark Encounter, several of my interview subjects cited Noah's scoffers even though these scoffers are not part of the biblical narrative. Mason knew that "people made fun of him"[8] while Kurtis pointed out that nobody believed Noah.[9] For some of the interview subjects, the perceived mocking endured by Noah serves as a frame for their experiences as Bible literalists and as supporters of the Ark Encounter. Olivia employed this frame when I asked why she thought the Creation Museum devoted an entire display to Methuselah. She hypothesized that the Creation Museum did this because the idea that somebody could live to 969 years old "stands out even to non-Christian and it becomes a mocking point."[10] There is some sense, therefore, that these material representations of biblical narratives serve as a means of countering skeptics. Just seeing a thing, even a reconstruction, contributes more to its believability than does the text alone. This is made rather explicit in Isabella's response to the question about how the Ark Encounter changed her understanding of the biblical flood narrative. She cites atheistic and anti-religious radio shows that question how Noah was able to accomplish building an ark. For this subject the Ark Encounter provided her with answers to the objections of these atheistic scoffers.[11]

There are many interpretations of biblical materials that, while not adhering strictly to the text, do exhibit the transitivity that Malley proposes but are nonetheless not acceptable in evangelical circles. For instance, one does not find too many evangelicals who accept the notion that the sons of God (*bene ha'elohim*) of Gen 6:1–4 were actually space aliens conducting experiments on earth's

---

4. Brian Malley, *How the Bible Works: An Anthropological Study of Evangelical Biblicism*, Cognitive Science of Religion Series (Walnut Creek, CA: AltaMira Press, 2004), 73.
5. Malley, 73.
6. Malley, 84.
7. Malley, 84.
8. Mason, in discussion with the author, April 2017.
9. Kurtis, discussion.
10. Olivia, in discussion with the author, May 2017.
11. Isabella, discussion.

prehuman life-forms.[12] There must, therefore, be something that establishes the authority of an evangelical writer to offer acceptable transitive readings of the Bible. Recalling that Fish argued that reading (and writing) is governed by interpretive communities, then the degree to which an evangelical writer conforms to the rules of a particular interpretive community will govern how authoritative his or her readings are considered. For Ken Ham and AiG, this authority is established by following the writing conventions of the biblical literalist community. This means, first and foremost, adhering to the language of literalism. Though this concept is contested, and though few fundamentalists are "pure literalists,"[13] literalism generally includes the concept of the plain meaning of the text and reading the text as it was meant to be read (which is itself a thorny interpretative task). Malley suggests any literalist outcome in reading is less important than claims to literalism. More important is letting the text speak for itself rather than applying a formal hermeneutic to the text.[14] In this respect, AiG adheres very closely to the reading practices of the audience it attracts. This is evident in Ken Ham's description of his exegesis, which he claims should be an effort to determine meaning based on the "plain words," genre, context, and other scriptural references.[15] For Ham, meaning should arise from the text rather than having views forced upon it. This he terms as *eisegesis*, which he defines as the practice of bringing external ideas to scripture, and describes it as a "spiritual virus" that "infects . . . thinking in such a way that people are no longer able to consistently determine absolute truth."[16] By laying claim to the exegetical label, Ham is claiming for himself the authoritative mantle of higher criticism grounded in the notion that the Bible can be analyzed scientifically according to its language and context. This gives AiG the aura of objectivity.

Time Traveling the Bible

David Chidester points out that "if you want to get real, touching, not seeing, is believing."[17] In her article on performing creationism, Jill Stevenson argues that Creation Museum displays seek to bring life to the Bible.[18] An important premise of

---

12. This is, essentially, the position of Claude Vorilhon (Rael) who claims to have received this novel interpretation of the Bible directly from a space alien in France. Rael built the International Raelian Movement around this interpretation of the text.
13. Malley, *How the Bible Works*, 94.
14. Malley, 92.
15. Ham, *Six Days*, 187.
16. "Eisegesis," Answers in Genesis, accessed May 10, 2019, https://answersingenesis.org/hermeneutics/eisegesis/.
17. David Chidester, *Authentic Fakes: Religion and American Popular Culture* (Berkeley, CA: University of California Press, 2005), viii.
18. Stevenson, "Embodying Sacred History," 97.

James Bielo's work on the Ark Encounter is that "materializing the Bible" creates an intimacy with the text that reaches "across space-time" to allow for "direct access to the past."[19] Seeing is believing and the Bible benefits from material representation in order to reinforce the reality of the text for those who read it. Based upon my conversations with Creation Museum and Ark Encounter patrons, and what I have read in online reviews of each attraction, Chidester is correct in asserting that the material object promotes a certain sense of realism. However, I would not entirely discount, as he does, the impact of sight. The impact of seeing in physical form that which usually exists as words on a page—translated into mental images—turns out to be quite powerful, and rather emotional.

Some patrons maintain that there is a qualitative difference between reading the biblical text and seeing the displays represented in non-textual formats. For example, Patiodadio wrote about the difference between reading about the ark in the Bible and seeing it come to life.[20] Here is a clear demonstration that text alone is not enough to support what patrons consider an authentic and realistic image of the ark. The fact that the Noah's Ark replica makes the Bible come alive is an oft repeated statement in reviews of this type. Motorcity70 states that the Ark Encounter brought the Old Testament to life.[21] Jesus_Love_Me2 seems to hint that, prior to visiting the Ark Encounter, the idea of Noah's Ark had an unreal quality and for his family of believers the Ark Encounter made it real and personal.[22] That it only became very real in that moment speaks to the ability of the material object to overcome deficiencies in the text. The relationship between the material presentation and the Bible, and perhaps its necessity, was best expressed by BobUSMC who views the Creation Museum and the Ark Encounter as fixing a perceived material deficit for Christians. Despite recognizing that there are Christian and Jewish material cultures, BobUSMC maintains that there is a paucity of physical representations of God's influence and work in the world.[23] While one can question BobUSMC's perspective on the perceived absence of Christian material culture, his comment does, nonetheless, point to the important function of the Creation Museum and the Ark Encounter as pilgrimage sites that offer something tangible that can be felt and experienced.

19. Bielo, *Ark Encounter*, 35.
20. Patiodadio, "Great family day," TripAdvisor, July 15, 2016, https://www.tripadvisor.com/ShowUserReviews-g39995-d10110346-r393063042-Ark_Encounter-Williamstown_KentucKY.html.
21. Motorcity70, "Amazing!" TripAdvisor, August 11, 2016, https://www.tripadvisor.com/ShowUserReviews-g39995-d10110346-r404287187-Ark_Encounter-Williamstown_KentucKY.html.
22. Jesus_Love_Me2, "Wow!" TripAdvisor, August 30, 2016, https://www.tripadvisor.com/ShowUserReviews-g39995-d10110346-r412799021-Ark_Encounter-Williamstown_KentucKY.html.
23. BobUSMC, "Confirmation for Christians," TripAdvisor, October 3, 2016, https://www.tripadvisor.com/ShowUserReviews-g39995-d10110346-r424633573-Ark_Encounter-Williamstown_KentucKY.html.

While the perceived authenticity of the material displays is seen as giving life to the narrative, some visitors additionally report being transported either back in time or to a place out of time. Tim Beal, in his examination of roadside religion noted that such attractions are efforts at creating sacred space. Though of a scale different than most of the places visited by Beal, both the Creation Museum and the Ark Encounter seek to sacralize space as well. Playing with size, through both enlargement and miniaturization, creates a space where the normal rules no longer apply giving the visitor a sense of being in an "'other' fantasy world."[24] While the Creation Museum and the Ark Encounter, as "biblical recreation,"[25] do function as an escape from the corrupt and fallen world, to relegate them entirely to the realm of fantasy would betray the sense of "real" reality that comes with the concept of sacred space.

Though difficult to discern in patron comments, romantic notions about a more biblical past underlie the emotional impact of this short-term visit with Noah. Both the Creation Museum and the Ark Encounter emerged from a dissatisfaction with modern culture and its perceived abandonment of the Bible. The Ark Encounter is a vessel that functions like a time machine introducing the visitor to a man and his family who did take God's Word seriously. This is a balm for today's world-weary Christian who witnesses their own trials and tribulations played out in Noah's life and participate, by proxy, in Noah's vindication. Noah's vindication in the eyes of his doubters is the vindication that Creation Museum and Ark Encounter patrons crave. Psalm9242017 draws a stark distinction between the Creation Museum as a place out of time and the present day by noting that visiting the Creation Museum was like walking in the Bible and that leaving the Creation Museum transported one back to the present.[26] Impristine exclaims that a visit to the Ark Encounter was like leaving the twenty-first century.[27] In this, the Creation Museum and the Ark Encounter function like Disney attractions in creating simulacra, a copy without an original that has the force of the real. For others, modern life distorts how we read the Bible and a little dose of the ancient is the corrective. KenB writes on TripAdvisor that it is really difficult not to read the Bible from the perspective of the modern world; however, the Ark Encounter is a fantastic tool for transporting the visitor back in time for a taste of the ancient worldview.[28] Many commentators

---

24. Beal, *Roadside Religion*, 9.

25. Beal, 27.

26. Psalm9242017, "God Is Awesome!" TripAdvisor, March 11, 2017, https://www.tripadvisor.com/ShowUserReviews-g39743-d619562-r466368258-Creation_Museum-Petersburg_KentucKY.html.

27. Impristine, "Ark encounter," TripAdvisor, October 17, 2016, https://www.tripadvisor.com/ShowUserReviews-g39995-d10110346-r428711114-Ark_Encounter-Williamstown_KentucKY.html.

28. Ken B., "This Changes Everything," TripAdvisor, July 11, 2016, https://www.tripadvisor.com/ShowUserReviews-g39995-d10110346-r391524932-Ark_Encounter-Williamstown_KentucKY.html.

argue that visiting the Ark Encounter is really like being there[29] and that it felt like going back with Noah.[30] Shirley R exclaimed that the people look and act so authentically that she felt like she was interacting with Noah and his family.[31]

For others, certain modern intrusions can spoil the authenticity. The Ark Encounter features a cafeteria called Emzara's Café (Emzara being the name that Ark Encounter designers settled on for Noah's wife). Emzara's Café serves typical American fare, including hamburgers, fries, and pizza. For those looking for an authentic ancient Near Eastern experience, the modern American food is like a fly in the ointment. On this topic mycatfatsoo expected more authentically biblical or Middle Eastern food (like flatbread)[32] and others suggested the addition of period foods instead of burgers and fries.[33] While these statements reveal an expectation of being transported back in time, they betray an image of ancient Near Eastern history fabricated from images of the modern Middle East with its shawarma and falafel sandwiches. In reality, a cafeteria stocked according to the average diet of an ancient Palestinian would have contained bread, cooked legumes, goat or sheep milk, and fruits like figs and grapes.

For others, the commercial activities occurring inside the ark replica (snack and drink vendors and the gift shop) damage the attraction's credibility as an authentic representation of Noah and his culture. Diane L points out that vendors and their high-priced drinks and snacks detract from the experience.[34] On the issue of authenticity, a wooden structure this big exceeds the engineering principles of wood alone. In order to remain standing, and to accommodate building codes, modern construction techniques were employed. For some, finding hints of these modern techniques lessened the ark's authenticity. Bud A, a self-described evangelical Christian, points to these features with some contempt, claiming that

---

29. Bronie_1997, "The Spiritual Meets the Physical," TripAdvisor, August 9, 2016, https://www.tripadvisor.com/ShowUserReviews-g39995-d10110346-r403262686-Ark_Encounter-Williamstown_KentucKY.html.

30. Starmar1955, "Structural beauty!" TripAdvisor, August 12, 2016, https://www.tripadvisor.com/ShowUserReviews-g39995-d10110346-r404580241-Ark_Encounter-Williamstown_KentucKY.html.

31. Shirley R., "Breath Taking!!!!" TripAdvisor, August 25, 2016, https://www.tripadvisor.com/ShowUserReviews-g39995-d10110346-r410783838-Ark_Encounter-Williamstown_KentucKY.html.

32. mycatfatsoo, "Lots of Walking," TripAdvisor, September 10, 2016, https://www.tripadvisor.com/ShowUserReviews-g39995-d10110346-r416959702-Ark_Encounter-Williamstown_KentucKY.html.

33. slm E., "Excellent Exhibits & Event Venue!" TripAdvisor, July 14, 2016, https://www.tripadvisor.com/ShowUserReviews-g39995-d10110346-r392530059-Ark_Encounter-Williamstown_KentucKY.html.

34. Diane L., "Very Pricey Interpretation of God's Word," TripAdvisor, September 26, 2016, https://www.tripadvisor.com/ShowUserReviews-g39995-d10110346-r422602842-Ark_Encounter-Williamstown_KentucKY.html.

visitors will be disappointed at the use of Tyvek to waterproof the ark instead of gopher wood and pitch.[35] This quote also illustrates how cultural traditions creep into biblical narratives and become part of the reader's understanding of the text. Here the patron writes as though the average Ark Encounter visitor would know gopher wood when they see it despite the fact that the wood represented by the term "gopher" (Heb. *gopher*, Gen 6:14) remains unidentified.

Give It a Chance

In Chapter 5 I detailed how AiG, the Creation Museum, and the Ark Encounter employ rhetorical devices that are common among conspiracy theorists and pseudoarcheologists. Specifically, AiG pushes the notion that perspectives like theirs do not get a fair hearing in the public because of the power and influence of secular scientists. From this, creationists developed a strategy to "teach the controversy" by arguing that it is only fair that all sides of an issue receive attention—an idea that resonates with many fair-minded Americans. Creationist attempts to teach creationism in public school science classes leverage this strategy.

Appeals to fairness, and calls for open-mindedness, are evident in patron comments on the Creation Museum and the Ark Encounter. In fact, some reviewers argue that the Creation Museum handles its topics more fairly than its secular opponents. For instance, writing about the Creation Museum on July 5, 2015, Denise F suggests that the Creation Museum is fairer than the Smithsonian because it presents both sides of the issue.[36] The idea that the Creation Museum is a response to the unfair exclusion of creationism from scientific circles finds expression in a June 14, 2015, TripAdvisor review of the Creation Museum. HPhil J complains about how secular museums promote evolutionary theory to the exclusion of other theories of origins.[37]

Typically, visitors view the Creation Museum's presentation as a counterbalance to what they view as the dominant secular evolutionary theory. Occasionally, however, there are reviewers who find that the Creation Museum treats opposing evolutionary theory with fairness. A particularly eloquent expression of this approach to fairness comes from a reviewer writing about the Creation Museum on January 31, 2015. Hakwanderer writes on TripAdvisor that the Creation

---

35. Bud A., "Lots to Read; Nothing to See," TripAdvisor, August 22, 2016, https://www.tripadvisor.com/ShowUserReviews-g39995-d10110346-r409077511-Ark_Encounter-Williamstown_KentucKY.html.

36. Denise F., "Destination Vacation to the Creation," TripAdvisor, July 5, 2015, https://www.tripadvisor.com/ShowUserReviews-g39743-d619562-r285891873-Creation_Museum-Petersburg_KentucKY.html.

37. Phil J., "Great Petting Zoo, Beautiful Gardens," TripAdvisor, June 14, 2015, https://www.tripadvisor.com/ShowUserReviews-g39743-d619562-r280250604-Creation_Museum-Petersburg_KentucKY.html.

Museum does a better job of presenting science than a lot of people are willing to recognize (despite its creationist agenda) and actually treats evolutionary theory with an even hand.[38] This reviewer, who self-identifies as being raised in the Judeo-Christian tradition, appears to be addressing a concern, leveled by many secular scientists, that the Creation Museum's understanding of evolution is flawed and skewed toward the AiG theological agenda. Hakwanderer suggests that, while the Creation Museum appeals to fairness in order to claim a seat at the table, and despite the fact that AiG claims unfair treatment, they nonetheless treat evolutionary theory in a fair manner. A certain element of "having your cake and eating it too" is evident in this discourse. AiG, through the Creation Museum, is very critical of evolutionary theory and the science supporting it while, at the same time, craving scientific legitimation from the very community it criticizes.[39] In doing so, as Ella Butler points out, the Creation Museum both "inhabits and *dismantles* the tools of science."[40]

In online reviews of the Creation Museum and the Ark Encounter, appeals to open-mindedness, a concept closely related to fairness, are also very prevalent. In these reviews, open-mindedness is a suggested trait for those considering a visit to the Creation Museum. For example, Idjit wrote on January 7, 2015, that, even if you do not take the Old Testament literally, open-mindedness is central to the experience.[41] In the so-called culture wars, appeals to open-mindedness have been a feature of the political left, who contrast themselves with the closed-minded right. An appeal to open-mindedness, this time coming from the Christian right, is another example of how the creationists are appropriating the rhetorical techniques of the left. Thus, failure to approach the Creation Museum with an open mind becomes tantamount to hypocrisy on the part of museum opponents, many of whom likely number among those who champion open-mindedness regarding other social issues. One reviewer recommends going to the Creation Museum with an open mind simply to learn about different perspectives on the world.[42] Few of the reviewers demanded that the visitor accept creationist beliefs, but rather, they appealed to the visitor to just approach the topic with a sense of open-mindedness.

---

38. Hakwanderer, "A Skeptic's Visit," TripAdvisor, January 31, 2015, https://www.tripadvisor.com/ShowUserReviews-g39743-d619562-r251899113-Creation_Museum-Petersburg_KentucKY.html.

39. Joshua C. Tom, "Social Origins of Scientific Deviance: Examining Creationism and Global Warming Skepticism," *Sociological Perspectives* 61, no. 3 (June 2018): 355, https://doi.org/10.1177/0731121417710459.

40. Butler, "God Is in the Data," 231.

41. Idjit, "You May Not Be a 'Believer,'" TripAdvisor, January 7, 2015, https://www.tripadvisor.com/ShowUserReviews-g39743-d619562-r248181830-Creation_Museum-Petersburg_KentucKY.html.

42. Reshee, "I'm Probably Not It's Target Demographic," TripAdvisor, August 31, 2015, https://www.tripadvisor.com/ShowUserReviews-g39743-d619562-r305541209-Creation_Museum-Petersburg_KentucKY.html.

Other reviewers, however, use the concept of close-mindedness like a cudgel in an attempt to depict creationism's opponents as inflexible. In the words of Jason M, the close-minded, atheists, or anybody offended when God is mentioned in the public square ought to stay away.[43]

Appealing to open-mindedness is a rhetorical technique that flips the script. Secular science presents itself as a means of examining the world that is open to falsification and new ideas—practically the definition of open-mindedness—provided that the new ideas can be supported through the scientific method. The rhetorical technique being employed at the Creation Museum is a two-part strategy. First, AiG argues that, rather than being open-minded, secular scientists are actually dogmatic, close-minded, and work from faulty premises.[44] This leads to depicting secular scientists as slavish to a Darwinian dogma and being unwilling to consider other perspectives or ideas, like creation science, for instance. The second part of the strategy is convincing others that the Creation Museum, and other creation science organizations, represents the truly open-minded defenders of inquiry who have been rejected by close-minded secular scientists.[45] Open-mindedness is here touted as a virtue with close-mindedness acquiring a negative moral connotation.

This is a rather peculiar, and flawed, understanding of open-mindedness. First, open-mindedness is, according to William Hare, a willingness to revise and reconsider one's view.[46] To claim that secular scientists are close-minded because they refuse to give creation science a hearing is a distortion. In fact, much of the early history of Darwinism and evolutionary theory was a consideration of evolution in light of biblical theories of creation and the vast majority of scientists found the biblical evidence not compelling. Open-mindedness demands nothing more than this. A willingness to reconsider one's view does not mean the challenger of that view automatically gets a hearing, which seems to be the perspective of those who argue that creation sciences should be taught with evolution in public schools. Rejecting an idea that does not have sufficient evidence is not a sign of close-mindedness; rather, it is a sign of critical thinking.

For some Creation Museum visitors, it appears that appeals to open-mindedness spring from indignation that non-creationists would declare others wrong on this issue. For instance, Laura M argues that a sense of fairness would demand that

---

43. Jason M., "Interesting and Fun," TripAdvisor, August 15, 2014, https://www.tripadvisor.com/ShowUserReviews-g39743-d619562-r222106899-Creation_Museum-Petersburg_KentucKY.html.

44. "Defense—'Scientific' Arguments," Answers in Genesis, accessed May 10, 2019, https://answersingenesis.org/age-of-the-earth/defensescientific-arguments/; "Matt Walsh and a Young Earth," Answers in Genesis, accessed May 10, 2019, https://answersingenesis.org/creationism/young-earth/matt-walsh-and-young-earth/.

45. "Secularist Intolerance against Scientific Paper."

46. Harvey Siegel, "Open-Mindedness, Critical Thinking, and Indoctrination: Homage to William Hare," in *Philosophical Inquiry in Education* 18, no. 1 (2009): 29.

we not declare anybody wrong if they disagree with scientific conclusions.[47] For others, appeals to open-mindedness sound rational and reasonable and are meant to appeal to everybody's innate sense of fairness. One interview subject, when asked if she would emphasize any particular thing about the Creation Museum said: "I would say give, especially for non-believers, give it a chance. Give it a shot. Go there with an open mind, and see what you take away from it. And try not to go there expecting to see a bunch of stuff that you necessarily disagree with. Go there with an open mind."[48] Even if this subject did not express it in this manner, this appeal reveals a particularly evangelical way of looking at the Bible. For many in the evangelical community, in addition to reading the Bible, there is a potential transformative power that comes from being in close proximity to the Word. Thus, appeals for visiting the Creation Museum with an open mind, which sound innocuous enough, are ultimately meant to encourage readers to place themselves in close proximity to God's Word at the Creation Museum so that the Holy Spirit can work a transformation in the life of the visitor.

That the Bible has power that operates independently of its reading is evident in evangelical culture in many ways. One striking example of this is represented in the 1997 film *The Apostle*. In one memorable scene, a character simply listed in the credits as "Troublemaker" (Billy Bob Thornton), who has been nursing a grudge against Sonny, aka. The Apostle E.F. (Robert Duvall), drives a bulldozer to Sonny's church and threatens to knock it down. Sonny and his fellow congregants prevent this by laying bibles on the ground around the bulldozer. That the bibles have power as objects is revealed in Sonny's comment: "If you go to that church go over that holy book first . . . if you do, I don't want to sit where you're sitting." To further emphasize the point, when Troublemaker leaves the cab of the bulldozer in order to pick up the Bible, Sonny squats on the ground beside him, takes the Troublemaker's hand, and effects a spiritual change in him by laying his hand on the text. At no point in this process did the Troublemaker read from the text.[49]

Though this scene from *The Apostle* is fictionalized, it does reflect perspectives on Bible power that are evident in evangelical culture. Candida Moss and Joel Baden explain this within the context of the MotB by pointing to the stories collected in John Fea's *The Bible Cause: A History of the American Bible Society*. Included therein is a story about an American Bible Society agent who hid a Bible in a farmer's barn. The farmer, in spiritual turmoil, eventually finds the Bible, repents, and finds salvation. In another story, a recalcitrant young man uses Bible pages to clean his razor blade until, one day, his close physical contact to the text help effect a spiritual change. While this might sound rather magical, it is

---

47. Laura M., "Where Is the Book on Scientific Fact?" TripAdvisor, August 12, 2013, https://www.tripadvisor.com/ShowUserReviews-g39743-d619562-r171898021-Creation_Museum-Petersburg_KentucKY.html.

48. Olivia, discussion.

49. Adele Reinhartz, *Scripture on the Silver Screen* (Louisville, KY: Westminster John Knox Press, 2003), 123–25.

explained in evangelical culture as the work of the Holy Spirit. In conversations with Steve Green, the driving force behind the MotB, Moss notes that, for Green, "the tangible presence of scriptural texts contains its own kind of religious power" and Moss notes that "the power of the word of God to transform the hearer has a particular history in American Protestantism."[50] This is not, however, just the power in the words received via reading; this is power received via simple contact and proximity. This partly explains why situating the Bible within the context of Bible scholarship and a purportedly neutral context seems not to trouble Steve Green and the MotB. Just the mere presence of the Bible in the MotB invites the Holy Spirit to work its transforming powers on museum patrons.

Is this as effective, however, when the Bible is in pieces? If visitors go to the Creation Museum expecting an encounter with the complete Bible, they are likely to come away disappointed. Instead, what the Creation Museum and the Ark Encounter present is the Bible in fragments with most of those being fragments of Genesis. It is striking, as Trollinger and Trollinger note, that the visitor encounters very few complete bibles at the Creation Museum.[51] The most concentrated collection of actual bibles occurs in a special display of rare Bible manuscripts called the *Verbum Domini* ("The Word of the Lord"). According to the Creation Museum, the *Verbum Domini* consists of twenty-seven rare manuscripts and fragments, including the *Codex Climaci Rescriptus*, described by AiG as a nearly complete fourth-century Aramaic text of the Bible.[52] Other bibles on display in the *Verbum Domini* include a 1611 King James "HE" Bible (so named because it contains a typo of Ruth 3:15 that reads "he went into the city" instead of "she went into the city) and a 1552 Tyndale New Testament with woodcut illustrations.[53] According to a Creation Museum article on the *Verbum Domini*, the artifacts on display are from the "famed Green Collection," the same collection that would form the heart of the MotB, and were personally dedicated by Steve Green.

The bibles in the *Verbum Domini* have their own display room and are not found in the main museum display. Visitors do not encounter complete bibles in the displays, nor do they seem (based on my own observations) to browse the displays with Bible in hand. Even though visitors may not have the text in hand, and are only getting the Bible in fragments, text is still very important at the Creation Museum and the Ark Encounter—it surrounds the visitor. Trollinger and Trollinger describe the amount of text, presented on placards and wall displays, to be exhausting.[54] The Trollingers suggest that the overwhelming amount of text

---

50. Moss and Baden, *Bible Nation*, 159.
51. Trollinger and Trollinger, *Righting America at the Creation Museum*, 116.
52. "Rare Bible Manuscripts at Creation Museum," Creation Museum, accessed July 16, 2018, https://creationmuseum.org/press/rare-bible-manuscripts-on-display-at-creation-museum/.
53. "Rare Bible Manuscripts at Creation Museum."
54. Trollinger and Trollinger, *Righting America at the Creation Museum*, 121.

intentionally encourages skimming, the consequence of which is overlooking or ignoring context.[55]

Though the Bible exists in pieces at the Creation Museum and the Ark Encounter, visitors nonetheless frame the attractions from the perspective of the whole Bible. People do not talk about the Creation Museum as presenting just Genesis, for example, but are more likely to talk about the Creation Museum as representing the entire Bible. In fact, one online reviewer named Dee H was quite expansive in her conflation of the Bible with the Creation Museum, describing the Creation Museum as representing the Bible from beginning to end.[56] Others found that the Creation Museum so authentically represented the Bible that they felt transported into the text, like WomanofGOD_12, who walked through the Bible.[57]

From its 40-foot-tall Gutenberg Bible doors to its Hebrew Bible experience, the MotB is also a walk through the Bible. In fact, with dozens of bibles on display, the MotB is much more about the Bible as an object than the Creation Museum and the Ark Encounter. As with the Creation Museum and the Ark Encounter, the MotB has both a story to tell about the Bible and a story to tell using the Bible. These stories, largely about religious freedom, are the subjects of the next chapter.

---

55. Trollinger and Trollinger, 121.

56. Dee H., "Wonderful Museum," TripAdvisor, January 23, 2012, https://www.tripadvisor.com/ShowUserReviews-g39743-d619562-r123515083-Creation_Museum-Petersburg_KentucKY.html.

57. WomanofGOD_12, "Wonderful," TripAdvisor, April 24, 2012, https://www.tripadvisor.com/ShowUserReviews-g39743-d619562-r128558384-Creation_Museum-Petersburg_KentucKY.html.

Chapter 11

PLAYING IT SAFE AT THE MUSEUM OF THE BIBLE

430,000 Square Feet of Religious Freedom

I visited the MotB in the middle of the longest government shutdown in American history. The government shutdown started on Saturday, December 22, 2018, as a result of a budget impasse over President Trump's demand for 5.7 billion dollars to fund a border wall between the United States and Mexico. As is often the case in contentious social debates, both those in favor of and those against the border wall employed the Bible to justify their positions. Wayne Grudem, professor and general editor of the *ESV Study Bible*, maintained that building a border wall is a morally good action consistent with biblical ethics.[1] Representative Luis Gutierrez (Democrat, Illinois) invoked the Bible by asserting that a wall might have hampered Mary and Joseph as they sought refuge in Egypt.[2] In response, Pastor Robert Jeffress justified the border wall by pointing out that even heaven has a wall.[3] From slavery to the Civil War to current debates about the border wall, the Bible has played a role in some of the messiest and most tragic eras and events in American history. The MotB, however, attempts to tread a middle path through all this, rarely confronting in any meaningful manner the national heartaches that have resulted from certain readings of the Bible. There is an irony that, while the Bible was being employed in a furious partisan debate that shut down the government, the MotB was open, and was playing it safe.

---

1. Wayne Grudem, "Why Building a Border Wall Is a Morally Good Action," Townhall, accessed February 1, 2019, https://townhall.com/columnists/waynegrudem/2018/07/02/why-building-a-border-wall-is-a-morally-good-action-n2496574.

2. Tim Marcin, "DHS Chief Kirstjen Nielsen Claims Jesus, Mary and Joseph Would Be Welcomed in the U.S.," Newsweek, December 20, 2018, https://www.newsweek.com/dhs-kirstjen-nielsen-jesus-mary-joseph-usa-democrat-lawmaker-1267571.

3. Ian Schwartz, "Rev. Jeffress: Trump Fulfilling His 'God-Given Responsibility' By Building The Wall, Heaven Has A Wall," Real Clear Politics, accessed February 1, 2019, https://www.realclearpolitics.com/video/2018/12/22/rev_jeffress_trump_fulfilling_his_god-given_responsibility_by_building_the_wall_heaven_has_a_wall.html.

As argued earlier, the Creation Museum is unabashedly a walk-through sermon. Though it wears the badge of "museum" in order to lend itself an aura of authority and authenticity, there is, nonetheless, a clear theological agenda. The MotB, on the other hand, uses the museum genre to better effect, even having an accessioned collection, and couches their displays in seemingly neutral language. Nonetheless, the placard and display text that guides visitors through the museum is not the only way to manipulate the narrative. What is included, what is excluded, and the context of the displays in relation to other exhibits contribute to MotB's story. In short, at the MotB the Bible is presented as a document supporting freedom and any evidence to the contrary is downplayed. With its emphasis on religious freedom, the MotB offers powerful support for the recent rhetoric of religious freedom used in the Green family's religious objections to the 2010 Affordable Care Act.

To understand the message being conveyed at the MotB, it is important to understand the Green family and their place in recent social and political debates on religious freedom in America. The arts-and-crafts retail giant, Hobby Lobby, was started by David and Barbara Green on a six-hundred-dollar loan in 1970. Still privately owned by the Green family, Hobby Lobby employs about 37,500 people in more than 850 Hobby Lobby stores.[4] The Greens have never been shy about their Christian religious beliefs and have used the Hobby Lobby brand to promote those beliefs. For example, patrons will know that Hobby Lobby is closed on Sunday and that the Green family publishes Bible story images in hundreds of newspapers during the holidays.[5]

It was not until the passing of the Affordable Care Act in 2010, with its contraception mandate, that the Green family's religious convictions came to the fore of the American political scene in a public way. Citing violations of religious freedom, in 2012 the Green family filed a lawsuit against the Obama administration over the contraception mandate in the Affordable Care Act. Following a July 2013 preliminary injunction releasing Hobby Lobby from the contraception mandate, the Obama administration appealed the case to the Supreme Court (*Burwell v. Hobby Lobby, Inc.*). On June 30, 2014, in a 5–4 decision, the Supreme Court ruled in favor of Hobby Lobby citing the 1993 Religious Freedom Restoration Act (which was written for the purpose of protecting Native American lands).[6]

Though I did not find explicit reference *to Burwell v. Hobby Lobby, Inc.* at the MotB it is clear that the lawsuit is the governing structure for the permanent second floor display titled *The Impact of the Bible* where the concepts of tyranny and freedom are the display's primary themes. The *Impact of the Bible* display begins with the Bible's arrival in the New World with the Pilgrims, continues through the

---

4. "Our Story," Hobby Lobby, accessed May 30, 2019, https://www.hobbylobby.com/about-us/our-story.

5. Moss and Baden, *Bible Nation*, 4.

6. "Burwell v. Hobby Lobby Stores, Inc.," SCOTUSblog, accessed May 30, 2019, https://www.scotusblog.com/case-files/cases/sebelius-v-hobby-lobby-stores-inc/.

founding of America and the Civil War, the civil rights era, popular culture, and concludes with the status of the Bible in the world today.

Within the first 10 feet of the *Impact of the Bible* exhibit entryway the visitor sees no less than five references to the Mayflower Compact. As the first governing document of colonists arriving in North America, it is here held up as a model of a government established "in the presence of God" and is clearly meant to support the argument that America was founded as a Christian nation where "church and state would both be governed by biblical teachings."[7] The founding of America by those seeking religious freedom is a prevalent theme in these initial displays. Many arrived, according to MotB, with their own versions of the Bible and "some professed their intentions to convert Native Americans to Christian beliefs."[8] On a placard about Benjamin Rush, a Philadelphia signer of the American Declaration of Independence, the museum declares that Rush "frequently stated the importance of the Bible in sustaining the moral character of the American republic."[9]

There are many ways that the early history of America could have been introduced. For example, instead of the Puritans and the Mayflower Compact, the MotB could have started with the earlier founding of the Colony of Virginia (1606) and the business interests of the Virginia Company. This, of course, does not suit the narrative the MotB wants to create as their selective reading of America's founding better serves the argument that America was founded as a Christian nation. In the *Impact of the Bible* exhibit this narrative is supported by demonstrating the degree to which the Bible influenced the growth and founding of the young nation. Lurking behind all of this is *Burwell v. Hobby Lobby*, a Christian sense of persecution in America, and struggles over American identity that both the AiG and the MotB seek to influence and address.

The first section of the *Impact of the Bible* exhibit features display placards with the header "Tyranny and Tolerance." Here the theme of religious freedom in the settling of America is highlighted. On a placard titled "Coming to America" the MotB notes, "Among them were many English dissenters seeking religious freedom."[10] Another display discusses the founding of Rhode Island on the principle of using "biblical arguments to support tolerance" as a haven for those seeking religious freedom.[11] These are just a few examples of many where the theme of religious freedom is woven into the tapestry of the MotB's understanding of America's early history.

In recent years, certain segments in American society have claimed that being required to do things like provide no-cost contraception for women and make wedding cakes for gay couples is a violation of their religious freedom.[12]

---

7. Wall text, *New World,* MotB, Washington, D.C.
8. Wall text, *Coming to America,* MotB, Washington, D.C.
9. Display text, *George Washington,* MotB, Washington, D.C.
10. Wall text, *Coming to America,* MotB, Washington, D.C.
11. Wall text, *New England: Establishment and Resistance,* Washington, D.C.
12. Ariane de Vogue, "Supreme Court Rules for Colorado Baker in Same-Sex Wedding Cake Case," CNN, accessed May 17, 2019, https://www.cnn.com/2018/06/04/politics/maste

This, essentially, was the Hobby Lobby's argument in *Burwell v. Hobby Lobby*. In a video published by the Heritage Foundation on March 27, 2014, Steve Green noted that the very first freedoms in America were religious freedoms, an idea that is central to the MotB *Impact of the Bible* exhibit.[13] President Trump's executive order 13798, issued on May 4, 2017, titled "Promoting Free Speech and Religious Liberty," affirmed an executive policy to vigorously enforce Federal law's robust protections for religious freedom.[14] Indeed, protecting religious freedom now appears four times in the "About Us" website description of the US Department of Health and Human Services' Office for Civil Rights.[15] Such moves are predicated upon the idea that Christians in America are persecuted and oppressed and must, therefore, have their religious liberty protected. This is further fueled by the prognostications delivered by many figures on the religious right about a current and continuing attack on American Christianity as evidenced by Fox News' so-called war on Christmas. At the MotB, in the *Impact of the Bible* exhibit, the language of persecution is used in at least one place. After the first third of the *Impact of the Bible* display the museum visitor is asked to participate in a Bible in America survey. The ongoing results of the survey circulate in front of the visitor on a large curved screen. One question asks visitors if they agree that "individuals and religious groups in America should be able to read, interpret, and live out their religious texts (no matter what religion) without fear of persecution." Of course, the vast majority of respondents (92 percent) agree. A second question on this topic asks people to agree or disagree that "there is a threat to religious freedom in America." A third asks visitors if they agree that the "Bible supports the defense of religious freedom for all." This is, again, a false equivalence. To the degree that there is religious persecution in America, it is not directed at Christians. We can cite examples of Muslims or Sikhs suffering in post-9/11 America, but the power and privilege held by Christians as individuals and in American systems points to the opposite of persecution. Though couched in objective and inclusive language, these particular questions function as a dog whistle for those who have bought into the idea that Christians in America are being oppressed.

rpiece-colorado-gay-marriage-cake-supreme-court/index.html; "Masterpiece Cakeshop, Ltd. v. Colorado Civil Rights Commission," Oyez, accessed May 17, 2019, https://www.oyez.org/cases/2017/16-111; "Religious Exemptions and Accommodations for Coverage of Certain Preventive Services Under the Affordable Care Act," Federal Register, November 15, 2018, https://www.federalregister.gov/documents/2018/11/15/2018-24512/religious-exemptions-and-accommodations-for-coverage-of-certain-preventive-services-under-the.

13. The Heritage Foundation, *Hobby Lobby's Steve Green on Religious Liberty*, accessed February 4, 2019, https://www.youtube.com/watch?v=mIIeVCttTkg.

14. "Promoting Free Speech and Religious Liberty," Federal Register, May 9, 2017, https://www.federalregister.gov/documents/2017/05/09/2017-09574/promoting-free-speech-and-religious-liberty.

15. Office for Civil Rights (OCR), "About Us (OCR)," HHS.gov, September 6, 2015, https://www.hhs.gov/ocr/about-us/index.html.

The MotB implicitly lends support to this oppression narrative; however, the mere existence of the MotB suggests just the opposite. When the MotB was first announced, commentators commented on the irony following from claims that evangelical Christianity is under attack with this proposal to build a large museum, grounded in the evangelical theology of the Green family, just steps of the National Mall. For example, Sarah Posner wrote:

> The museum will be a living, breathing testament to how American evangelicalism can at once claim it is under siege from secularists, the LGBT rights movement, or feminism—yet also boast of acquiring a prime private perch, strategically located at the nation's epicenter of law and politics, and nestled among its iconic public monuments.[16]

The MotB attempts to lend legitimacy (and gain sympathy) to this narrative by placing the Christian fight for religious liberty in America on the same playing field with other oppressions, like those faced by enslaved Africans and Jim Crow–era people of color, who fought against real, devastating, oppression. By way of example, a set of displays in the *Impact of the Bible* exhibit bear the subheading "Civil Rights and Beyond." One placard with the subheading titled "Science and the Bible: The Scopes Trial" describes the central question of the Scopes trial as a battle between faith and secularism and how one maintains faith in a scientifically changing world.[17] Although there is not a lot to quibble about regarding the content of this placard, placing it within the context of the civil rights movement is bound to create a subtle link between these two subjects in the visitor's mind and suggests that struggles over the Bible's authority in the mid-twentieth century were equivalent to the struggles faced by the civil rights movement. This is also especially evident in a display on human rights. Here, large displays, each measuring about 3 foot by 7 foot, stand in a circle (imagine a mini Stonehenge). On the back of each display is a large photo of a civil rights leader and a caption. One of these figures is Abraham Joshua Heschel who is accompanied by the caption "Freedom of Religion." Also featured are Frederick Douglass and Josephine Bakhita (representing freedom from slavery), Eleanor Roosevelt and Desmond Tutu (representing freedom from injustice), and Dorothy Ray and "The Bible and the Poor" (representing freedom from want). On the opposite side of each is a video screen showing microdocumentaries on how the Bible influenced each person. The choice of Abraham Joshua Heschel is interesting because, as a theologian who marched with Dr. Martin Luther King, Jr., his inclusion lends further authority and weight to the suggestion that the fight for religious freedom in America is equivalent to the oppressions targeted by the civil rights movement.

---

16. Sarah Posner, "The Inside Story of Hobby Lobby's New Bible Museum on the National Mall," Talking Points Memo, accessed February 10, 2019, https://talkingpointsmemo.com/theslice/hobby-lobby-museum-of-the-bible.

17. Wall text, *Science and the Bible: The Scopes Trial,* MotB, Washington, D.C.

What is absent from this display is just as telling as what is there. It is hard to imagine telling the story of the Bible's use against oppression without highlighting liberation theology. Absent are figures like Gustavo Gutierrez (1928–), who coined the term liberation theology and whose book *A Theology of Liberation* (1973) is foundational to the movement. Likewise, James Cone (1938–2018), the father of black liberation theology in America, is absent as well. The closest the MotB comes to highlighting liberation theology is a small display about the *communidades de base*, a post–Second World War Latin American Bible discussion movement rooted in consideration of the poor and the powerless accompanied by a poster about the 1980 assassination of Archbishop Oscar Romero. The text of this display steers clear of the term "liberation theology" and mentions no other supporters of this movement. Liberation theology is not an obscure footnote in the history of twentieth-century biblical theology but is a movement that shaped social unrest in many countries. Liberation theology even gained mainstream attention in the United States during the 2008 presidential campaign of Barack Obama, who attended the church of Jeremiah Wright, a supporter of black liberation theology.

The furor that arose over then candidate Obama's attendance at this church illustrates the likely reasons liberation theology was excluded from MotB's civil rights displays. Since its inception, many right-wing commentators have painted liberation theology as a warmed-over socialism and Marxism placed within a Christian context, a "Marxist class struggle with a sprinkling of holy water."[18] In recent years, the unsubstantiated claim that liberation theology was seeded into Latin American churches by the KGB has also been circulating among right-wing groups.[19]

The MotB does little more than gloss over the role the Bible played in perpetuating injustice. Without doubt, the MotB mentions that the Bible was brought to native culture by missionaries wielding Bibles and that the Bible was used to justify slavery. Making this admission gives MotB a veneer of objectivity and balance. However, throughout the *Impact of the Bible* display it is the Bible, and white people fighting for it, that feature as heroes. A long, stitched fabric wall tapestry reflects the struggles faced by European colonizers in North America. One set of images depicts a battle between European settlers and Native Americans—battles and wars that we know happened. However, the manner in which the figures are displayed reveals much about the implicit assumptions of museum designers. The battle takes place in a wooded area that appears to be littered with pages from a book. The visitor is not told what these pages are, but it would be a fair guess to read this as a battle over the Bible. In this battle the European colonists are presented as more passive while the images of active killing are assigned to Native

---

18. John L. Allen, Jr., "Did the Kgb 'Create' Latin America's Liberation Theology?" *Crux*, May 5, 2015, https://cruxnow.com/church/2015/05/05/did-the-kgb-create-latin-americas-liberation-theology/.

19. Ion Mihai Pacepa, "The Secret Roots of Liberation Theology," *National Review*, April 23, 2015, https://www.nationalreview.com/2015/04/secret-roots-liberation-theology/.

Americans wielding axes and bows. Two colonists are depicted using guns, but the muzzles of their guns are hidden by a tree trunk. The single depiction of hand-to-hand combat shows a colonist in a defensive position, with his back against a tree, while a dagger-wielding Native American grasps him by the throat. This is nothing more than the noble white man, schooled in restraint and civilization, facing off against the savage in need of a Christianizing influence.

The MotB takes a color-blind approach to presenting this complicated history. In doing so, the MotB, founded by the Green family and rooted in a normative white evangelical American Christianity, fails to confront and problematize the role this segment of Christianity, and the Bible, has played in perpetuating these injustices. It is not enough, as the MotB does, to report the facts. For instance, MotB rightly points out that the Bible was used to support both slavery and abolition. However, MotB displays have a curious neutrality on the topic coupled with a very subtle downplaying of the Bible's role in supporting slavery. For example, an information placard titled "The Bible and Slavery" describes how abolitionists and slave owners used the authority of the Bible. In discussing the abolitionist perspective, MotB cites Deut 24:7 as a biblical argument used by abolitionists against "man-stealing." The plaque then states that "proslavery factions, with equal fervor, turned to specific passages in the Bible that condoned the practice in ancient Israel and seemed to sanction it in the New Testament."[20] Note that the discussion of abolitionist arguments received a very specific biblical citation while the reader is not directed to any specific proslavery passages in the Bible. This very subtle move enhances the Bible as a force for good while downplaying its potential as an oppressive text. Furthermore, the phrase "in ancient Israel" suggests to the visitor that the biblical sanction for slavery is limited to a particular culture in a specific time in history. The proslavery factions obviously did not read the Bible in this manner; this is the "how" and the "why" that the MotB fails to confront.

Other displays very subtly downplay the role of the Bible in supporting slavery. A poster titled "Religious Freedom: A New Awakening" states, "The religious vitality also opened the door to social change and ignited a campaign to abolish slavery in the United States. Southern slaveholders, however—some of them also involved in the revivals—interpreted the Bible as affirming slavery."[21] This general approach, evident throughout the *Impact of the Bible* display, presents biblical support for slavery as an afterthought. In another example on the "African American Experience," a display poster reads, "The Bible quickly came into play as a justifying creed for slave owners, a source of solace for slaves, and a spark that shaped what would emerge as forms of worship in the new African American context."[22] Here, the good and the bad are placed on the same level with little evaluation made between the two. Moreover, this quote whitewashes the history of

---

20. Wall text, *The Bible and Slavery,* MotB, Washington, D.C.
21. Wall text, *Religious Freedom: A New Awakening,* MotB, Washington, D.C.
22. Wall text, *African American Experience,* MotB, Washington, D.C.

the Bible's use in slavery by emphasizing the good things that, like solace for slaves and African American forms of worship, emerged from this experience.

The Slave Bible and Questions about the Good Book

By presenting issues of interest to people of color and women, the MotB passes itself off as sensitive to minority and gender issues. For example, on November 28, 2018, the MotB opened a temporary exhibit titled *The Slave Bible: Let the Story Be Told*. Published in London in 1807, "The Slave Bible" was an abridged version of the Bible used to educate slaves about Christianity. Bible passages that might have incited revolt, such as the Hebrew Exodus from Egypt, were omitted from the text. The MotB's *The Slave Bible* exhibit is centered on an original copy of the text. Various posters describe the history of the Slave Bible and offer an outline of Bible passages that were omitted from the text.

Without being unduly unfair to MotB, it is worth commenting on both the temporary nature of the display and its location in the museum. In some sense, what is valued by an institution is reflected in what they choose to institutionalize. *The Slave Bible* exhibit does not occupy either a permanent or a central place in the museum. The temporary exhibit space is located in the basement on floor B1. This is not to say that this space is dark, damp, and filled with spiders. In fact, the whole museum, including B1, is impressively done. However, as pointed out in some museum patron comments, there are symbolic statements in being both transient and off the beaten path. As one visitor wrote on a comment card, "I am shocked this particular exhibition is on the *bottom* floor . . . lol, REALLY?" (emphasis in the original). Another wrote, "This exhibit should be *front* and *center* on the first floor" (emphasis in the original).

The Slave Bible display asks for patron participation in the form of comment cards. These cards are each themed to a particular question. For example, one card asks, "What questions does the Slave Bible raise about how the Bible is used today?" Another asks, "Would you call the Slave Bible the 'Good Book'?" While a third asks if the Bible is still authoritative if portions are removed. Patrons write their responses to these questions and then hang the cards on rows of hooks attached to the wall. While the MotB goes to great lengths to maintain a neutral tone, pointing out that the Bible has been used to support despicable ideas and actions, the MotB does little to confront what it is about the Bible and its readers (in various contexts) that produce such harmful readings. On *The Slave Bible* exhibit patron comment cards, one finds evidence of oppositional readings and calls for accountability on this point. In response to the question, "What questions does the Slave Bible raise about how the Bible is used today?" one patron wrote, "The origins of our American Christianity is [sic] the same 'Christianity' that enabled the 'slave Bible.'" When it comes to issues like slavery and civil rights, it is not enough to state that some used the Bible to support abolition while others used the Bible to support slavery. In taking the neutral ground, the MotB misses a powerful opportunity to take a stand and reflect on the nature of the text and its readers and how they both work together to create oppression. Other commentators push the MotB in this direction. One patron wrote, "Surprised that this information has been made public and is, yet still alive for many of the white-anglo-saxon denomination." There is thus a clear recognition among some museum patrons that the readings that produced the Slave Bible are not a thing of the past and that Bible-justified oppression still occurs. Another visitor cried through the display because of its shocking content and the realization that not much has changed. In a similar train of thought, another wrote, "It shows that people do not change. Today, people use the bible to oppress women and wives; police women's bodies and justify racism."

Some object to the questions being posed on the comment cards, noting that they are either loaded or are the wrong question. In response to the question, "Would you call the Slave Bible the 'Good Book'?" a patron wrote, "The better question that I'm pondering is, 'Are we still reading the slave book 2.0.?'" Another wrote that

> the above questions direct viewers away from the horrors of colonization. Slaves had their own religion before they were kidnapped from Africa and stuffed in the holds of ships. Christianity was forced on them. . . . Ask visitors questions like: Do you feel slaves were robbed of their religion? Do you feel like the Bible was a big contributor? Ask visitors an open question: What do you think about the Bible and slavery?

By raising the question of colonization, this visitor does more to suggest a systemic relationship between white supremacy, the Bible, and oppression than does *The Slave Bible* exhibit.

The MotB is somewhat selective in the oppressions it focuses on and works hard to equate perceived religious freedom oppressions and slavery, Jim Crow, and the civil rights movement. Some patrons write, however, that Bible-based oppression does not end there. One person wrote, "In the Slave Bible, man used only parts of the real Bible so that they could manipulate slaves. I feel that is still happening today. Especially with sexuality. People will take certain verses without context and 'justify that being gay is wrong.'" Others suggest that more attention needs to be paid to the relationship between the Bible and the poor and the incarcerated.

There were some other patron responses to these questions that counter the concerns listed above. One patron suggested that the Slave Bible was the result of a compromise between people pursuing their own agendas. On one hand, this patron writes, "British slave owners wanted NO education of & missionary work among their slaves" while "Christian missionaries wanted to do both." The Slave Bible was thus a compromise that allowed slave owners to protect "their lifestyle" while allowing "missionaries . . . an opportunity to educate & 'Christianize' the slaves." This patron's analysis focuses solely on the interests of the enslaving and oppressing class and betrays not a single concern for the interests of the enslaved. In fact, this patron's comments open with a reminder that "slavery was legal then" and closes with the question, "What compromise would you have made?" as though the level of oppression is a matter of compromise. Another patron reminds us that "slavery started in Africa from tribal wars." Comments like this pop up on occasion in social debates about reparations and serves as an emollient for the guilt of benefiting from an economic system rooted in slavery. The prior comment asking the reader to remember that slavery was legal then is likewise a similar guilt-reducing technique. Furthermore, such comments ignore the impact that European colonization had on Africa, how the introduction of guns upset social and economic structures, and how colonization forced some among the native populations into collaboration with European slave traders.[23]

Finally, on the questions, "Would you call the Slave Bible the 'Good Book'?" and if the Bible is still authoritative with portions removed, an interesting debate on the Bible as sacred text emerges. Many patrons agreed that an edited Bible or a Bible with portions removed is not authoritative. Some argued that the Bible is meant to be one book and one word. Thus, removing portions of the text reduces its authority because it has been manipulated. Others, however, maintained that God's power is not limited to a complete Bible and that He can even perform his work through incomplete editions of the text. According to one patron, "The Word of God is powerful no matter what" and the good of slaves learning to read from the Slave Bible mitigated some of its shortcomings. She concluded with the statement that "nothing can take away the 'power' of God's word." Others maintained that even though the Slave Bible was incomplete, it still allowed the reader to connect with God. In one instance a debate on these two positions played itself out on one of the comment cards. In response to the question, "Would you call the Slave Bible the 'good book'?" a person responded, "Yes, because it still contains the word of God." This is a position that finds support in other comments. However, this person appears to have been of two minds because she also wrote, "No, because it was manipulated by those in power for their own good." At some point somebody took exception to this and wrote, "You're a terrible person!" To cap the debate, a third person wrote, at the bottom of the card "Wow!"

Accusations of being a terrible person on this issue illustrate what is at stake for the Bible and its readers. To say that the Slave Bible is not the good book mitigates responsibility with the soothing claim that the Slave Bible was not the real Bible. The unspoken implication being that had the whole, or "real," Bible been used, then such abuses might not have been conscionable. Accepting that the Slave Bible was still the good book leaves the Bible on the hook and forces questions about the text's role in supporting an oppressive institution like slavery. As "You're a horrible person!" demonstrates, accepting the Slave Bible as the good book suggests that

---

23. Steven Mintz, Introduction to *African-American Voices: A Documentary Reader, 1619-1877*, ed. Steven Mintz (Malden, MA: Wiley-Blackwell, 2009), 9; Sylviane A. Diouf, "Introduction," in *Fighting the Slave Trade: West African Strategies*, ed. Sylviane A. Diouf (Athens, OH: Ohio University Press, 2003), 15.

the Bible supports or endorses slavery which then becomes an indictment of poor moral character.

On the topic of racism, the Creation Museum and the Ark Encounter are less ambiguous. While the MotB employs language that walks a middle path between approval and disapproval, the Creation Museum and the Ark Encounter do not hide their dismay with the use of Bible to support racism. At the Ark Encounter, on a poster titled "Was the Bible Used to Promote Racism?" ark designers clearly call such incidents sad and a misuse of the Bible. Kudos for a better effort; nonetheless, AiG still falls short of fully confronting the Bible's history in perpetuating racism. In arguing that it is a misuse of the Bible to support racist ideas, AiG paraphrases from the Bible: "We are all created by God" (Gen 2:7), "We are all made in God's image" (Gen 1:26–27), "We are all one race" (Acts 17:26), and "We are all loved by God" (John 3:16). This display ends with calls to remember that "we are all members of one human race."[24] While a heart-warming platitude, it is another example of whitewashing the Bible's place in oppressing people based on race. This display does not mention Philemon, which fails to question the institution of slavery or the Torah's many laws governing slavery. While one might object by pointing out that ancient Near Eastern slave laws were not grounded in race, it is still the case that the text was used to justify race slavery and, thus, the potential to read it in that manner clearly exists. Better questions, for both AiG and MotB, would have explored what it is about the text, and its Christian readers, that inspired racist readings. This work is not done in either attraction.

Asking people to adopt the perspective that "we are all members of one human race" ignores the very real impact that these oppressions have had, and continue to have, on people of color. That we are all members of one human race is the AiG equivalent to the well-meaning, but ultimately harmful, assertion, "I don't see color" often made by people who want to be seen as progressive on racism. This color-blind racism still serves the interest of the powerful as it encourages one to ignore the powerful impact that skin color still has on the lives of people.[25]

The Bible and Women's Authority

The MotB attempts to create a powerful connection between the establishment of religious freedom and the pursuit of black civil rights in America. Curiously, links to other civil rights movements are weak or are absent. For instance, MotB does some work on suffrage and the woman's rights movement. A display poster titled "Biblical Authority: Women and the Bible" touches upon the women's rights movement and Elizabeth Cady Stanton's (1850–1902) *The Woman's Bible* (1895). The poster ends by noting, "Today, religious groups continue to discuss what the

---

24. Wall text, *Was the Bible Used to Promote Racism?* MotB, Washington, D.C.
25. Eduardo Bonilla-Silva, *Racism Without Racists: Color-Blind Racism and the Persistence of Racial Inequality in America*, 5th ed. (Lanham: Rowman & Littlefield, 2018).

Bible teaches about woman's authority."[26] To say that there is merely an ongoing discussion downplays the serious social issues that are at stake should the Greens' evangelical vision of America come to fruition. *Burwell v. Hobby Lobby* is a window into how the Greens' religiosity informs their approach to women's issues.

On the issue of women, it is again telling what the MotB chooses to leave out. While information about suffragists, Stanton, and Susan B. Anthony appear, the visitor would not know, based on these displays, that any work on women's rights, as it relates to the Bible and Christianity, has occurred since. The MotB could have pointed to the Bible's influence in the founding of the Jewish feminist publication titled *Lilith*. Additionally, the MotB could have devoted space to Phyllis Trible, Elizabeth Schussler Fiorenza, Mary Daly, or Rosemary Radford Ruether and their contributions to a feminist biblical hermeneutics. Instead, the MotB asks a question that takes a subtle dig at Stanton. On the Bible in America survey, visitors are asked to respond to a loaded statement about Elizabeth Cady Stanton. The statement reads, "Elizabeth Cady Stanton reinterpreted parts of the Bible to make it less male-dominated in the 1890s. Ongoing reinterpretation of the Bible is acceptable." The results: so far 61 percent agree with that statement. Of course, this is a rather poor explanation of *The Woman's Bible*, and the term "reinterpret," especially for this audience, predisposes people to a particular answer.

Stanton and a group of marching suffragists are the subject of a tapestry display. The left side of the display features an image of Stanton facing the viewer. The right side of the tapestry features a parade of women holding banners marching away from the viewers. The banners read "The Lord Giveth the Word, the Women That Publish the Tidings Are a Mighty Host (Psalms 68:11)," "Votes for Women" and "We Demand Justice." As we saw with the earlier tapestry featuring a violent battle between pilgrims and Indians, the bodily positions of the characters reveal much about the implicit assumptions of display designers. This is also the case with the Stanton and suffragist tapestry. While Stanton is shown facing the viewer, six other women, marching in parade procession, move away from the patron. This creates both a physical and an ideological distance. Had the women been depicted marching toward the viewer, a better sense of closing the gap would have resulted, leaving the impression that the goals of the suffragists and those of the viewer could be bridged. Instead, the women move away and toward the margins. Moreover, facing the women's backs makes them anonymous, making them easier to ignore, and obscuring their identity and their humanity. In light of MotB's failure to bring feminist engagement with the Bible up to date, one cannot help but conclude that this tapestry should be read as a subtle commentary on modern feminism in that the women's march depicted here is the beginning of feminist separation from society.

In this tapestry, Elizabeth Cady Stanton, an important figure in early modern feminism, is facing the viewer haloed in light. While this might seem to counter the prior analysis of the ideological import of suffragists marching away from

---

26. Wall text, *Biblical Authority: Women and the Bible,* MotB, Washington, D.C.

the viewer, this actually reveals an important fact about how MotB displays are designed and function. Adopting the appellation of museum, and being within a stone's throw of Smithsonian museums, the MotB wants to support the authority of the Bible with a seemingly balanced and objective presentation. Because of this, many important historical figures who engaged with the Bible in a manner that runs counter to the evangelical goals of the Green family cannot simply be ignored. Doing so would damage MotB's right to stand among the nation's great museums. The MotB accomplishes this goal by offering just enough information on people like Elizabeth Cady Stanton, Martin Luther King, Jr., or Oscar Romero to lay claim to objectivity without revealing just how radical (from a modern evangelical perspective) many of these people and movements were.

Traditional gender stereotypes also find their way into MotB exhibits. The children's display titled *Courageous Pages* uses the Bible to reinforce stereotyped gender roles. *Courageous Pages* is predicated on telling the stories of people in the Bible who were strong and courageous in upholding God's Word. In doing so, the vast majority of the stories are those of boys and men, including depictions of David versus Goliath, Samson versus the Philistines, Joseph versus his brothers, and Daniel in the lion's den. These depictions include artistic rendering and games. For example, in the David versus Goliath dexterity game kids fling stones at the giant. In another, kids help Joseph (represented by a ball) move through a maze filled with pitfalls. One of the few activities that feature a female is a game titled "Get Esther to the King." Focused on the Hebrew Bible book of Esther, kids attempt to maneuver a ball through the various events in Esther's life in order to get her to the king.

The choice to tell Esther's story, which features a female Jew saving her people, actually reinforces gender stereotypes rather than challenging them. There are many examples of courageous women in the Bible who exemplify leadership, including the judge and prophet Deborah and Jael, both of whom were critical to Israel's deliverance from the Canaanites of Hazor. Instead, MotB presents the story of a woman who sets a leadership example by acting within the bounds of patriarchal culture. Esther comes to king Ahasuerus' (Xerxes I) attention because of her beauty and her actions arise from obedience and subservience. In this, she stands in strong contrast to queen Vashti who refused to let Ahasuerus objectify her by parading her in front of his courtiers. For this, she loses her position as queen of Persia because Ahasuerus fears her actions will become a model for other Persian woman who might be inspired to "look with contempt on their husbands" (Esth 1:17). After all, as Ahasuerus decrees, "every man should be master in his own house" (Esth 1:22). Esther, because of her beauty, was raised from the king's harem to assume the position of queen. When Mordecai learns of Haman's plot against the Jews, Esther has to be cajoled into taking action. When she does act, she plies Ahasuerus with food and wine for two days before asking him to rescind the order to murder the Jews. By emphasizing this story over others that could have been used to demonstrate courage, the MotB provides a model of a woman who acts within the bounds of patriarchal authority, using stereotypical feminine wiles, instead of pushing at and challenging those boundaries.

The only other significant reference to a female Bible character in the *Courageous Pages* exhibit is of an unnamed woman. Second Kings 5: 1–19 tells the story of Naaman, a general for the king of Aram, who was cured of his leprosy because he took the advice of his wife's unnamed female Israelite slave. As with the story of Esther, this is a woman who does not work from a position of power, but rather one of service in a domestic sphere, manipulating the situation rather than directly confronting power.

In light of the Green family's stated agenda, the MotB serves as a potentially more potent conveyor of evangelical messages about the Bible than does the Creation Museum or the Ark Encounter. AiG wears its theology on its sleeve and does nothing to hide its agenda. This makes it far easier for the casual visitor to more easily discern the ideological context of AiG displays and to evaluate them accordingly. This, as I learned myself, is much more difficult to do with MotB. I spent many hours in the museum before the ideological thrust of the displays started becoming clearer to me. The average visitor, having a lot of trust in the seemingly objective, Smithsonian-like approach of the MotB, likely remains unaware of the perspectives on the Bible they are absorbing. Thus, the more neutral observer is more likely to absorb the messages being presented here than the same neutral observer would at the Creation Museum and the Ark Encounter.

Chapter 12

STRANGERS IN THEIR OWN LAND[1]

On May 19, 2017, David Roberts published an insightful article titled "Donald Trump and the Rise of Tribal Epistemology" on Vox.com. This article begins by analyzing a series of 2009 transcripts of *The Rush Limbaugh Show* that focused on "Climategate," the incident in which the emails of climate scientists were hacked and published without context. These show transcripts, published in late 2009, bear some form of the title "Universe of Lies." One particular banner image, published in the *Vox* article and linking to the website of *The Rush Limbaugh Show*, depicts an astounded-looking Limbaugh looking down on the image of a globe around which are wrapped the words "Universe of Lies."[2] The right side of this banner image bears a round graphic that reads "4 Corners of Deceit," "Government, Academia, Media, Science." *Vox* quotes one of Limbaugh's transcripts:

> We live in two universes. One universe is a lie. One universe is an entire lie. Everything run, dominated, and controlled by the left here and around the world is a lie. The other universe is where we are, and that's where reality reigns supreme and we deal with it.[3]

Looking back from 2019, one can see that questions about expertise, suspicion of secular science, and "fake news" were hovering around the margins well before the election of Barack Obama and the 2009 "Universe of Lies" transcripts moved them into the mainstream. With the election of Donald Trump as president in 2016, the ideas of vast academic conspiracies, discounting of expertise, and "fake news" have fully emerged into the national consciousness.

---

    1. Arlie Russell Hochschild, *Strangers in Their Own Land: Anger and Mourning on the American Right* (New York: The New Press, 2018).

    2. David Roberts, "Donald Trump and the Rise of Tribal Epistemology," *Vox*, March 22, 2017, https://www.vox.com/policy-and-politics/2017/3/22/14762030/donald-trump-tribal-epistemology.

    3. Roberts, "Donald Trump and the Rise of Tribal Epistemology."

In a 2012 interview with the *Guardian*, Andrew Snelling, PhD, director of research at AiG, said, "We don't have to be afraid of the real evidence."[4] In a 2017 article published on the AiG website, Ken Ham wrote that the real fake news are the evolutionary claims that life arose as a result of strictly material processes.[5] In this article, Ham laments the years that he and his organization have been targeted by fake news. He posits that the media is now doing to Donald Trump what it has done to AiG for years, that is, spreading falsehoods and misinformation. Ham continues by noting that the left-wing media is engaged in censorship and is anti-free speech. For Ham this is the continuation of a culture and spirit war that actually began in Gen 3 when the serpent tempted Eve. The American moral crisis is the result of abandoning the authority of God's Word.[6]

The Christian organizations behind attractions like the Creation Museum, the Ark Encounter, and the MotB have been working to create social structures that parallel those of secular society. This includes education and entertainment venues, like the attractions examined in this book, but also extends to things like Christian health sharing plans like Medi-Share, social networking sites like Christians Like Me, and streaming video services like God Tube. These, and more, continue to create a growing system that increasingly allows motivated Christians to create Christian-themed analogs to secular education and entertainment venues while further separating from secular or objectionable elements in American culture.[7]

Throughout this book on Bible interpretation at the Creation Museum, the Ark Encounter, and the MotB, the reader will no doubt have noticed that I occasionally dip my toes into the current political moment. It became increasingly clear as I worked through this project that this was not just a matter of how certain interpretative communities read the Bible but that these readings were informed by—and inform—the noteworthy social moment we find ourselves in. Despite claims that the Bible does not need interpretation (young-earth creationists) or that it can stand in a seemingly neutral museum context (the MotB), the Bible is clearly being employed in a rhetoric spanning the blue grasses of Kentucky to the pavements of our nation's capital.

Additionally, I have found that in these storytelling institutions efforts to frame an authoritative narrative about the Bible requires more than just the Bible. The Bible as a text is powerful because its mere presence is thought to facilitate the Holy Spirit's work. At the same time, the text alone is inadequate because AiG and the MotB tap the authoritative rhetoric of the museum and co-opt the reputation of the scientific method in order to legitimate their presentation. What has emerged

---

4. Neil Denny, "'We Don't Have to Be Afraid of the Real Evidence'—Creation Museum," *The Guardian*, June 6, 2012, sec. Science, http://www.theguardian.com/science/2012/jun/06/evidence-creation-museum.

5. "The Real Fake News," Answers in Genesis, accessed May 24, 2019, https://answersingenesis.org/blogs/ken-ham/2017/03/21/real-fake-news/.

6. "The Real Fake News."

7. Bielo, *Ark Encounter*, 22.

is a complex network of interpreters engaging people at the grassroots level (Ken Ham) to moneyed interests with influence at the highest levels of government (the Green family). The functioning of this network relies upon both fostering and harnessing a nostalgic, romanticized, and idealized vision of the Bible and its place in history that I called *biblical hiraeth*. *Biblical hiraeth*, this longing, homesickness, and nostalgia for a biblical past and a Bible-guided future, is fueled by the perceived authenticity that AiG and the MotB bring to their attractions. As has been noted about religious tourism generally, people visit these places as "shared memory spaces" and as places of community building. Moreover, the Creation Museum and the Ark Encounter in an effort to create an authentic experience transports visitors out of their own time to a place where Godly men, like Noah, were the true exemplars of righteousness and where the wicked were unambiguously punished.

This study has examined two important sources of authority building. First are the AiG and the MotB claims about biblical authority and the role that the Bible ought to play in governing American society. Second is the authority of AiG and MotB as interpreters of the Bible. AiG does not see itself as a Bible interpreter. For AiG, letting the Bible stand on its own means reading according to a particular set of rules. For the MotB, the focus is less on the right way to read the Bible and more on the Bible as an object. The MotB builds authority using the apparatus of the academic study of ancient texts and artifacts, wants those to stand on their own, and does not overtly force a position on the patron. Likewise, the Creation Museum fosters a "you decide" approach with the God's Word/man's word rhetorical structure; however, any argument about letting the patron decide between these two options is merely a façade. The Creation Museum is a theological sermon through and through. Any presentation of the Bible is an act of interpretation. To merely display a Bible on a plinth involves interpretative decisions, including what version of the Bible to display, what page (if any) to have the Bible opened to, to what other items are present in the room.

AiG, of course, goes far beyond letting the Bible speak for itself and uses the Bible to construct an argument. As explored in detail above, many elements found in AiG displays are not derived from the Bible. Through the concepts of educated guesses and artistic license the interpretive hand of AiG is clearly visible. For example, as it is not described in the text, the manner in which to depict Adam's sexy body is a work of interpretation. Likewise, as the Bible is silent on this, depicting Noah as a shipwright is a manner of interpretation. The Bible is also silent on the fruit Adam and Eve were forbidden to eat, thus, depicting the fruit as berries is a matter of guesswork. Many more examples of this abound.

This is where the authority fostered by people like Ken Ham and the authoritative nature of the museum and science come into play. Because there is an inherent trust in the scientific method and museums as institutions, things that are presented as educated guesses and artistic license acquire an aura of authority they would not otherwise have. Thus, the evidence I gathered suggests that most people are going to attend the Ark Encounter and take seriously ideas about animals walking on treadmills removing waste from the ark because of Ham's authority as a Bible interpreter and because of the scientific context in which such claims are made.[8] This is evident in the things interview subjects said and wrote about the ingenious things Noah did to operate the ark. For instance, one reviewer wrote that the Ark Encounter presents the technology of Noah's day easily demonstrating how animal and human needs were met.[9] While some patrons note that these things "might" have been done or are interesting ideas, many others seem to accept them as fact. For instance, Larry D wrote that the Ark Encounter was true in its details and true to the Bible in every respect.[10] Such speculations, for example, about the skin color of the ark occupants, feeding and watering systems, waste disposal systems, are becoming part of the visitor's knowledge about the Bible.

This is likewise true of the MotB, where it is, dare I say, a bit more insidious. While AiG targets a sympathetic audience (recall that Ken Ham wants to reach Christians who have abandoned a literal reading of Genesis) the MotB hopes to pull in the more casual tourist to the nation's capital. Hewing more closely to the museum expectations of Washington, D.C., makes the rhetorical argument of the MotB much harder to identify. As a consequence, the visitor is more likely to absorb the MotB argument about Christian oppression and violations of religious freedom without being aware of it. In either case, in the educated guesses of AiG or the more subtle argument of the MotB, their perspectives on the Bible is likely to become part of the visitor's horizon of expectations.

I think one of the broad implications of this is that visitors to the Creation Museum and the Ark Encounter may arrive expecting to be better educated about the Bible but may actually leave less informed. The Creation Museum and the Ark Encounter (and the MotB as well) do little to contextualize the rich, complicated, and ambiguous nature of the Bible and the contested nature of its interpretation. This fits with the AiG approach to the Bible as a text that speaks clearly, without inconsistency, and in a unified manner. Thus visitors would not learn that this thing called the Bible at the Creation Museum is not monolithic, that there are different versions of it with different contents, and that the ancient manuscripts reveal contradictions, changes, and editorializing.

While there are those who adopt the dominant-hegemonic presentation of AiG and the MotB, incorporating this presentation into their knowledge of the Bible, there are others who negotiate or resist. For example, some of my interview subjects suggested that AiG went too far beyond the Bible. For instance, a patron who described himself as an evangelical Christian criticized the inconsistency in Ham's demand to not read into the Bible and the artistic license on display at the

---

8. Bielo, 29. As Bielo notes, this authority is "fundamentally about trust."

9. amymY7050UF, "Magnificent!!!" TripAdvisor, July 14, 2016, https://www.tripadvisor.com/ShowUserReviews-g39995-d10110346-r392727344-Ark_Encounter-Williamstown_KentucKY.html.

10. Larry D., "All aboard," TripAdvisor, July 29, 2016, https://www.tripadvisor.com/ShowUserReviews-g39995-d10110346-r399001257-Ark_Encounter-Williamstown_KentucKY.html.

Ark Encounter.[11] Likewise, perhaps because it is drawing a more diverse audience, there are signs of resistance at the MotB. Though I did not interview MotB patrons, *The Slave Bible* exhibit comment cards provided a window into patron opinions. I found there a number of messages that seemed to indicate concern that society has not moved past the Bible abuses illustrated in *The Slave Bible* exhibit. Though slavery may not be the specific issue, other battles for civil rights are relevant. As one patron wrote, "I feel that is still happening today. Especially with sexuality. People will take out certain verses without context to justify that being gay is wrong."

Finally, what does all this mean for reception studies of the Bible? I had two goals in mind at the outset for this study. First, I wanted to examine Bible interpretation in non-textual material objects. It was in patron responses to AiG material objects, like the replica of the ark, that I discovered the Bible benefits from material representation. Some patrons wrote that much of the Bible's description of the ark was hard to imagine, or even hard to believe, until they saw the material object in person. Numerous times patrons commented on how the biblical narratives seemed more real as a result of their visit. For some the Bible verses came to life[12] while others, like Impristine, were able to leave the twenty-first century behind.[13]

Second, I wanted to hear directly from the patrons who I imagined as reading the Bible as presented by Ken Ham through his material displays. In all honesty I was initially panicked by the nature of the material I was recording in interviews. Going into this project I expected to encounter people who would demonstrate a high level of biblical literacy and who could reflect upon the Bible, what they know about the Bible, and consider this knowledge in light of their experiences at the Creation Museum and the Ark Encounter. When this was not the case, I worried about what I was going to pull from this data—until it occurred to me that the very vague and general responses I was getting from patrons actually was central to the story. It was clear that for most of the people I talked to, the Bible was a central and important part of their lives, even if they never heard of Methuselah. They even rate their overall knowledge of the Bible higher than their specific responses to questions seemed to merit. I even talked to Sunday school teachers who could not answer some basic questions about the Bible. In one instance, Emma was preparing to lead a Sunday school class on Genesis and did not know who Methuselah was and could recall few details about the flood narrative (and

---

11. Bud A., "Lots to Read; Nothing to See," TripAdvisor, August 22, 2016, https://www.tripadvisor.com/ShowUserReviews-g39995-d10110346-r409077511-Ark_Encounter-Williamstown_KentucKY.html.

12. Julie D., "Noah's Ark," TripAdvisor, October 29, 2016, https://www.tripadvisor.com/ShowUserReviews-g39995-d10110346-r432708715-Ark_Encounter-Williamstown_KentucKY.html.

13. Impristine, "Ark encounter," TripAdvisor, October 17, 2016, https://www.tripadvisor.com/ShowUserReviews-g39995-d10110346-r428711114-Ark_Encounter-Williamstown_KentucKY.html.

despite this, she told me that she thought that the Creation Museum's presentation of Genesis narratives aligned fully with the biblical narratives).[14] This suggests two things. First, the potential impact of AiG and MotB Bible interpretations on the patron may be greater than I imagined. Second, I think the general conception of having a biblical worldview is more important to patrons than knowing many of the specific textual details. To grasp this, Brian Malley's examination of transitivity in biblical interpretation is particularly useful. Recall that transitivity "allows propositions to be regarded as interpretations of a text even when they are not identical to the text."[15] In fact, as Malley maintains, no specific connection to the text is required as long as there is *some* connection.[16]

Here, finally, I return to the concept of *biblical hiraeth*. I believe patrons judge the presentation of AiG less upon chapter and verse and more upon a feeling about the Bible derived in these places. More often than not, patrons generally are not speculating on specific Bible passages. Rather, they are reflecting on how it felt to be at the Creation Museum and the Ark Encounter. It is like the longed-for homecoming that even inspires some to tears. However, even though patrons do not realize it, this is a simulated home in the sense of Baudrillard's simulacra, a place that only ever really existed in the minds of Creation Museum and Ark Encounter designers and in the imaginations of patrons. Nonetheless, it is uniquely real for many visitors, an idealized vision of a Bible society, for a group of people who feel like strangers in their own land.

---

14. Emma, in discussion with the author, April 2017.
15. Malley, *How the Bible Works*, 84
16. Malley, 85.

BIBLIOGRAPHY

Abraham, Ibrahim. "Would You Adam and Eve It? Social Scientific Contributions to the Study of the Reception of Scripture in Consumer Society." *The Bible and Critical Theory* 10, no. 2 (2015). http://novaojs.newcastle.edu.au/ojsbct/index.php/bct/article/view/602.

Allen, John L. Jr. "Did the KGB 'Create' Latin America's Liberation Theology?" *Crux*. Accessed May 31, 2019. https://cruxnow.com/church/2015/05/05/did-the-kgb-create-latin-americas-liberation-theology/.

Answers in Genesis. "Adam, Morality, the Gospel, and the Authority of Scripture." Accessed March 2, 2017. https://answersingenesis.org/bible-characters/adam-and-eve/adam-morality-gospel-and-authority-of-scripture/.

Answers in Genesis. "Answering Claims About the Ark Project." Accessed April 18, 2017. https://answersingenesis.org/ministry-news/ark-encounter/answering-claims-about-the-ark-project/.

Answers in Genesis. "Are Human Hands More Primitive Than Chimps'?" Accessed October 19, 2018. https://answersingenesis.org/human-evolution/human-hands-primitive-chimps/.

Answers in Genesis. "Bara-What?" Accessed February 25, 2017. https://answersingenesis.org/creation-science/baraminology/bara-what/.

Answers in Genesis. "Creation Museum to Expand as Part of a Three-Year Plan." Accessed April 11, 2017. https://answersingenesis.org/blogs/ken-ham/2016/02/04/creation-museum-expand-part-three-year-plan/.

Answers in Genesis. "Creation's Original Diet and the Changes at the Fall." Accessed July 2, 2018. https://answersingenesis.org/animal-behavior/what-animals-eat/creations-original-diet-and-the-changes-at-the-fall/.

Answers in Genesis. "Creative Designer Honors the Creator." Accessed January 31, 2017. https://answersingenesis.org/ministry-news/creation-museum/creative-designer-honors-the-creator/.

Answers in Genesis. "Darwin Exhibit at the American Museum of Natural History." Accessed March 6, 2017. https://answersingenesis.org/reviews/darwin-exhibit-at-american-museum-of-natural-history/.

Answers in Genesis. "Defense—'Scientific' Arguments." Accessed May 10, 2019. https://answersingenesis.org/age-of-the-earth/defensescientific-arguments/.

Answers in Genesis. "Do Genesis 1 and 2 Contradict Each Other?" Accessed February 17, 2019. https://answersingenesis.org/contradictions-in-the-bible/do-genesis-1-and-2-contradict-each-other/.

Answers in Genesis. "Dr. Andrew Snelling." Accessed August 2, 2018. https://answersingenesis.org/bios/andrew-snelling/.

Answers in Genesis. "Dr. David Menton." Accessed August 2, 2018. https://answersingenesis.org/bios/david-menton/.

Answers in Genesis. "Dr. Georgia Purdom." Accessed August 2, 2018. https://answersingenesis.org/bios/georgia-purdom/.

Answers in Genesis. "Dr. Henry Morris Has Died." Accessed January 20, 2017. https://answersingenesis.org/blogs/ken-ham/2006/02/25/dr-henry-morris-has-died/.

Answers in Genesis. "Dragons: Fact or Fable?" Accessed March 23, 2017. https://answersingenesis.org/dinosaurs/dragon-legends/dragons-fact-or-fable/.

Answers in Genesis. "Eisegesis." Accessed May 10, 2019. https://answersingenesis.org/hermeneutics/eisegesis/.

Answers in Genesis. "Era of Christian Attractions Is Calling People Back to Christ." Accessed February 22, 2017. https://answersingenesis.org/ministry-news/ark-encounter/era-of-christian-attractions-calling-people-back-to-christ/.

Answers in Genesis. "Evolution Without Molecules-to-Man Evolution." Accessed March 15, 2017. https://answersingenesis.org/natural-selection/speciation/evolution-without-molecules-to-man-evolution/.

Answers in Genesis. "History of Answers in Genesis." Accessed September 9, 2016. https://answersingenesis.org/about/history/.

Answers in Genesis. "How Many Kinds?" Accessed August 16, 2018. https://answersingenesis.org/blogs/ken-ham/2012/11/01/how-many-kinds/.

Answers in Genesis. "How Young Is Too Young?" Accessed February 15, 2018. https://answersingenesis.org/train-up-a-child/raising-godly-children/how-young-is-too-young/.

Answers in Genesis. "Is Genesis 1 Literal, Literalism, or Literalistic?" Accessed March 1, 2017. https://answersingenesis.org/hermeneutics/is-genesis-1-literal-literalism-or-literalistic/.

Answers in Genesis. "Is the Bible Enough?" Accessed November 4, 2016. https://answersingenesis.org/bible-questions/is-the-bible-enough/.

Answers in Genesis. "Matt Walsh and a Young Earth." Accessed May 10, 2019. https://answersingenesis.org/creationism/young-earth/matt-walsh-and-young-earth/.

Answers in Genesis. "Methuselah's Hands ... Found!" Accessed September 16, 2016. https://answersingenesis.org/ministry-news/creation-museum/methuselahs-hands-found/.

Answers in Genesis. "More False Accusations Against the Ark Refuted!" Accessed March 29, 2017. https://answersingenesis.org/blogs/ken-ham/2016/01/26/more-false-accusations-against-ark-refuted/.

Answers in Genesis. "News Release: Ark Encounter (12/1/2010)." Accessed February 23, 2017. https://answersingenesis.org/ministry-news/ark-encounter/news-release-ark-encounter-12-1-2010/.

Answers in Genesis. "Our Index Finger—Pointing to the Creator." Accessed October 19, 2018. https://answersingenesis.org/human-body/our-index-finger/.

Answers in Genesis. "Our Real Motive for Building Ark Encounter." Accessed February 22, 2017. https://answersingenesis.org/ministry-news/ark-encounter/our-real-motive-for-building-ark-encounter/.

Answers in Genesis. "Over 3 Million Tuned In for Historic Bill Nye and Ken Ham Debate." Accessed May 30, 2019. https://answersingenesis.org/creation-vs-evolution/over-3-million-tuned-in-live-for-historic-bill-nye-and-ken-ham-evolutioncreation-debate/.

Answers in Genesis. "Putting the Ark into Perspective." Accessed August 15, 2018. https://answersingenesis.org/noahs-ark/putting-the-ark-into-perspective/.

Answers in Genesis. "Secularist Intolerance Against Scientific Paper." Accessed May 10, 2019. https://answersingenesis.org/who-is-god/creator-god/secularist-intolerance-against-scientific-paper-briefly-mentions-creator/.

Answers in Genesis. "Store Home." Accessed June 18, 2018. https://answersingenesis.org/store/?sitehist=1529337769738.

Answers in Genesis. "Taking a Look at Jonathan Edwards." Accessed December 8, 2017. https://answersingenesis.org/ministry-news/ministry/taking-a-look-at-jonathan-edwards/.
Answers in Genesis. "The Message, Not the Literal Meaning, Is What Matters." Accessed March 29, 2019. https://answersingenesis.org/theistic-evolution/god-and-evolution/the-message-not-the-literal-meaning-is-what-matters/.
Answers in Genesis. "The Noah Movie Is Disgusting and Evil—Paganism!" Accessed January 19, 2017. https://answersingenesis.org/blogs/ken-ham/2014/03/28/the-noah-movie-is-disgusting-and-evil-paganism/.
Answers in Genesis. "The 'Pilgrim' Who 'Preaches' From a Grave." Accessed December 1, 2017. https://answersingenesis.org/ministry-news/ministry/the-pilgrim-who-preaches-from-a-grave/.
Answers in Genesis. "The Real Fake News." Accessed May 24, 2019. https://answersingenesis.org/blogs/ken-ham/2017/03/21/real-fake-news/.
Answers in Genesis. "The Templeton Connection." Accessed September 1, 2017. https://answersingenesis.org/blogs/ken-ham/2014/12/06/the-templeton-connection/.
Answers in Genesis. "Tim Chaffey." Accessed October 21, 2016. https://answersingenesis.org/bios/tim-chaffey/.
Answers in Genesis. "To Be a Pilgrim." Accessed February 15, 2018. https://answersingenesis.org/christianity/to-be-a-pilgrim/.
Answers in Genesis. "Top 15 Illustration Problems in Genesis 1–11." Accessed November 10, 2017. https://answersingenesis.org/bible-history/15-illustration-problems-genesis/.
Answers in Genesis. "Toward a Practical Theology of Peer Review." Accessed May 23, 2019. https://answersingenesis.org/creation-science/toward-a-practical-theology-of-peer-review/.
Answers in Genesis. "Unicorns in the Bible?" Accessed December 27, 2018. https://answersingenesis.org/extinct-animals/unicorns-in-the-bible/.
Answers in Genesis. "Unlocking the Truth of Scripture." Accessed March 1, 2017. https://answersingenesis.org/hermeneutics/unlocking-the-truth-of-scripture/.
Answers in Genesis. "We Just Don't Noah." Accessed April 18, 2017. https://answersingenesis.org/noahs-ark/we-just-dont-noah/.
Answers in Genesis. "When Did Methuselah Die?" Accessed September 16, 2016. https://answersingenesis.org/bible-timeline/genealogy/when-did-methuselah-die/.
Ark Encounter. "Lehman Brothers Visit the Ark Site." Accessed May 19, 2019. https://arkencounter.com/blog/2014/06/11/lehman-brothers-visit-the-ark-site/.
Ark Encounter. "Making the Ark Encounter Animals." Accessed August 14, 2018. https://arkencounter.com/blog/2016/11/01/making-ark-encounter-animals/.
Ark Encounter. "Mything the Boat." Accessed February 23, 2017. https://arkencounter.com/blog/2011/02/23/mything-the-boat/.
Ark Encounter. "Noah Is Stylin'." Accessed March 13, 2017. https://arkencounter.com/blog/2016/04/19/noah-is-stylin/.
Ark Encounter. "What Kind of Jewelry Did Noah's Family Wear?" Accessed March 13, 2017. https://arkencounter.com/blog/2016/06/09/what-kind-jewelry-did-noahs-family-wear/.
Ark Encounter. "When Is A Window Not A Window?" Accessed February 23, 2017. https://arkencounter.com/blog/2012/09/07/when-is-a-window-not-a-window/.
Atlantis Rising Magazine Library. "About Us." April 10, 2010. https://atlantisrisingmagazine.com/about/.

Barthold, Lauren Swayne. "Gadamer, Hans-Georg." *Internet Encyclopedia of Philosophy*. Accessed June 12, 2017. http://www.iep.utm.edu/gadamer/.

Babylon Rising. "God vs God—The Days of Noah." Accessed April 7, 2019. http://www.babylonrisingblog.com/Godvsgod1.html.

"BBC—Will & Testament: A Creationist with a Phd." Accessed August 2, 2018. http://www.bbc.co.uk/blogs/ni/2012/08/a_creationist_with_a_phd.html.

Beal, Timothy. "Reception History and Beyond: Toward the Cultural History of Scriptures." *Biblical Interpretation* 19, no. 4 (December 1, 2011): 357–72. https://doi.org/10.1163/156851511X595530.

Beal, Timothy. *Roadside Religion: In Search of the Sacred, the Strange, and the Substance of Faith*. Boston, MA: Beacon Press, 2005.

Bible and Culture Collective. *The Postmodern Bible*. New Haven, CT: Yale University Press, 1995.

Bielo, James S. *Ark Encounter: The Making of a Creationist Theme Park*. New York: New York University Press, 2018.

Bielo, James S. "Creationist History-Making: Producing a Heterodox Past." In *Lost City, Found Pyramid: Understanding Alternative Archaeological and Pseudoscientific Practices*, edited by Jeb J. Card and David S. Anderson, 81–101. Tuscaloosa: University of Alabama Press, 2016.

Bielo, James S. *Words Upon the Word: An Ethnography of Evangelical Group Bible Study*. Qualitative Studies in Religion. New York: New York University Press, 2009.

Bonilla-Silva, Eduardo. *Racism Without Racists: Color-Blind Racism and the Persistence of Racial Inequality in America*. 5th ed. Lanham, MD: Rowman & Littlefield, 2018.

Boym, Svetlana. "The Future of Nostalgia." In *The Svetlana Boym Reader*, edited by Cristina Vatulescu, Tamar Abramov, Nicole G. Burgoyne, Julia Bekman Chadaga, Jacob Emery, and Julia Vaingurt, 217–33. New York: Bloomsbury Academic, 2018.

Bros, Peter. "The Case for the Flood: Exposing the Scientific Myth of the Ice Age." In *Forbidden History: Prehistoric Technologies, Extraterrestrial Intervention, and the Suppressed Origins of Civilization*, edited by J. Douglas Kenyon, 44–52. Rochester, VT: Bear & Co., 2005.

Butler, Ella. "God Is in the Data: Epistemologies of Knowledge at the Creation Museum." *Ethnos* 75, no. 3 (September 2010): 229–51. https://doi.org/10.1080/00141844.2010.507907.

Card, Jeb J. "Steampunk Inquiry: A Comparative Vivisection of Discovery Pseudosciences." In *Lost City, Found Pyramid: Understanding Alternative Archaeological and Pseudoscientific Practices*, edited by Jeb J. Card and David S. Anderson, 19–32. Tuscaloosa: University of Alabama Press, 2016.

Chaffey, Tim. "How Should We Interpret the Bible, Particularly Genesis 1–11?" In *Six Days: The Age of the Earth and the Decline of the Church*, 221–37. Green Forest, AR: Master Books, 2013.

Chattaway, Peter T. "Darren Aronofsky Talks to CT about 'Noah.'" *ChristianityToday.com*. Accessed February 8, 2017. http://www.christianitytoday.com/ct/2014/march-web-only/darren-aronofsky-interview-noah.html.

Chhabra, Deepak, Robert Healy, and Erin Sills. "Staged Authenticity and Heritage Tourism." *Annals of Tourism Research* 30, no. 3 (July 2003): 702–19. https://doi.org/10.1016/S0160-7383(03)00044-6.

Chidester, David. *Authentic Fakes: Religion and American Popular Culture*. Berkeley, CA: University of California Press, 2005.

Christou, Doulos Iesou. *Stop Mything Noah's Ark*. https://www.youtube.com/watch?v=NQDgnFgx2Js.
Crăciun, Magdalena. *Material Culture and Authenticity: Fake Branded Fashion in Europe*. London: Bloomsbury, 2014.
Creation Museum. "Creationists Do Better Science." Accessed August 2, 2018. https://creationmuseum.org/blog/2016/07/21/creationists-do-better-science/.
Creation Museum. "Dragon Legends." Accessed March 23, 2017. https://creationmuseum.org/dinosaurs-dragons/legends/.
Creation Museum. "Rare Bible Manuscripts at Creation Museum." Accessed July 16, 2018. https://creationmuseum.org/press/rare-bible-manuscripts-on-display-at-creation-museum/.
Creation Museum. "Story of Adam and Eve." Accessed July 2, 2018. https://creationmuseum.org/eden/adam-eve/.
Creation Museum. "The Wonders Room." Accessed September 7, 2017. https://creationmuseum.org/blog/2006/10/02/the-wonders-room/.
"Creationism, Science and Peer Review." Accessed September 28, 2018. http://creation.com/creationism-science-and-peer-review.
Dalton, Russell W. *Children's Bibles in America: A Reception History of the Story of Noah's Ark in US Children's Bibles*. Scriptural Traces: Critical Perspectives on the Reception and Influence of the Bible 5. London: Bloomsbury T&T Clark, 2016.
Davey, Nicholas. "Gadamer's Aesthetics." In *The Stanford Encyclopedia of Philosophy*. Fall 2018 Edition, edited by Edward N. Zalta. Metaphysics Research Lab, Stanford University, 2018. https://plato.stanford.edu/archives/win2016/entries/gadamer-aesthetics/.
de Vogue, Ariane. "Supreme Court Rules for Colorado Baker in Same-Sex Wedding Cake Case." *CNN*. Accessed May 17, 2019. https://www.cnn.com/2018/06/04/politics/masterpiece-colorado-gay-marriage-cake-supreme-court/index.html.
Denny, Neil. "'We Don't Have to Be Afraid of the Real Evidence'—Creation Museum." *The Guardian*, June 6, 2012, sec. Science. http://www.theguardian.com/science/2012/jun/06/evidence-creation-museum.
Diouf, Sylviane A. "Introduction." In *Fighting the Slave Trade: West African Strategies*, edited by Sylviane A. Diouf, 1–14. Athens, OH: Ohio University Press, 2003.
Downing, Barry. *The Bible and Flying Saucers*. New York: Marlowe and Company, 1997.
Eve, Raymond A. and Francis B. Harrold. *The Creationist Movement in Modern America*. Boston, MA: Twayne Publishers, 1990.
Federal Register. "Promoting Free Speech and Religious Liberty." Accessed May 9, 2017. https://www.federalregister.gov/documents/2017/05/09/2017-09574/promoting-free-speech-and-religious-liberty.
Federal Register. "Religious Exemptions and Accommodations for Coverage of Certain Preventive Services Under the Affordable Care Act." Accessed November 15, 2018. https://www.federalregister.gov/documents/2018/11/15/2018-24512/religious-exemptions-and-accommodations-for-coverage-of-certain-preventive-services-under-the.
Fish, Stanley. *Is There a Text in This Class? The Authority of Interpretive Communities*. Cambridge, MA: Harvard University Press, 1980.
Gadamer, Hans-George. *Truth and Method*. 2nd ed. Translated by Joel Weinsheimer and Donald G. Marshall. New York: The Seabury Press, 1975.
Gallup Inc. "In U.S., Belief in Creationist View of Humans at New Low." Accessed July 24, 2018. https://news.gallup.com/poll/210956/belief-creationist-view-humans-new-low.aspx.

Genesis Park. "Behemoth or Bust." Accessed September 28, 2018. https://www.genesispark.com/essays/behemoth-or-bust/.

Genesis Park. "The Fiery Flying Serpent." Accessed September 28, 2018. https://www.genesispark.com/essays/fiery-serpent/.

Grudem, Wayne. "Why Building a Border Wall Is a Morally Good Action." *Townhall*. Accessed February 1, 2019. https://townhall.com/columnists/waynegrudem/2018/07/02/why-building-a-border-wall-is-a-morally-good-action-n2496574.

Hall, Stuart. "Encoding, Decoding." In *The Cultural Studies Reader*, edited by Simon During. New York: Routledge, 1999.

Ham, Ken. "Ken Ham: The Unbiblical Noah Is a Fable of a Film." *Time*, March 28, 2014. http://time.com/42274/ken-ham-the-unbiblical-noah-is-a-fable-of-a-film/.

Ham, Ken. *Six Days: The Age of the Earth and the Decline of the Church*. Green Forest, AR: Master Books, 2013.

Ham, Ken. "What Really Happened to the Dinosaurs?" In *The New Answers Book: 25 Top Questions on Creation/Evolution and the Bible*, edited by Ken Ham, 149–176. Green Forest, AR: Master Books, 2006.

Ham, Ken A. and Paul S. Taylor. *The Genesis Solution*. Grand Rapids, MI: Baker Book House, 1988.

Hege, Brent. "Contesting Faith, Truth, and Religious Language at the Creation Museum: A Historical-Theological Reflection." *Theology and Science* 12, no. 2 (April 3, 2014): 142–63. https://doi.org/10.1080/14746700.2014.894730.

Heller, Karen. "A Giant Ark Is Just the Start: These Creationists Have a Bigger Plan for Recruiting New Believers." *Washington Post*, May 24, 2017, sec. Style. https://www.washingtonpost.com/lifestyle/style/a-giant-ark-is-just-the-start-these-creationists-have-a-bigger-plan-for-recruiting-new-believers/2017/05/24/b497bd14-2920-11e7-be51-b3fc6ff7faee_story.html.

Hess, Richard. "Methuselah." In *Anchor Bible Dictionary, Volume 4, K-N*, edited by David Noel Freedman et al., 800–801. New York: Doubleday, 1992.

Hess, Richard. "The Meaning of Mîn in the Hebrew Old Testament, Part 1." *BioLogos*. Accessed December 7, 2018. /blogs/archive/the-meaning-of-min-part-1.

Hetherington, Marc J. and Jonathan Daniel Weiler. *Authoritarianism and Polarization in American Politics*. New York: Cambridge University Press, 2009.

"Higher Criticism." *New World Encyclopedia*. Accessed November 30, 2018. http://www.newworldencyclopedia.org/entry/Higher_criticism.

"Hiraeth: Word of the Week." Accessed May 21, 2019. https://sites.psu.edu/kielarpassionblog2/2016/04/02/hiraeth/.

Hobby Lobby. "Our Story." Accessed May 30, 2019. https://www.hobbylobby.com/about-us/our-story.

Hochschild, Arlie Russell. *Strangers in Their Own Land: Anger and Mourning on the American Right*. New York: The New Press, 2018.

Holland, Norman Norwood. *The Nature of Literary Response: Five Readers Reading*. New Brunswick: Transaction Publishers, 2011.

Holland, Norman Norwood. "Unity Identity Text Self." *PMLA* 90, no. 5 (October 1975): 813. https://doi.org/10.2307/461467.

Horgan, John. "What Thomas Kuhn Really Thought about Scientific 'Truth.'" *Scientific American Blog Network*. Accessed March 8, 2017. https://blogs.scientificamerican.com/cross-check/what-thomas-kuhn-really-thought-about-scientific-truth/.

Hurn, Samantha. "Introduction." In *Anthropology and Cryptozoology: Exploring Encounters with Mysterious Creatures*, 1–11. New York: Routledge, 2017.

Jackson, Gregory S. *The Word and Its Witness: The Spiritualization of American Realism.* Chicago, IL: University of Chicago Press, 2009.

Jameson, Fredric. *Postmodernism, or, the Cultural Logic of Late Capitalism.* Durham, NC: Duke Univ. Press, 2005.

Jauss, Hans Robert and Elizabeth Benzinger. "Literary History as a Challenge to Literary Theory." *New Literary History* 2, no. 1 (1970): 7–37. https://doi.org/10.2307/468585.

Jauss, Hans Robert and Paul De Man. *Toward an Aesthetic of Reception.* Translated by Timothy Bahti. Vol. 2. Theory and History of Literature. Minneapolis: University of Minnesota Press, 1982.

Jewish Women's Archive. "Adah 1: Bible." Accessed March 23, 2017. https://jwa.org/encyclopedia/article/adah-1-bible.

Jewish Women's Archive. "Adah 1: Midrash and Aggadah." Accessed March 23, 2017. https://jwa.org/encyclopedia/article/adah-1-midrash-and-aggadah.

Joseph, Frank. "Ancient High Tech and the Ark of the Covenant." *Atlantis Rising Magazine Library*, January 1, 2008. https://atlantisrisingmagazine.com/article/ancient-high-tech-and-the-ark-of-the-covenant/.

JRC. "20 Question Bible Quiz—Bible Trivia—James River Church." Accessed February 2, 2017. https://jamesriver.org/blog/bible-quiz.

Keenan, William J. F. and Elisabeth Arweck. "Introduction: Material Varieties of Religious Expression." In *Materializing Religion: Expression, Performance, Ritual*, 1–20. Hampshire: Ashgate, 2006.

Kehoe, Alice B. "Scientific Creationism: World View, Not Science." In *Cult Archaeology and Creationism: Understanding Pseudoscientific Beliefs about the Past*, edited by Francis B. Harrold and Raymond A. Eve, 11–20. Iowa City, IA: University of Iowa Press, 1987.

Kelly, Casey R. and Kristen Hoerl. "Genesis in Hyperreality: Legitimizing Disingenuous Controversy at the Creation Museum." *Argumentation and Advocacy*, Winter 2012, 1–21.

Kenyon, J. Douglas. "Exposing a Scientific Cover-Up: Forbidden Archaeology Coauthor Michael Cremo Talks about the 'Knowledge Filter' and Other Means for Cooking the Academic Books." In *Forbidden History: Prehistoric Technologies, Extraterrestrial Intervention, and the Suppressed Origins of Civilization*, edited by J. Douglas Kenyon, 22–28. Rochester, VT: Bear & Co., 2005.

Lincoln, Bruce. *Discourse and the Construction of Society: Comparative Studies of Myth, Ritual, and Classification.* New York: Oxford University Press, 1989.

Luu, Chi. "Very British Villains (and Other Anglo-Saxon Attitudes to Accents)." *JSTOR Daily*. January 18, 2017. https://daily.jstor.org/very-british-villains-and-other-anglo-saxon-attitudes-to-accents/.

Lynch, John. "'Prepare to Believe': The Creation Museum as Embodied Conversion Narrative." *Rhetoric and Public Affairs* 16, no. 1 (2013): 1–27. https://doi.org/10.14321/rhetpublaffa.16.1.0001.

MacKenzie, John M. *Museums and Empire: Natural History, Human Cultures and Colonial Identities.* Manchester: Manchester University Press, 2010.

Malley, Brian. *How the Bible Works: An Anthropological Study of Evangelical Biblicism.* Walnut Creek, CA: AltaMira Press, 2004.

Malley, Brian. "Understanding the Bible's Influence." In *The Social Life of Scriptures: Cross Cultural Perspectives on Biblicism*, edited by James S. Bielo, 194–204. New Brunswick, NJ: Rutgers University Press, 2006.

Malpas, Jeff. "Hans-Georg Gadamer." In *The Stanford Encyclopedia of Philosophy*. Fall 2018 Edition, edited by Edward N. Zalta. Metaphysics Research Lab, Stanford University, 2018. https://plato.stanford.edu/archives/win2016/entries/gadamer/.

Man, Paul de. Introduction to *Toward an Aesthetic of Reception*, by Hans Robert Jauss, vii–xxix. Minneapolis, MN: University of Minnesota Press, 1982.

"Man's Pre-Flood Potential." *Ark Encounter*. Accessed February 23, 2017. https://arkencounter.com/blog/2012/01/06/mans-pre-flood-potential/.

Marcin, Tim. "DHS Chief Kirstjen Nielsen Claims Jesus, Mary and Joseph Would Be Welcomed in the U.S." *Newsweek*, December 20, 2018. https://www.newsweek.com/dhs-kirstjen-nielsen-jesus-mary-joseph-usa-democrat-lawmaker-1267571.

Merritt, Elizabeth. "Trust Me, I'm a Museum." *American Alliance of Museums*. February 3, 2015. https://www.aam-us.org/2015/02/03/trust-me-im-a-museum/.

Meyer, Birgit. "How Pictures Matter: Religious Objects and the Imagination in Ghana." In *Objects and Imagination: Perspectives on Materialization and Meaning*, edited by Øivind Fuglerud and Leon Wainwright, 160–82. New York: Berghahn Books, 2015.

Miller, Kevin. "Former Virginia Tech Professor Opened Floodgates of Creation Debate." *Roanoke Times*. Accessed January 20, 2017. http://www.roanoke.com/news/former-virginia-tech-professor-opened-floodgates-of-creation-debate/article_c64307bf-5f70-5192-a313-98d1e85782cb.html.

Mintz, Steven. *Huck's Raft: A History of American Childhood*. Cambridge, MA: Belknap Press of Harvard University Press, 2004.

Mintz, Steven. Introduction to *African-American Voices: A Documentary Reader, 1619–1877*, edited by Steven Mintz, 1–39. Malden, MA: Wiley-Blackwell, 2009.

Mitchell, W. J. T. *What Do Pictures Want? The Lives and Loves of Images*. Chicago, IL: University of Chicago Press, 2005.

Mohler, Albert. "The Scandal of Biblical Illiteracy: It's Our Problem." Accessed April 19, 2018. http://albertmohler.com/2016/01/20/the-scandal-of-biblical-illiteracy-its-our-problem-4/.

Morris, Henry M. *Evolution and the Modern Christian*. Philadelphia, PA: The Presbyterian and Reformed Publishing Co., 1967.

Morris, Henry M. *The Genesis Record: A Scientific and Devotional Commentary on the Book of Beginnings*. Grand Rapids, MI: Baker Book House, 1976.

Morse, Holly. "What's in a Name? Analysing the Appellation 'Reception History' in Biblical Studies." *Biblical Reception* 3 (2014): 243–64.

Moss, Candida R. and Joel S. Baden. *Bible Nation: The United States of Hobby Lobby*. Princeton, NJ: Princeton University Press, 2017.

Nickelsburg, George W. E. and James C. VanderKam. *1 Enoch: A New Translation Based on the Hermeneia Commentary*. Minneapolis, MN: Fortress, 2004.

Numbers, Ronald L. *The Creationists*. New York: A. A. Knopf, 1992.

Office for Civil Rights (OCR). "About Us (OCR)." *HHS.gov*, September 6, 2015. https://www.hhs.gov/ocr/about-us/index.html.

Oyez. "Masterpiece Cakeshop, Ltd. v. Colorado Civil Rights Commission." Accessed May 17, 2019. https://www.oyez.org/cases/2017/16-111.

Pacepa, Ion Mihai. "The Secret Roots of Liberation Theology." *National Review*. April 23, 2015. https://www.nationalreview.com/2015/04/secret-roots-liberation-theology/.

Parris, David. *Reception Theory and Biblical Hermeneutics*. Eugene, OR: Pickwick Publications, 2009.

Petro, Pamela. "Dreaming in Welsh." *The Paris Review*, September 18, 2012. https://www.theparisreview.org/blog/2012/09/18/dreaming-in-welsh/.

Pew Forum. "Americans' Beliefs About the Nature of God," April 25, 2018. http://www.pewforum.org/2018/04/25/when-americans-say-they-believe-in-god-what-do-they-mean/.
Pew Forum. "U.S. Religious Knowledge Survey." September 28, 2010. https://www.pewforum.org/2010/09/28/u-s-religious-knowledge-survey/.
Posner, Sarah. "The Inside Story of Hobby Lobby's New Bible Museum on the National Mall." *Talking Points Memo.* Accessed February 10, 2019. https://talkingpointsmemo.com/theslice/hobby-lobby-museum-of-the-bible.
Reinhartz, Adele. *Scripture on the Silver Screen.* Louisville, KY: Westminster John Knox Press, 2003.
Roberts, David. "Donald Trump and the Rise of Tribal Epistemology." *Vox.* March 22, 2017. https://www.vox.com/policy-and-politics/2017/3/22/14762030/donald-trump-tribal-epistemology.
Ryan, Michael. *Cultural Studies: A Practical Introduction.* Hoboken, NJ: John Wiley and Sons, 2010.
Sahlins, Marshall David. *Islands of History.* Chicago, IL: University of Chicago Press, 2004.
"Scholars Initiative." Accessed August 2, 2018. http://www.museumofthebible.org/research/scholars-initiative.
Schwartz, Ian. "Rev. Jeffress: Trump Fulfilling His 'God-Given Responsibility' By Building The Wall, Heaven Has A Wall." Accessed February 1, 2019. https://www.realclearpolitics.com/video/2018/12/22/rev_jeffress_trump_fulfilling_his_god-given_responsibility_by_building_the_wall_heaven_has_a_wall.html.
Scott, Eugenie Carol. *Evolution vs. Creationism: An Introduction.* Westport, CT: Greenwood Press, 2009.
SCOTUSblog. "*Burwell v. Hobby Lobby Stores, Inc.*" Accessed May 30, 2019. https://www.scotusblog.com/case-files/cases/sebelius-v-hobby-lobby-stores-inc/.
Sherwood, Yvonne. *A Biblical Text and Its Afterlives: The Survival of Jonah in Western Culture.* Cambridge: Cambridge University Press, 2000.
Siegel, Harvey. "Open-Mindedness, Critical Thinking, and Indoctrination: Homage to William Hare." *Philosophical Inquiry in Education* 18, no. 1 (2009): 26–34.
Skiba, Rob. "Archon Invasion, Robs Channel." Accessed May 23, 2019. http://robschannel.com/archon-invasion.
Slevin, Peter. "Genesis on Display at Creationist Disneyland." *The Seattle Times.* Accessed May 27, 2007. http://www.seattletimes.com/nation-world/genesis-on-display-at-creationist-disneyland/.
Stausberg, Michael. *Religion and Tourism: Crossroads, Destinations, and Encounters.* New York: Routledge, 2011.
Stearns, Peter N. *Childhood in World History.* 3rd ed. New York: Routledge, 2017.
Stetzer, Ed. "The Epidemic of Bible Illiteracy in Our Churches." Accessed April 19, 2018. https://www.christianitytoday.com/edstetzer/2015/july/epidemic-of-bible-illiteracy-in-our-churches.html.
Stevenson, Jill. "Embodying Sacred History." *TDR/The Drama Review* 56, no. 1 (2012): 93–113.
Stichele, Caroline Vander. "The Head of John and Its Reception or How to Conceptualize 'Reception History.'" In *Reception History and Biblical Studies: Theory and Practice,* edited by Emma England and William John Lyons, 79–93. London: Bloomsbury T&T Clark, 2015.
Storrey, John. *Cultural Studies and the Study of Popular Culture: An Introduction.* Edinburgh: Edinburgh University Press, 2010.

Taylor, John P. "Authenticity and Sincerity in Tourism." *Annals of Tourism Research* 28, no. 1 (January 2001): 7–26. https://doi.org/10.1016/S0160-7383(00)00004-9.

Taylor, Steve. "Reading 'Pop-Wise': The Very Fine Art of 'Making Do' When Reading the Bible in Bro' Town." In *The Bible In/And Popular Culture: A Creative Encounter*, edited by Philip Culbertson and Elaine M. Wainwright, 157–72. Leiden: Brill, 2011.

The Heritage Foundation. *Hobby Lobby's Steve Green on Religious Liberty*. Accessed February 4, 2019. https://www.youtube.com/watch?v=mIleVCttTkg.

Tom, Joshua C. "Social Origins of Scientific Deviance: Examining Creationism and Global Warming Skepticism." *Sociological Perspectives* 61, no. 3 (June 2018): 341–60. https://doi.org/10.1177/0731121417710459.

Trollinger, Susan L. and William Vance Trollinger. *Righting America at the Creation Museum*. Baltimore: Johns Hopkins University Press, 2016.

Von Däniken, Erich. *Chariots of the Gods? Unsolved Mysteries of the Past*. Translated by Michael Heron. New York: G.T. Putnam's Sons, 1970.

Whitcomb, John C. and Henry M. Morris. *The Genesis Flood: The Biblical Record and Its Scientific Implications*. Philadelphia, PA: The Presbyterian and Reformed Publishing Co., 1961.

"Who Is Rob Skiba?" Accessed April 7, 2019. http://www.babylonrisingblog.com/FAQ.html.

Woetzel, Dave. "Cryptozoology & Creation Apologetics." Accessed March 21, 2017. http://www.genesispark.com/essays/cryptozoology-creation/,

Worthen, Molly. *Apostles of Reason: The Crisis of Authority in American Evangelicalism*. New York, New York: Oxford University Press, 2014.

INDEX

Abraham, Ibrahim   15, 17
academic credentials   61–2
Adah   101, 102–3, 105
Adam
  creation narrative   43–4, 49
  and Methuselah   87–8, 91
  sexiness   133–5
  sin   132
Adam and Eve (Durer)   134
aesthetic distance   93
Aichele, George   14
AiG. *See* Answers in Genesis
alternative histories   73–4
ambiguity   18, 53, 74, 96–7, 166. *See also* artistic license/educated guesses
Amish   109
animals
  care   46
  dinosaurs   38, 40, 41, 74, 81–3, 111, 131–2
  dragons   74, 81, 82–3
  Fairy Tale Ark   51, 110–12
  "the Fiery Flying Serpent"   82
  "kind"   24–5, 49
  modern   111, 121
  sea creatures   83
  unicorns   49–50
Answers (periodical)   22
Answers in Genesis (AiG). *See also* Ham, Ken
  cultural impact   6–7, 123–4, 166–8
  "Dragons: Fact or Fable?"   83
  establishment   22
  and higher education   41–2
  ideological position   12, 14
  as interpreter   4, 6, 30–1, 37, 53, 85–6, 98, 99–100, 165
  Nye/Ham debate   1
  Remarkable Rescue: Saved on Noah's Ark   120
  and secular science   60–2, 64, 79–80, 145

  supporters   3
  "Unlocking the Truth of Scripture"   31
  "We Just Don't Noah"   105–6, 135
anti-intellectualism   60, 65, 77–80
The Apostle (film: Duvall)   146
Arkansas Law   1981   25
Ark Encounter
  design and construction   23–5, 46–9, 74–5, 76, 142–3
  genre expectations   55
  and hermeneutical play   99–100
  opening   22–3
  physical location   2, 66
  simulacra   70–1, 141–2
  as theme park   18, 69–70, 71–2
  visitors' numbers   23
  visitors' reviews   16, 17, 37, 70, 130–2, 137, 138, 140–3, 148
  walk-through   18
Ark Encounter displays and shows
  "7 Ds of Deception"   51, 110–11, 118
  After the Flood   52
  The Door   51
  Fairy Tale Ark   51, 107, 110–12, 113, 118–22
  The Noah Interview (film)   18, 100–7
  Noah's Library   50
  "One World, Two Views" poster   53
  third-floor displays   51–2
Ark of the Covenant   76
Aronofsky, Darren. *See Noah* (film: Aronofsky)
artistic license/educated guesses
  AiG   135
  Ark Encounter   24, 50–2, 99, 104, 106–7, 127–9
  Creation Museum   132–5
  visitors' reviews   130–2, 165–7
artistic value   94–5
Arweck, Elisabeth   89, 96–7
Atlantis Rising Magazine   76–7

authenticity. *See also* realism
    Ark Encounter 23–5, 70–1, 131, 142–3
    Creation Museum 45–6, 109–10
    Fairy Tale Ark display 111–12, 120
    Methuselah display 89–90
authorial intent 6–7, 8–10, 14, 32–3
authority. *See also* biblical authority
    academic 61–2
    AiG 3–4
    Ark Encounter 74, 130–1
    building 164–6
    Creation Museum 56, 57, 58–9, 96
    MotB 60, 165
    museum 56–7, 164–5
    secular 3

Baden, Joel S. 60
bad objects 107, 118–22
Bakhita, Josephine 153
baramin 24–5, 49, 121
Barthes, Roland 13
Barton, Lucy 114
Baudrillard, Jean 16
Beal, Timothy 15, 67
Behemoth 81–2
Bible
    abandonment 5, 48, 51, 59, 62–3, 97, 111, 164
    authority (*see* biblical authority)
    God's Word/man's word heuristic 3, 40–1, 49, 57–8, 71–2, 165
    idealized image (*see* biblical *hiraeth*)
    misrepresentation (*see* fairy-tale arks)
    and oppression 153–5
    power 146–7
    resilience 41, 59
    sacred text 158–9
The Bible Cause: A History of the American Bible Society (Fea) 146
Bible Letters for Children (Barton) 114
Bible literacy 106, 125–7, 135, 166, 167–8
biblical authority 165. *See also specific characters, e.g.* Methuselah
    hegemonic narrative 12
    material displays 69–70, 106–7, 125, 130–1, 135–6, 137
    and old-earth reading 35
    sola scriptura 41
biblical characters 85–6

biblical creatures 81–3
biblical *hiraeth* 18, 55, 67–72, 97, 137, 165, 168
Bielo, James 30, 79, 83, 110, 125, 130–1, 137, 140
Biologos 39 n.4
Boym, Svetlana 71
Bros, Peter 78, 80
Bunyan, John 116
Burwell v. Hobby Lobby, Inc. 150, 151, 152, 160

catastrophe 43, 45
caves, as place of rebirth 44–5
Certeau, Michel de 7
Chaffey, Tim 32–3, 106, 135
Chattaway, Peter T. 93–4
Chhabra, Deepak 109–10
Chidester, David 139, 140
children
    inappropriate content 117–18
children's Bibles and stories 51
    bad objects 107, 118–22
    realism 110–13, 115–16
    softer approach 114–15
Chi, Luu 103
circumstantial evidence 29
civil rights movement 153–4
Clark, Gordon 40
Collins, Francis 39 n.4
Cone, James 154
confusion 46
corruption 43, 44, 45
cosmos 38
counterfeit 120–1
counter taxonomic discourses 119–20
Crăciun, Magdalena 120–1
Crawley, William 60
Creation (periodical) 22, 81
creationism 18, 21, 57–8, 77, 143, 144–5. *See also* old-earth creationism; young-earth creationism
creationism/evolution debate 1, 3–4, 27–30, 79
Creation Museum
    academic credentials 61
    Bible reading 30–3
    genre expectations 55
    layout 63–4
    and MotB compared 59–60

museum label   18, 56, 57, 58–9, 66, 69
Nye/Ham debate   1
physical location   2, 66
primary purpose   33–4
simulacra   70–1
spatial sermon   63–4
theme park features   69
visitors' numbers   3–4, 22
visitors' reviews   16, 17, 37, 70, 116–18, 123–4, 125–6, 137–8, 140, 141, 143–6, 148
walk-through   18
"you decide" approach   165
Creation Museum displays and shows
   "7 Cs of History"   43–6
   artistic license/educated guesses   132–5
   Biblical Relevance   41
   Cave of Sorrows   44–5, 62, 117–18
   "Cowboys and Dragons" poster   38, 82, 83
   Created Cosmos   38
   Culture in Crisis   42, 44, 62, 63–4, 117
   Dig Site   39–41, 43, 64–6
   Dragon Legends   37–8, 82, 83, 111
   Graffiti Alley   42, 63–4, 117
   Methuselah display   18, 45, 85–6, 87–90, 92–3, 96, 97–8, 125–6, 138
   miniature flood diorama   116
   post-Garden of Eve diorama   132
   Six Day Theater   43, 63
   Verbum Domini   147
   Voyage of the Ark   45–6
   Wonders of Creation   43
creation narrative   2 n.3, 34, 39–40, 43–4, 49, 83, 133, 134
creation science   4–5, 21, 25–8, 77, 79–80, 97 n.43, 145
Creation Science Foundation (CSF)   21, 22
Creation Science Ministries (CSM)   22.
   See also Answers in Genesis
Cremo, Michael   78–9, 80
Crouch, Nathaniel   113
CSF. See Creation Science Foundation
CSM. See Creation Science Ministries
cryptozoology   77–8, 80–4
cultural/moral degradation   5, 42–3, 44, 61, 62, 63–4, 97, 104, 164
cultural studies   14–17

Dalton, Russell W.   115
Darwin (Charles) and Darwinism   39, 66, 78
day   2 n.3, 49
   day-age theory   34, 43
Deborah   161
decoding. See encoding/decoding
demonstrative evidence   29
dinosaurs. See animals
discord   104–5
dominant/hegemonic reading   11, 12, 129, 166
Douglass, Frederick   153
Downing, Barry   76
dragons. See animals

earth's age   26, 59
Eco, Umberto   70
educated guesses. See artistic license/educated guesses
edutainment   124–5
Edwards, Brian H.   31
eisegesis   34, 94, 139
Emzara   101, 102, 105
encoding/decoding   10–13, 129
Encyclopedia of the Bible and Its Reception (De Gruyter)   17
Enoch   86, 87–8, 91
Esther   161
ethnography   16, 17
Evangelical culture   3, 146–7. See also Green family
Eve   43–4, 49, 132
evolution and evolutionary theory   145
   ancient humans   75
   and creationism   1, 3–4, 27–30, 40–1, 61, 64–5, 79, 143–4
   intraspecies   111
   limited form   25
Evolution and the Modern Christian (Morris), 29
evolutionary creationism   39 n.4
exegesis   94, 139

Facebook   16, 17, 106, 123, 124
fairness   57–8, 77–8, 143–4, 145–6
fairy-tale arks   51, 110–12, 115, 118–22
fake news   163–4
false images   118–21
fantasy   5–6, 13, 112

Fish, Stanley 8, 9–10, 139
flood geology 27, 52
flood narrative. *See also* Noah
   children 110–16
   displays 45–6 (*see also* Ark Encounter)
   historical event 50, 74, 128
   and Methuselah 87–8, 92
formalism 14
Frank, Joseph 76

Gadamer, Hans-Georg 7
   hermeneutic circle 94–5, 96
   hermeneutic play 99
   Wirkungsgeschichte 8–9
gap theory 34
gender relations 42
gender stereotypes 161–2
Genesis
   animal "kind" 24–5, 49
   and creationism 26–8, 46
   literacy 126
   Methuselah 86
   reading approach 12, 30–4
The Genesis Flood: The Biblical Record and Its Scientific Implications (Morris and Whitcomb) 26, 27–8
Genesis Rabbah 103
genres
   literary 30–1, 32
   physical objects 55
geopiety 67
Green family 150, 155, 160, 162, 165
Green, Steve 147, 152
Gutierrez, Gustavo 154

Hall, Stuart 10–13, 16, 96, 129–30
Ham, Ken 4, 18
   "Answering Claims about the Ark Project" 102
   on Ark Encounter 47–8
   on Aronofsky's Methuselah depiction 95–6
   career 21–2
   children's Bible storybooks 115–16
   division of science 28–30
   on exegesis and eisegesis 94, 139
   on fake news 164
   on literalism 30
   Morris influences 27–8
   and Nye debate 1–2
   radio following 22
   and secular science 29, 78, 79–80, 84
   views on US 5
   visitors' trust 106–7, 135
   young-earth creationist reading 33–4
Hancock, Graham 74, 75
hand 89–90
heritage tourism 109–10
Heritage USA 68
hermeneutic circle 94–6
hermeneutic play 99–100
Heschel, Abraham Joshua 153
Heuvelmans, Bernard 77–8, 80
higher education 41–2
historical narrative 30–1
historical periods 104–5
historical science. *See* origins science
history of effect (*Wirkungsgeschichte*), 8–9
Hodge, Bodie 87, 88, 111, 122
Holland, Norman 11, 13
homesickness/longing for home. *See* biblical *hiraeth*
Hopkins, Anthony 18, 90, 92
horizon of change 93
horizon of expectation 8, 9, 93–5, 96, 123, 134, 166
hydraulic sorting 27
hyperreality 70–1, 89

ideal body 133–4
identity 13, 30
idolatry 118–21
images
   Adam and Eve 132–5
   cartoon/fairy tale 51, 110–12, 118–21
   versus pictures 118
images-as-text 33
imagination 94
implied reader 9
injustice 154–5
interpretation
   evangelical vs critical 137–8
   and identity 13
   imaginative interpretation 94
   interpretative communities 10, 73–4, 86, 139, 164
Iser, Wolfgang 7–8, 9, 14
isolation 2, 66

Jacobs/Rosenbaum list   9–10
Jael   161
Jameson, Fredric   71
Jauss, Hans Robert   7–8, 14, 93, 94–5, 134
Jerusalem Talmud   103
Jesus Christ   3, 35, 45, 46, 55
Jones, Jonathan   90
Jude   88

Keenan, William J. F.   89, 96
Kehoe, Alice   4
King, Martin Luther (Jr)   161
Kuhn, Thomas   65
Kuyper, Abraham   40

Lanz, Gordon   64
Leitha, Dan   121
Leviathan   81, 82
Lewis, Frank   25
liberation theology   154
Lincoln, Bruce   119
literary genres   30–1, 32
literalism   30, 138, 139
"Literary History as a Challenge to Literary Theory" (Jauss), 7
Locke, John   114
Looy, Mark   22, 64
Lucifer's flood   34
Lynch, John   2, 63–4

Malley, Brian   137–8, 139, 168
Marsh, Patrick   69
material displays   89–90, 96, 138
material objects   7, 15–16, 89–90, 96, 110, 138, 139–43, 167. *See also* artistic license/educated guesses; realism
"bad objects"   107, 118–22
Material Varieties of Religious Expression (Keenan and Arweck)   96
Matthews, Mike   89
meaning
  and authorial intent   8–10, 14, 32–3
  plain meaning   31, 139
media   101–5
Methuselah
  Aronofsky's depiction   18, 90–4, 95–8
  flood provocateur   87–8, 90
  naming convention   86–7
  visitors' responses   125–6, 138
"Methuselah's Hands ... Found!" (Matthews)   89
Meyers, Carol   103
midrash   93–4
Mintz, Steven   113
Mitchell, W. J. T.   89, 118, 119
Mohler, Albert   127
Moody, Dwight   62
Morris, Henry M.   4, 26–8, 29, 30
Morse, Holly   14
Mortenson, Terry   64
Moss, Candida R.   60
MotB. *See* Museum of the Bible
Museum of the Bible (MotB)
  academic credentials   62
  and Creation Museum compared   59–60
  genre expectations   55
  heritage elements   110
  mission statement   60
  museum label   18, 153, 161, 166
  physical location   2–3, 66
  role of interpreter   4, 19
  Social Initiative   62
  visitors' reviews   16, 156–9
Museum of the Bible (MotB) displays and shows
  "African American Experience" poster   155–6
  Bible in America survey   152, 160
  "Biblical Authority: Women and the Bible" poster   159–60
  communidades de base   154
  Courageous Pages   161–2
  The Impact of the Bible   62–3, 150–6
  "Religious Freedom: A New Awakening"   155
  The Slave Bible: Let the Story Be Told   156–9, 167
  "Was the Bible Used to Promote Racism?" poster   159
  World of Jesus of Nazareth   110
museums
  genre expectations   55
  inherent trust   56–7, 64, 164, 165–6
"Mything the Boat: How the World Sees Noah's Ark" (Leitha)   121

Naaman, story of   162
Native Americans   154–5
natural history museums   56, 63, 64
negotiated reading   11, 129–31, 166–7
Noah
   depiction   100–3
   engineering acumen   50–1, 74–5, 76, 107
   and Methuselah   85, 88, 91–2, 94
   scoffers   105–6, 138
   selfishness   105
Noah (film: Aronofsky)   86, 90–4, 95–8, 124–5
Noah's Ark. *See* Ark Encounter
Numbers, Ronald L.   25
Nye, Bill   1

Obama, Barack   154
old-earth creationism   26, 34–5, 43
open floor plan   63
open-mindedness   57, 58, 144–6
operational science   28, 29, 65
oppositional reading   11–12, 130, 131–2, 156–8, 167
oppression   153–5, 157
origins science   28–9, 65

parable   31
perceived authenticity   109–10, 140–2
pictorial turn   89, 118
Pilgrim's Progress (Bunyan)   116
poetry   31
political right   4–5
popular culture   16, 17, 124–5. *See also* material objects
The Postmodern Bible (Aichele)   14
postmodernism   32–3, 65, 71
presuppositionalism   29, 39–40, 41
Price, George McCready   27, 77
pseudoarcheology   18, 73–80
pseudosciences   78
psychology   13
Purdom, Georgia   60, 61
Puritanism   112–13, 114, 116

racism   46, 52, 159
Ramm, Bernard   77
rationalization   5–6
Ray, Dorothy   153

reader-response criticism. *See also* reception criticism
   Fish's   9–10
   Iser's   7–8
reading positions   11–12, 129–30
realism. *See also* hyperreality
   Amish craftsmen   109
   children's illustrations and stories   110–16
   fairy-tale arks   51
   insistence on   120–1
   and material object   139–41
   miniature flood diorama display   116
   visitors' reviews   70
reception criticism   6–7
   cultural studies   14–17
   encoding/decoding   10–13
   psychology of reading   13
reception history (*Rezeptionsgeschichte*)   8, 14, 74
reception studies   6–8, 85–6, 167
religious freedom   150–6
religious material expressions   70, 96–7, 110, 132
religious persecution   152–3
religious recreation   67–8, 140–2
Rimmer, Harry   77
Romero, Oscar   154, 161
Roosevelt, Eleanor   153
ruin reconstruction   34
rural/urban dichotomy   101–2
Ryan, Michael   15–16

Sahlins, Marshall   100
science
   and AiG   3–4, 57–8, 60–2, 64–6, 84
   ancient mysteries writers   78–9
   and creationism   77–8
   cultural authority   39
   Ham's views   29–30, 79–80
   visitors' views   143–6
scientific creationism. *See* creation science
Scott, Eugenie   69
Scripture Prints: With Explanations in the Form of Familiar Dialogues (Sherwood)   115
Secrets of the Lost Races (Noorbergen)   75
self-presentation   99
Shaw, Ben   87
Sherwood, Mary   115

Sherwood, Yvonne   5, 125
sign vehicles   10, 129
sin   44, 92, 104
   Original Sin   114, 132
Sitchin, Zecharia   74, 75
skepticism   102
   scoffers   45, 80, 105–6, 138
Skiba, Rob   73
"The Slave Bible"   156–9
slavery   155–9
Slusher, Harold   77
Snelling, Andrew   164
social constructionism   65–6
social media. *See* Facebook; TripAdvisor reviews
social structures   164
sola scriptura   41
Stanton, Elizabeth Cady   159, 160–1
Stetzer, Ed   127
Storrey, John   16
The Structure of Scientific Revolutions (Kuhn)   65
subjectivism   10

tannin   83
teach the controversy approach   77, 143
technology (of ancients)   50–1, 52–3, 73, 74–6, 127–8
Templeton, Charles   41
theme park
   and biblical *hiraeth*   69–72
Thompson, Martyn   93
Toward an Aesthetic of Reception (Jauss)   7
Tower of Babel   46, 52–3
transitivity   138–9, 168
TripAdvisor reviews   16, 17, 106, 123–4
   Ark Encounter   70, 130, 131–2, 140, 141–3, 166–7
   Cave of Sorrows   117–18
   Creation Museum   58, 133, 137, 140, 143–6, 148
   Graffiti Alley   117–18
Trollinger, Susan L.   63, 147–8
Trollinger, William Vance   63, 147–8
Trump, Donald   2, 102, 149, 152, 163, 164
Truth and Method (Gadamer)   8
Turpin, Simon   30, 31
Tutu, Desmond   153

Unger, Eckhard   23
unicorns. *See* animals
United States
   and Bible   5, 62, 151, 165
   cultural and moral decline   5, 61, 63
   executive order 13798   152

Van Til, Cornelius   40
Vashti   161
visitor(s). *See also* biblical *hiraeth*
   AiG impact   6–7
   Bible literacy   106, 125–7, 135, 166, 167–8
   and open-mindedness   57–8
   trust on Ham and AiG   19, 106–7
visitor reviews
   Adam's sexiness   133
   to artistic license/educated guesses   106, 130–2, 165–7
   authenticity   142–3, 148
   "Bible comes alive"   140–2
   "biblical" references   137–8
   commercial activities   142
   fairness   143–4
   inappropriate for children   116–18
   open-mindedness   58, 144–6
   oppositional reading   131–2, 156–8, 167
   realism   37, 70
   social media   16, 17, 123–4
Von Däniken, Erich   74, 75

Wadsworth, Benjamin   113
"When Did Methuselah Die?" (Hodge)   87
Whitcomb, John C.   26
wilderness narratives   2, 3
Wirkungsgeschichte. *See* history of effect
Woetzel, Dave   81
The Woman's Bible   159, 160
women's rights movement   159–61
Wright, John Kirtland   67

young-earth creationism   21, 26–7
   and cryptozoology   81
   and science   29–30, 78–80, 84
Youth's Divine Pastime (Crouch)   110

Zovath, Mike   22

www.ingramcontent.com/pod-product-compliance
Lightning Source LLC
Chambersburg PA
CBHW070639300426
44111CB00013B/2165